IMAGES
of America

WESTFIELD

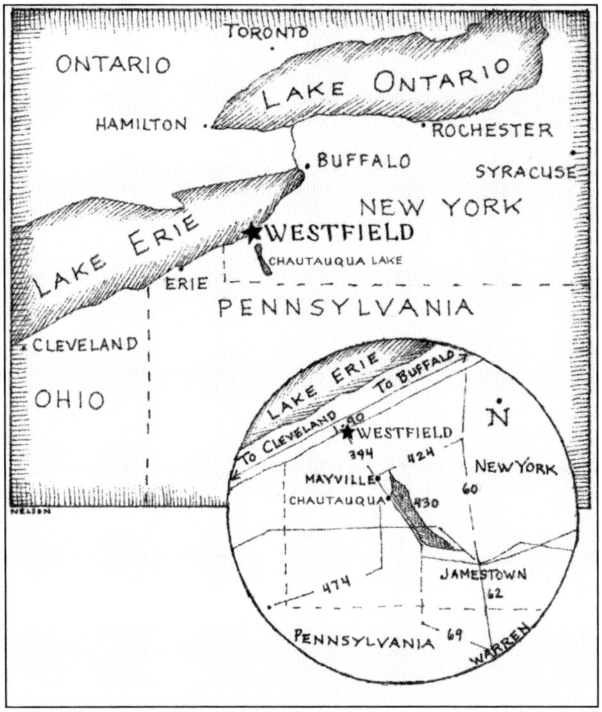

This map shows the town of Westfield in relation to the rest of the Chautauqua Region. (Jane Nelson.)

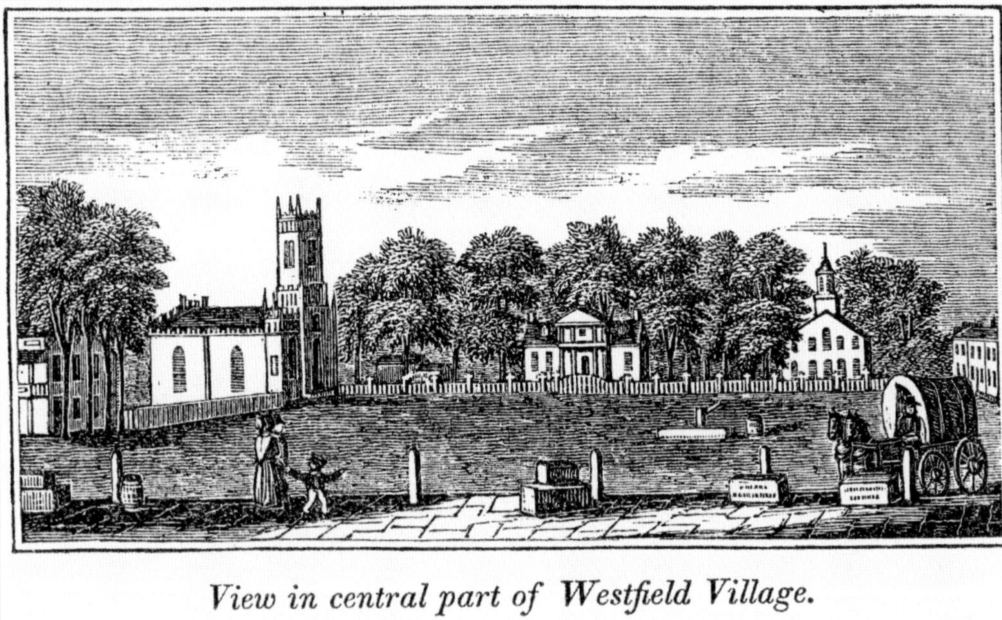

View in central part of ***Westfield Village.***

During the mid-1830s, the commons in the village of Westfield resembled the town squares in New England, the birthplace of many local settlers. (John Paul Wolfe.)

On the cover: A former resident recalled Westfield's Main Street as "kindly and protecting—a neighborly warmth a city never acquires." (Patterson Library.)

IMAGES
of America

WESTFIELD

Kathleen Crocker and Jane Currie

ARCADIA
PUBLISHING

ISBN 978-0-7385-4469-4

Published by Arcadia Publishing
Charleston, South Carolina

Printed in the United States of America

Library of Congress Catalog Card Number: 2005936974

For all general information contact Arcadia Publishing at:
Telephone 843-853-2070
Fax 843-853-0044
E-mail sales@arcadiapublishing.com
For customer service and orders:
Toll-Free 1-888-313-2665

Visit us on the Internet at www.arcadiapublishing.com

To Virginia Hopson Griffin—we cherish your friendship and your infectious love for your hometown of Westfield.

Contents

Acknowledgments 6

Introduction 7

1. Old Portage Road 9

2. Early Settlement 17

3. Barcelona 31

4. National Connections 47

5. The Grape Belt 59

6. Transportation and Recreation 75

7. The Village 89

8. Historic Treasures 115

Partial Bibliography 128

Acknowledgments

Thankfully, Byron, Ed, Pamela Berndt Arnold, Peggy Snyder, and Alex continue to be loving diehards. For their knowledge, time, expertise, and advice, we especially salute Sydney S. Baker, Jeff Bloomquist, David and Sandy Brown, Gert and Fran Brumagim, Stephanie Burdo, Linda Carlson, Jack E. Ericson, Jim Fincher, Pam Frank, Hayden Hanks, Nancy Hanks, Cristie Herbst, Judith Hess, Tom Hopson, Linda Hout, Dr. Lillian V. Ney, Mary Ellen Sheridan, the Welch family, John Paul Wolfe, and others who helped us showcase Westfield.

We are indebted to Westfield's knowledgeable historians, our friends whose assistance far exceeded our expectations: Nancy Nixon, Billie Dibble, and Deborah Williams, Patterson Library; and president James O'Brien and Ellen Schwanekamp, Chautauqua County Historical Society.

Courtesy lines identify those who shared images; unless indicated otherwise, the images are courtesy of the Patterson Library, Westfield.

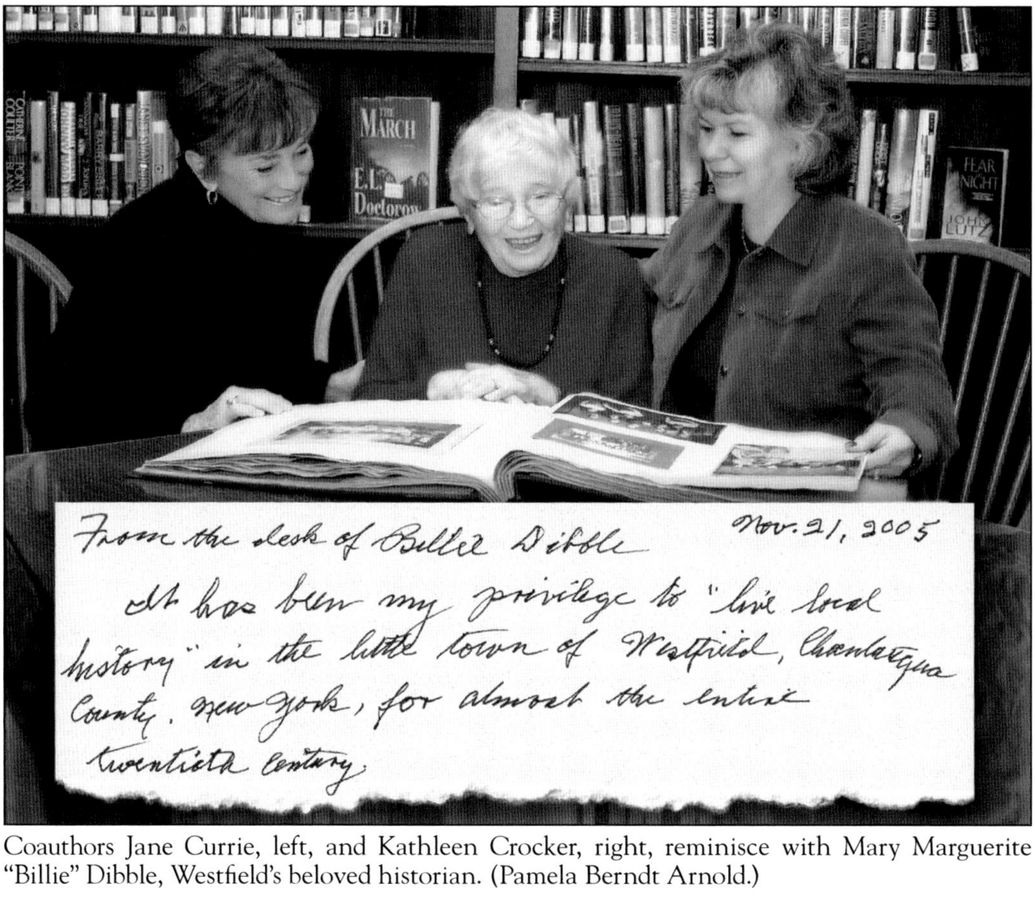

Coauthors Jane Currie, left, and Kathleen Crocker, right, reminisce with Mary Marguerite "Billie" Dibble, Westfield's beloved historian. (Pamela Berndt Arnold.)

Introduction

Originally called the Crossroads, Westfield is strategically located on the southern shore of Lake Erie, midway between Buffalo and Cleveland with easy access to Pennsylvania. In 1813, the town of Portland was formed from the towns of Portland, Ripley, and Westfield, and in 1829, the town of Westfield assumed its own identity, comprised of land from the western section of Portland and the eastern section of Ripley. Thus, Portland Harbor (present-day Barcelona) became the northernmost part of Westfield's Township, one of 26 in Chautauqua County. Westfield is heralded for many firsts: the county's first permanent settlement, first school, first church, and first post office. Nationally, it boasts the country's first Republican newspaper and the first public building to be lit by natural gas.

Since this book is designed to be an overview of the town of Westfield, founded in 1802, not a detailed history, we agonized over image selections. We decided to chronicle the area's development, touching on its national connections, its natural and man-made beauty, and its citizens and their contributions to everyday life. The 150-year-old *Westfield Republican* and picturesque Barcelona merit their own books. The same is true for Westfield's and Barcelona's grape industry, one of the largest in the world.

To ensure accuracy and to maintain the integrity of our own research, we waited until the project's final phase to delve into "Dibble's Dabbles," columns written by Mary "Billie" Dibble for the *Westfield Republican* for about a decade beginning in 1981. No better source exists of Westfield's intimate history, but readers should savor these themselves.

We hope readers preserve and research their own family histories to create memoirs for future generations. For, as Alex Haley, author of *Roots*, wrote, "In all of us there is a hunger, marrow deep, to know our heritage—to know who we are and where we came from."

—Kathleen Crocker and Jane Currie

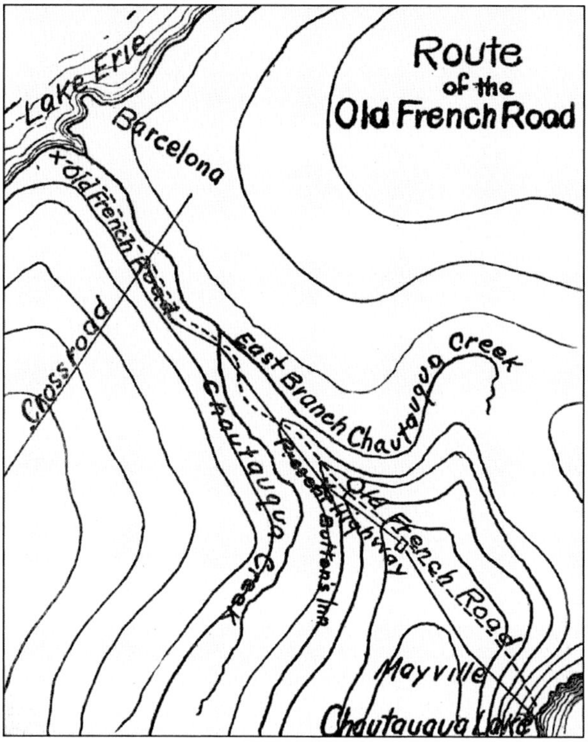

Historian Obed Edson credited explorers and early settlers for the name "the Old French Road" and "so Judge William Peacock called it." As a surveyor for the Holland Land Company, Peacock "had the best knowledge of [Chautauqua County's] early history and geography." (The Chautauquan, 1912–1913.)

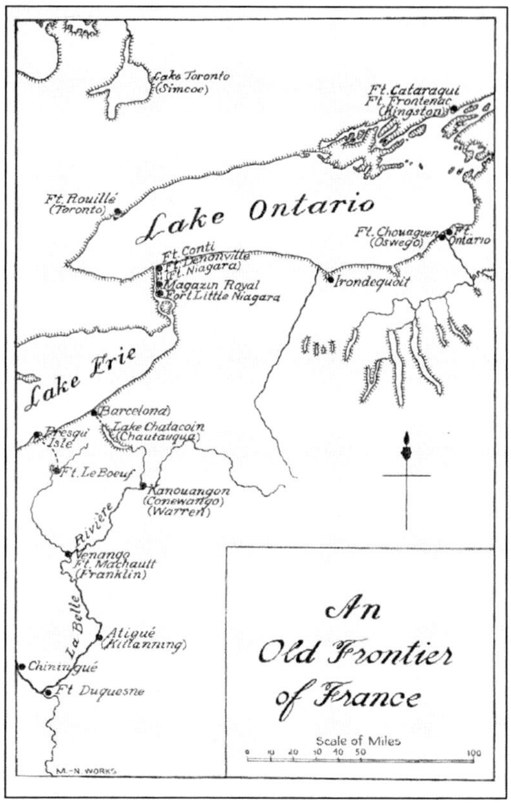

This map shows military posts established by the French in the 1700s on Lake Erie and southward. (*An Old Frontier of France*, Severance, 1917.)

One

Old Portage Road

According to Obed Edson, long before 1799, the French "had been accustomed to visit western New York and Pennsylvania, had explored the streams and journeyed upon the Indian trails there." One of those trails, the Portage Trail, was destined to play a significant role in American history.

France dispatched many scouting parties to the southern shores of Lake Erie to extend its empire on the American continent. These included Etienne Brulé in 1615; explorer Sieur de La Salle, who discovered Chautauqua Lake, in 1679; and engineer Chaussegros de Lery, who attempted to find the shortest military portage between Lake Erie and the headwaters of the Ohio River, in 1739.

The most important expedition, however, was made in 1749 by Capt. Pierre Joseph Blainville de Celoron and his party, who greatly impacted the area's future. Described by Edson as a "fleet of bark canoes, manned by half-naked Indians, Canadians in hunter's garb, and French soldiers in the uniform of their country," they landed at the mouth of the Riviere aux Pommes, later known as Chautauqua Creek, which had long been used by Native Americans en route from Lake Erie to the Ohio Valley. They established a temporary camp at the present-day Barcelona, but because of the shallowness of the lake and its unprotected harbor, it proved unsuitable.

In order to renew France's claim to the disputed territories west of the Allegheny Mountains and north of the Ohio River, the expedition faced severe challenges. The primitive Native American trail needed to be cleared and widened in order to transport their provisions, bartering goods, munitions, pine pirogues, bateaux, and birch bark canoes through the vast virgin forest to Chautauqua Lake, at whose outlet they planned to launch their canoes for the journey to Louisiana.

During their six-day trek, de Celoron's journal records struggles to climb the escarpment through the precipitous Chautauqua Gorge: "the heavily forested and hilly land in between proved a challenge . . . up the long steep slope of the divide through a heavy forest growth of oak, maple, beech, other native hard woods, mingled with pine and hemlock." De Celoron and his men toted and buried inscribed leaden plates along the way to stake their claim.

Four years later, Marquis Duquesne, the governor-general of Canada (or New France, as it was then called) wanted to assert France's sovereignty over the territory and prevent British expansion. Consequently, the enterprising French, who had cut the Old Portage Road, converted it into a military road and established a series of forts from Chautauqua Creek to Pittsburgh and southward along the Mississippi River. Skirmishes between the two nations to open up the Ohio Valley, "the gateway to North America's heartland," were documented by de Celoron's own maps and manuscripts purchased by the United States from France. These events were the beginnings of the global conflict known as the French and Indian War. The bottom map on the opposite page illustrates the secondary route adopted by the French in 1753 after they abandoned the Portage Road. The easier route led from Presque Isle (now Erie, Pennsylvania) with its deeper protected bay to Lebouf (Waterford, Pennsylvania) down to Fort Duquesne (Pittsburgh, Pennsylvania) via French Creek and the Allegheny River.

The Old Portage Road, now Route 394, remains a major artery in Chautauqua County and provides access to the Chautauqua Gorge, "a miniature Grand Canyon." On the edge of the Allegheny plateau, the gorge is located five miles from Lake Erie and extends about eight miles through woods and winding waters between Westfield and Mayville on Chautauqua Lake. It is a challenging mecca for hikers and outdoorsmen.

Some 1,500 feet above sea level and 700 feet above Lake Erie, the Chautauqua watershed separates into two entities. From the crest, water flows north into Lake Erie, cascades over Niagara Falls, and continues along the St. Lawrence River and empties into the Atlantic Ocean. Water that flows southward enters Chautauqua Lake and flows down the Allegheny and Ohio Rivers. To the north is a breathtaking view of the rolling fertile land and hills along Lake Erie, "stretching its pale-blue surface away toward Canada, and the famous vineyards filling the intervening space of eight miles with their fragrance and purple hue . . . and to the southeast, serene Chautauqua Lake and its adjacent rolling hills."

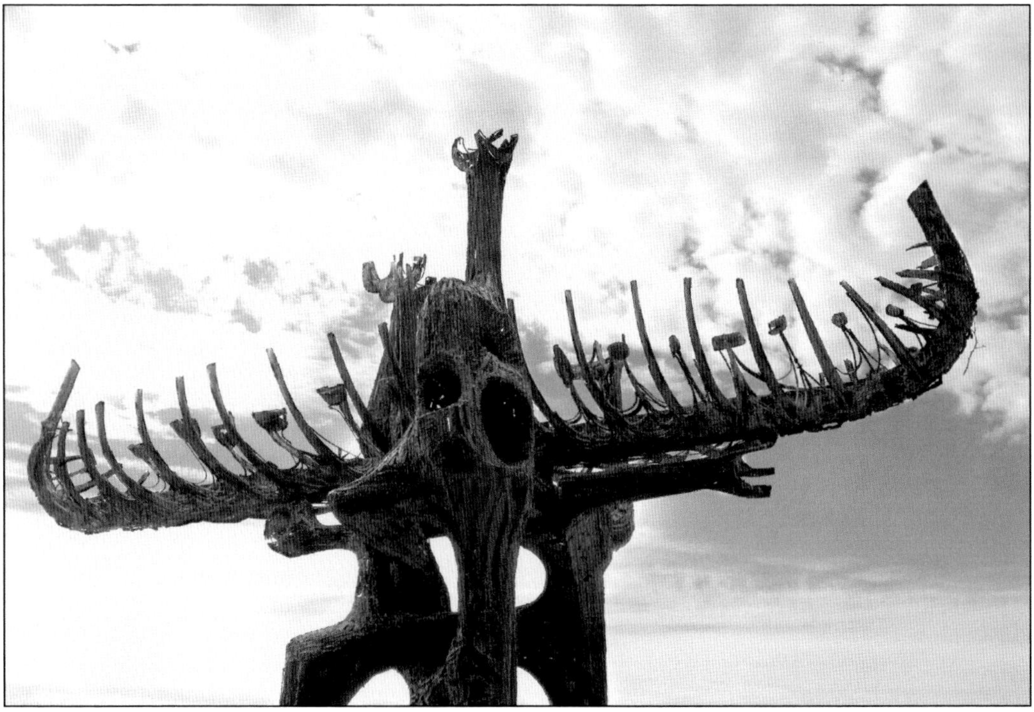

Created by Russell Vacanti, this 12-foot-tall bronze sculpture was recently relocated near the old Keelboat Landing on the Chadakoin River in Jamestown, New York. Commissioned by the Jamestown Rotary Club in the late 1960s, it celebrates Capt. De Celoron's 10-mile overland portage from Lake Erie to Chautauqua Lake in 1749. (Jane Currie.)

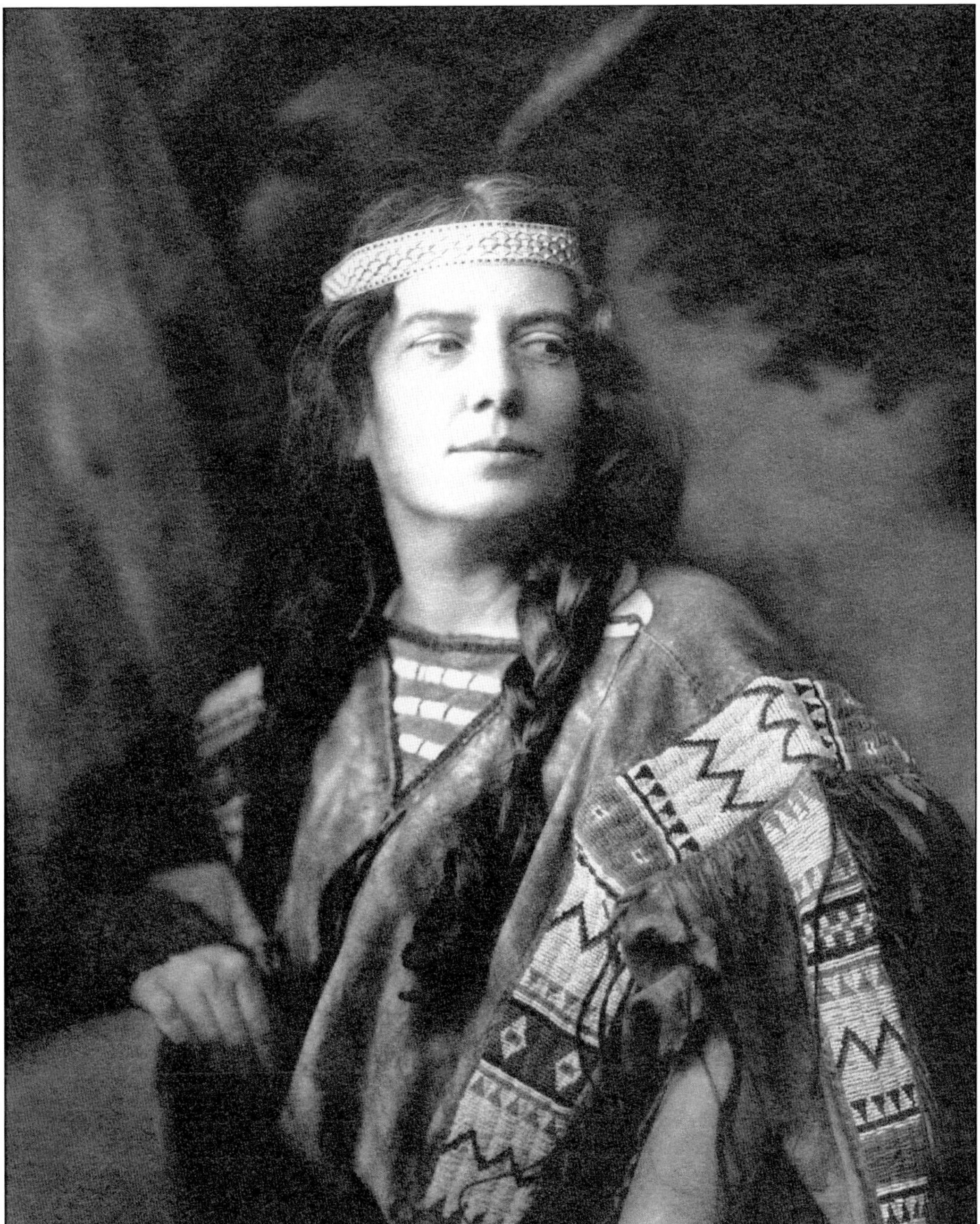

Born Ella Mabel Powers in 1872 near Buffalo, this "White Indian" lived in harmony with nature. Adopted by the Tonawanda Senecas, she became a lecturer and storyteller of Native American lore at the Chautauqua Institution where a Fire Circle in the ravine was dedicated to her. "Jahdahgwah," she professed, "has carried us from the life of self and things, into the life of Spirit. On the nature trail we have glimpsed God in Nature, in our Brother, in Ourself. Many more portages await us, for life is a series of portages, and each portage means a new sun-coming, new and undiscovered worlds, both within and without, wider vision, greater truth, larger love and more abundant life."

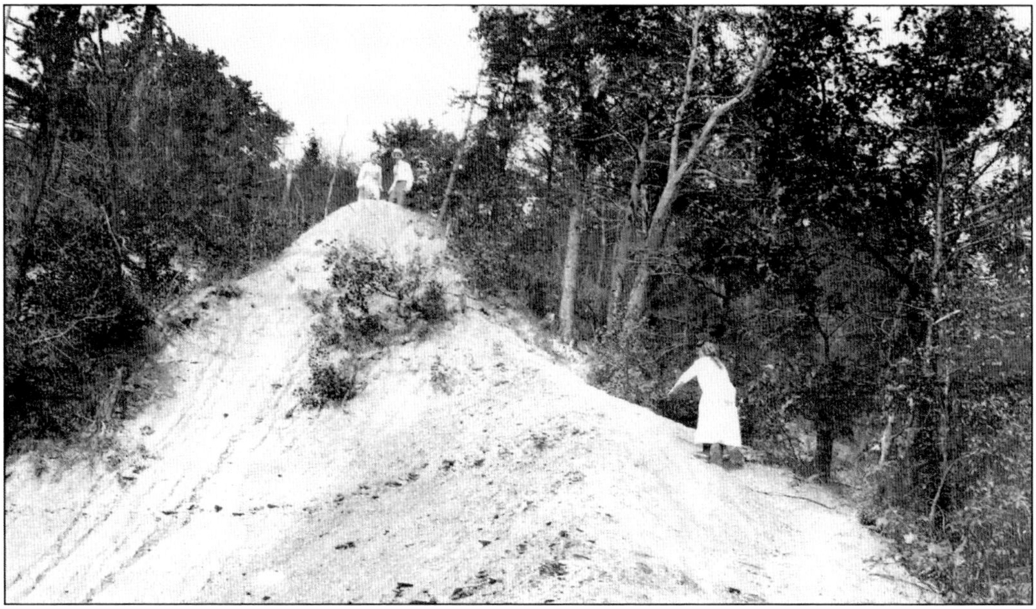

“Hogs Back” is a precipitous cliff that drops several hundred feet down to Chautauqua Creek. Resembling the razor-backed wild hog, Ella Mabel Powers considered its trail “a difficult, four-footed one; the average paleface puffs and grunts along the way . . . The Indian did his trail climbing with his head—not his heels. He lifted his thoughts. He let the Great Spirit run with him, leap with him, climb with him.” (Kathleen Crocker.)

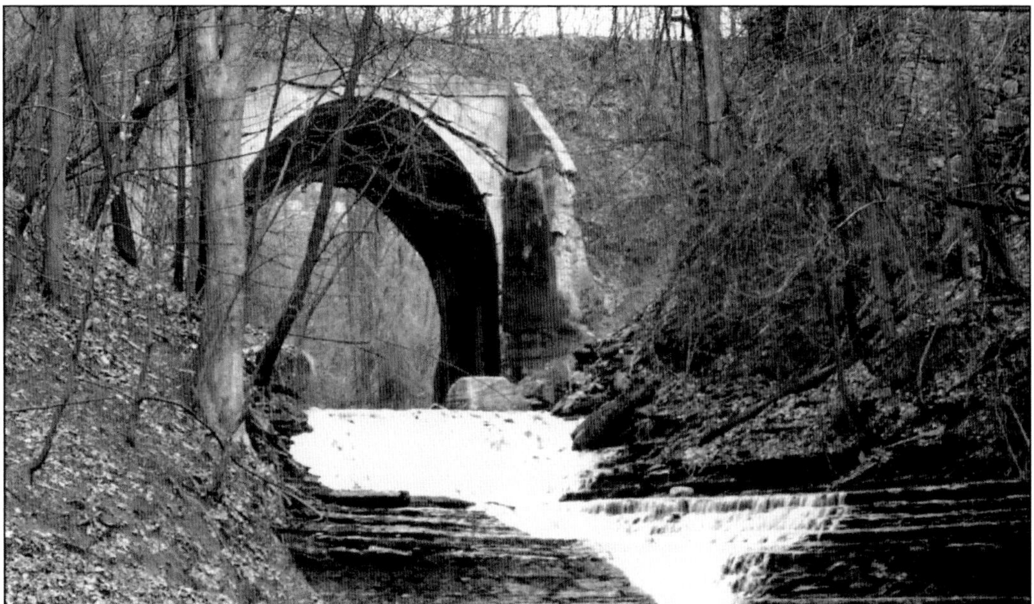

Hiking through the moss-covered ravines and narrow glens in the gorge, one is haunted by its past. Historian Obed Edson noted, “the voices of the wind are whispering in our ears, filling them with memories of our primitive state, and we wonder if the art of man has made [the gorge] as attractive as when virgin forest, unmarred by the desecrating hand of man, stood round it.” (Sydney S. Baker.)

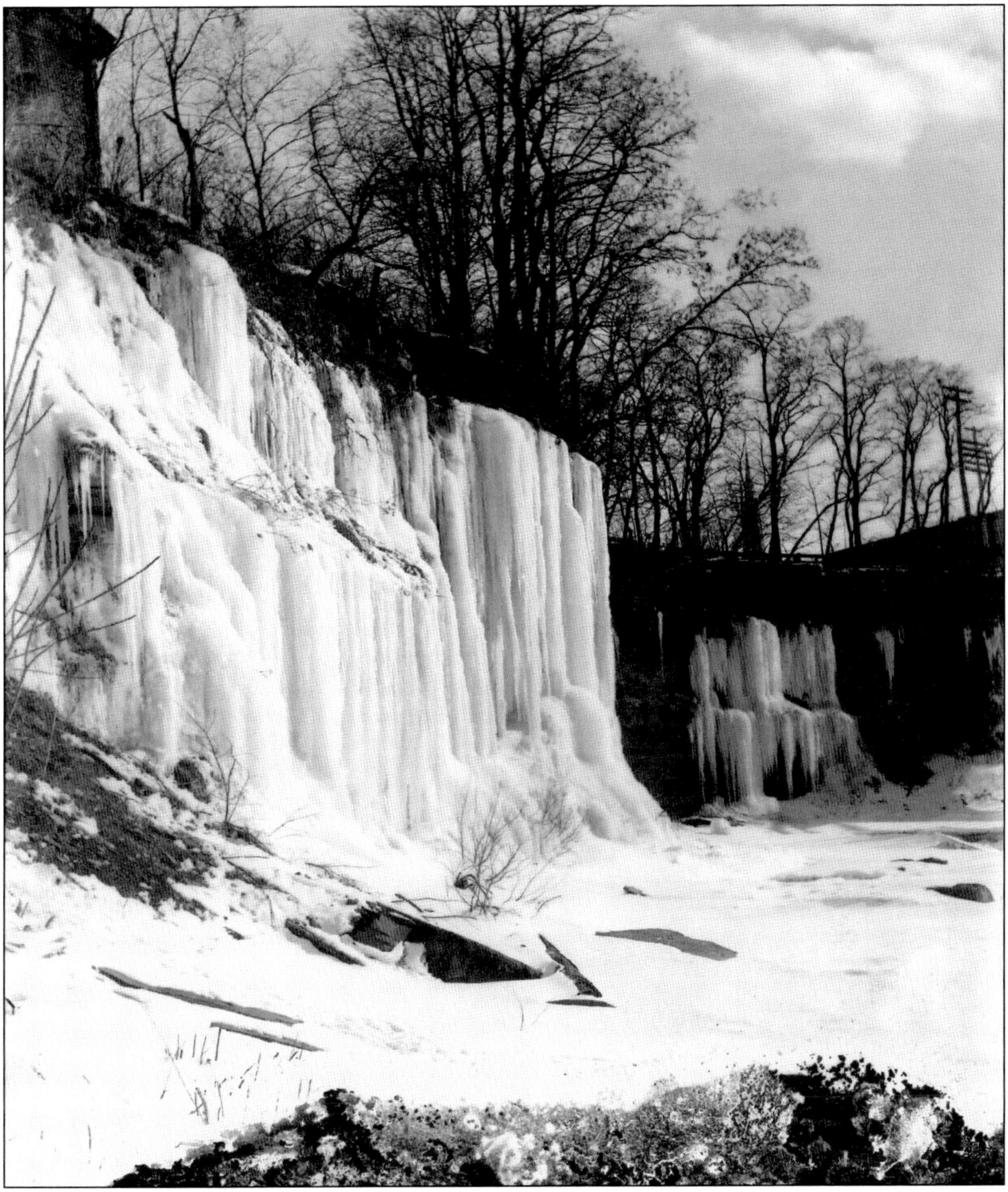

The Old Portage Road Bridge and aqueduct (on the previous page) and Buttermilk Falls (above) are ideal settings for artists and photographers. Journalist Patricia Appleyard Parker recalled the thrill of "plunging into the abyss" on the trolley track from Mayville into Westfield. From the station, "we descended, laden with picnic paraphernalia, into Little Chautauqua Gorge [where] the creek flows over shale rocks at the bottom of the steep, muddy hill. We walked through the water to the falls where our family had picnicked for at least three generations . . . Always, we swam under the falls and, after lunch, walked down the stream exploring, until it was time to leave . . . A few times, when we were teenagers, we camped overnight." (Sydney S. Baker.)

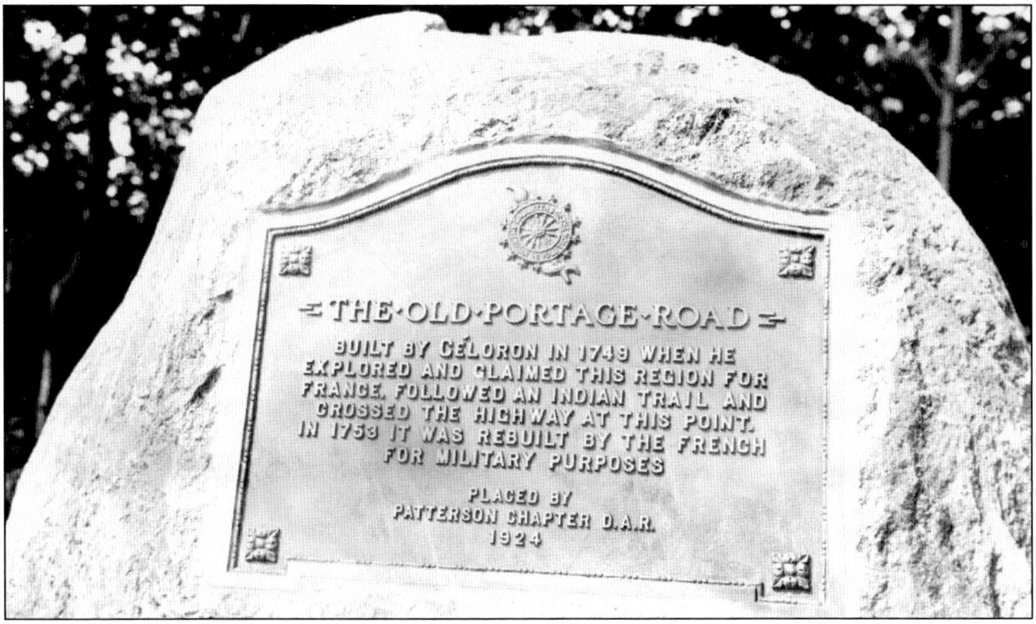

In 1924, the Patterson chapter of the Daughters of the American Revolution placed an inscribed boulder on the site where the old Native American trail and the French Portage Road intersected. The patriotic organization hoped to create "an enlightened public opinion and [afford] to young and old such advantage as shall develop in them the largest capacity for performing the duties of American citizens." (Jane Currie.)

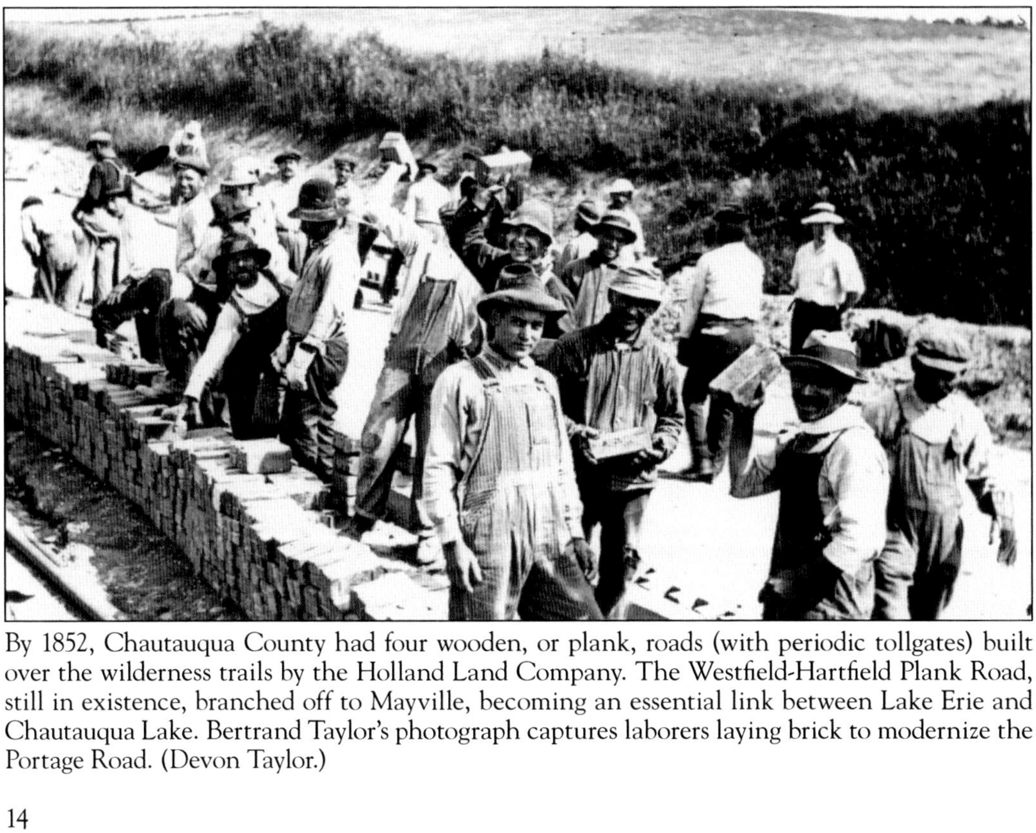

By 1852, Chautauqua County had four wooden, or plank, roads (with periodic tollgates) built over the wilderness trails by the Holland Land Company. The Westfield-Hartfield Plank Road, still in existence, branched off to Mayville, becoming an essential link between Lake Erie and Chautauqua Lake. Bertrand Taylor's photograph captures laborers laying brick to modernize the Portage Road. (Devon Taylor.)

Former carpetbagger Judge Albion Winegar Tourgee (1838–1905) achieved international acclaim for his novels, social commentaries in which he relentlessly opposed segregation. Disenchanted with the South, Tourgee moved his family to Mayville, where he continued to receive volumes of mail from discontented Southern veterans and African Americans. Westfield native Roy F. Dibble's 1921 biography of Tourgee presents an in-depth account of the county's adopted son. (Chautauqua County Historical Society.)

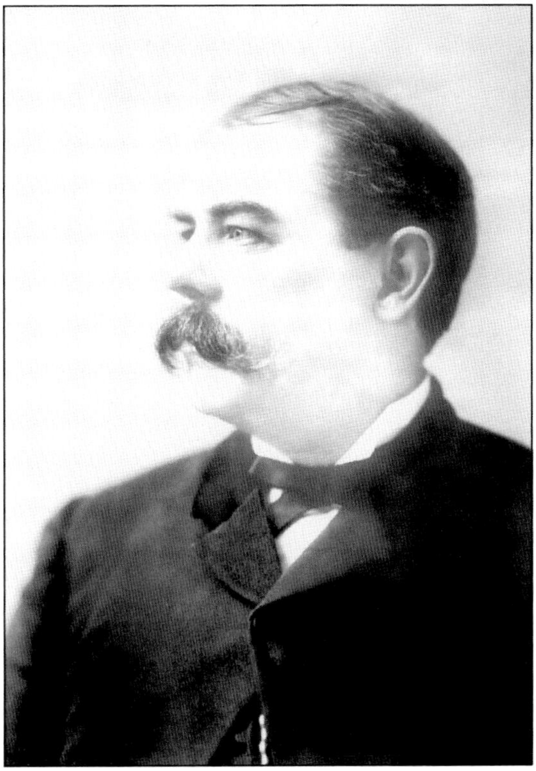

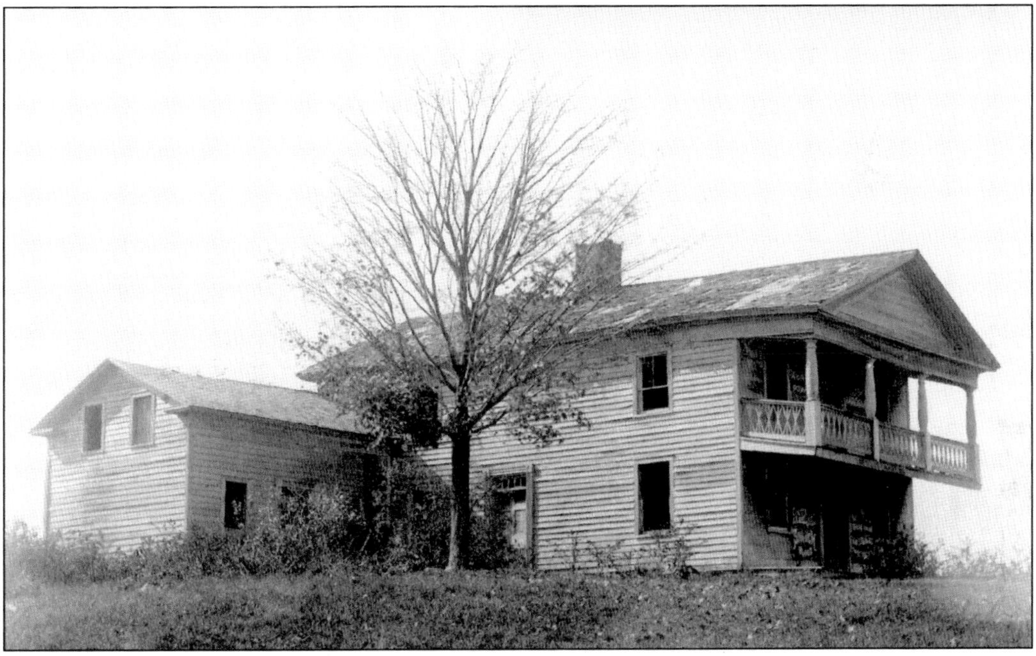

Built by Moses Chapman in 1823, Button's Inn was a hostelry and stagecoach stop immortalized by Judge Tourgee's 1887 novel, *Button's Inn*. "A fort and a residence, its upper story [overlapped] the lower as to prevent assault." Pre-railroad, it provided a "favorable resting-place . . . for those who climbed the ridge."

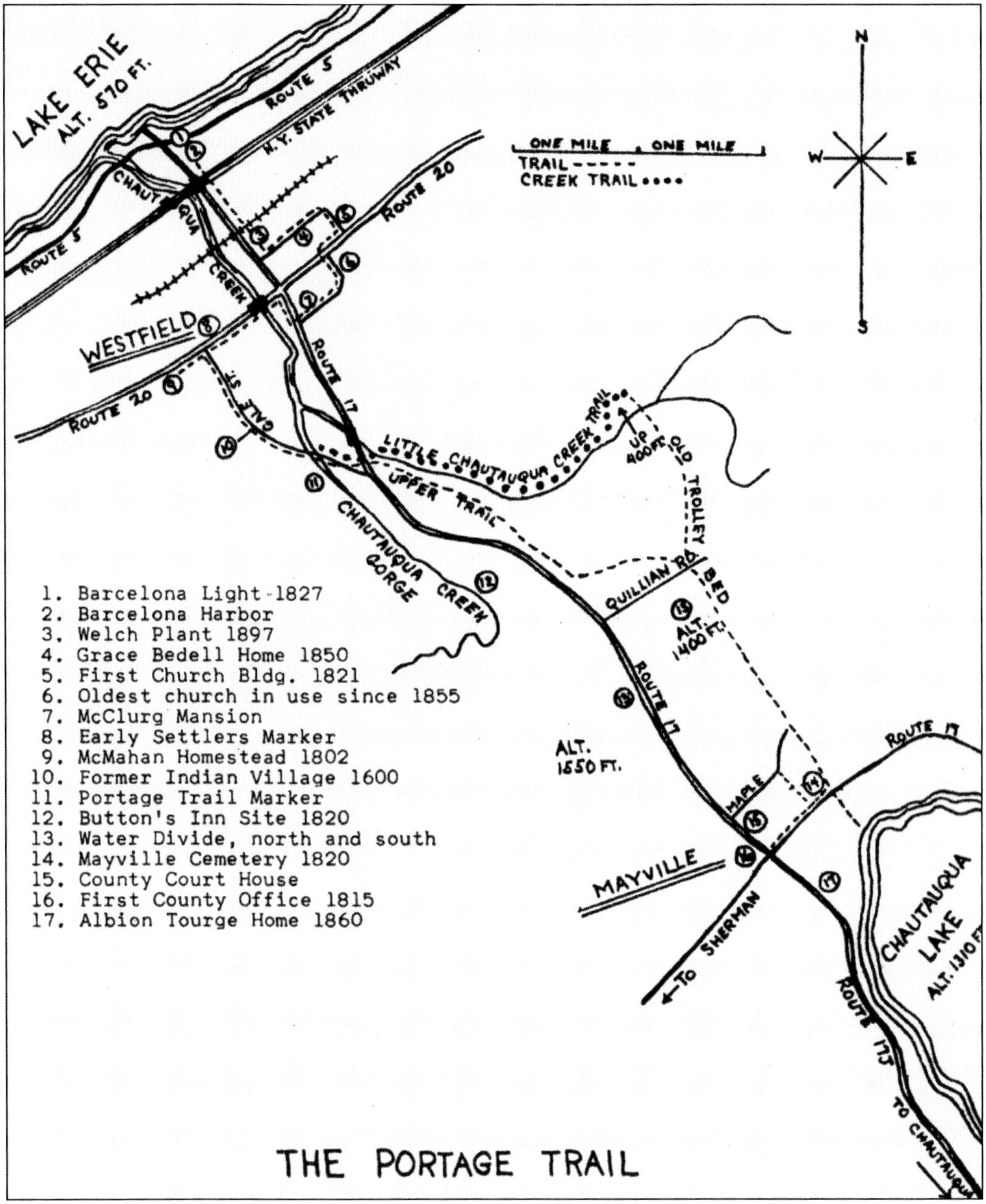

On August 12, 1972, a new Portage Trail opened. It was cleared by the Boy Scouts under the direction of Herbert F. Hern, a dedicated Boy Scout leader. *The Portage Trail*, a 28-page pamphlet published by the local council and researched by Hern, provides hiking enthusiasts with the trail's history, maps, and directions to access points on the approximately 10-mile public trail. Six to eight hours should be allowed to hike the trail leisurely, and private property along the top of the gorge should be respected. (Allegheny Highlands Council, Boy Scouts of America.)

Two

Early Settlement

Trails throughout the Chautauqua region indicated that Native Americans had roamed the area long before the white man's arrival. The forest was a hunter's paradise, providing sustenance for all outdoorsmen: plentiful panther, wolf, wildcat, partridge, ruffed grouse, wild turkey, ring-necked pheasants, quail, rabbit, squirrel, woodchuck, muskrat, fox, duck, geese, and deer.

In 1787, western New York's wilderness was considered less valuable than the eastern part of New York State bordering Massachusetts. To settle a border dispute, Massachusetts ceded to New York State 3.3 million acres, including the entire county of Chautauqua. In 1791, Robert Morris, a prominent Philadelphia financier, bought part of this tract for approximately $32 an acre, becoming the sole owner of Chautauqua County. He then sold his property to the Holland Land Company, a group of wealthy Dutch merchants. The Big Tree Treaty of 1797 secured a clear title of the territory from the resident Seneca Indians. Learning of the Holland Purchase, resolute pioneers, most "blest with health and strength," moved their families westward from the New England area to the pristine forests of western New York.

Rev. D. L. Hequembourg of Oregon wrote to a relative regarding Chautauqua County's settlement: "its isolated position and its dependence upon itself were . . . propitious circumstances, and gave it a homogeneous character and development . . . its zeal in the support of religious and educational institutions was a very striking feature . . . The tone of society was high and moral . . . a striking contrast [from] many of our settlements on the Pacific Coast in the rush for precious metals."

In essence, Westfield's pioneers were "an energetic, intelligent, and God-fearing people" or, as Forrest Crissey wrote:

> "Better than her rarest wine,
> Chautauqua's larger gift I sing—
> Her pioneers—a noble seed
> From which harvest rich and great,
> Of sturdy sons hath sprung to feed
> The school, the mart, the court, the state!"

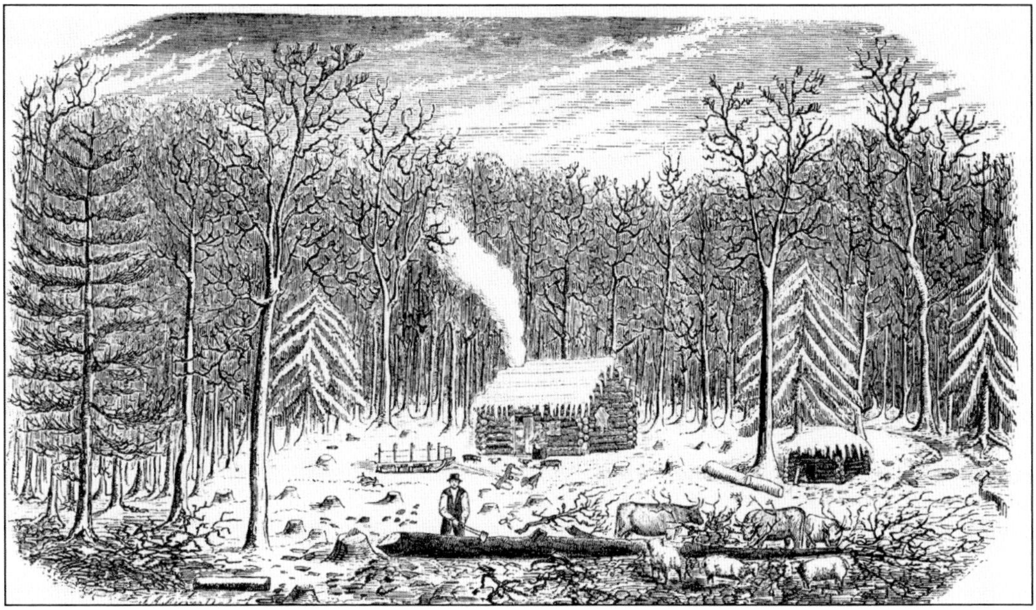

These two sketches from *Pioneer History of the Holland Land Purchase* illustrate "the conversion of Western New York from a wilderness to a theater of wealth, enterprise, and prosperity." Pioneers moving westward in oxen carts and horse carts first cleared the land to build crude cabins; planted corn, potatoes, beans, and pumpkins; and raised stock. They socialized with neighbors in logging, sewing, and quilting bees. (O. Turner.)

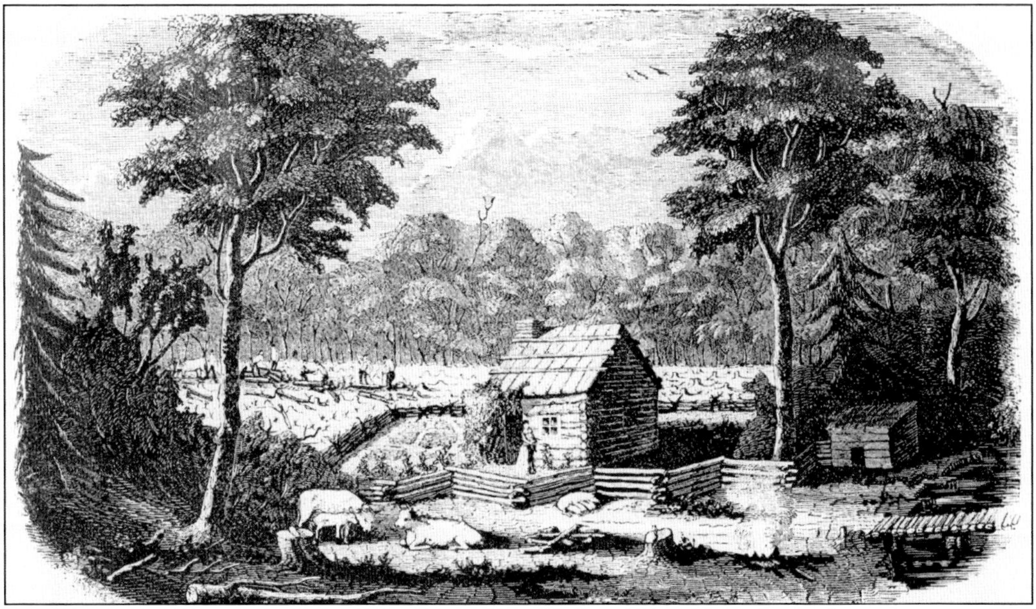

Over the years, pioneers became more independent but still enlisted their children to assist with household chores, to tend animals and gardens, and to help fill fruit cellars with bins of potatoes, canned fruits and vegetables, jellies, and pickles. Besides enlarged farms, flocks, herds, and orchards, the forest was replaced by a neighborhood complete with a meetinghouse, taverns, shops, and a schoolhouse. (O. Turner.)

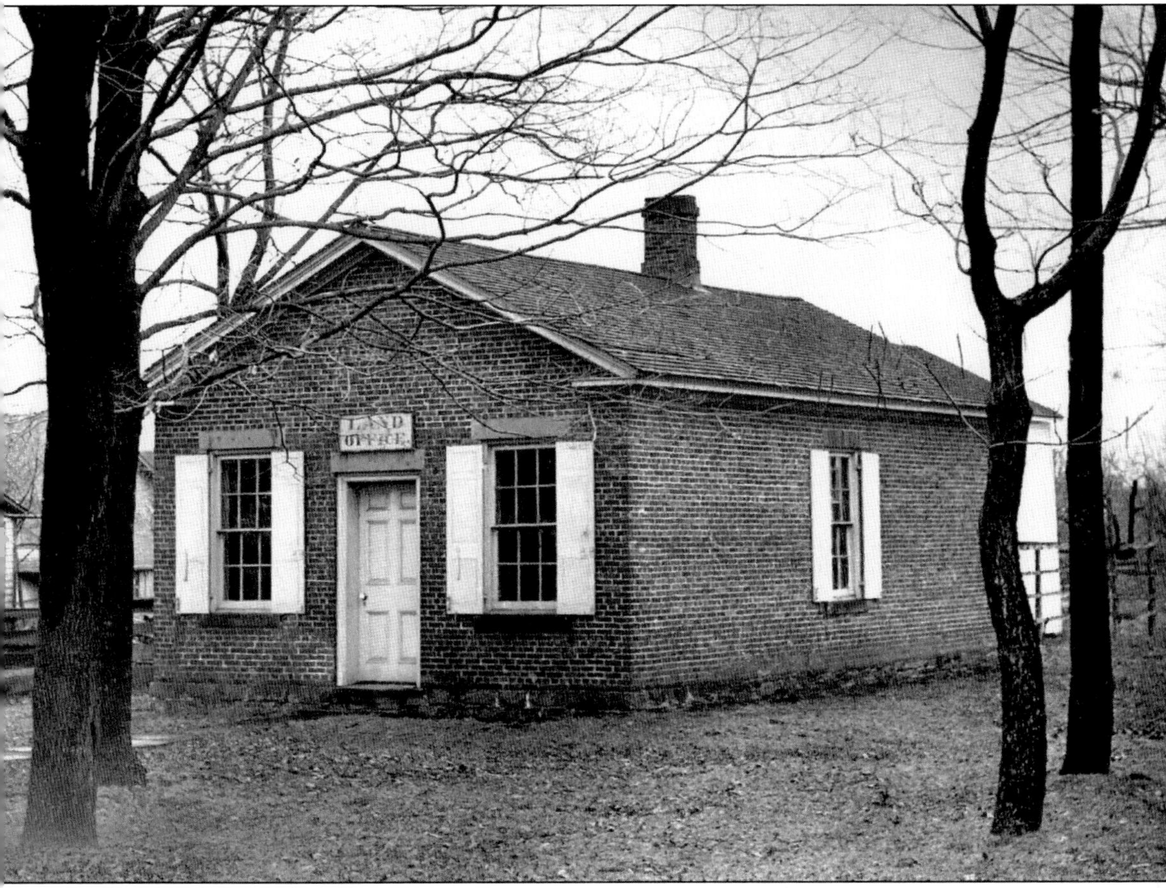

Pioneers purchased their tracts from the Holland Land Company. This office was later located at 85 North Portage Street. In *The Pioneer Settler Upon the Holland Land Purchase, and His Progress*, Alfred B. Street writes:

> "Through the deep wilderness, where scarce the sun
> Can cast his darts, along the winding path
> The Pioneer is treading. In his grasp
> Is his keen axe, that wondrous instrument,
> That like the talisman, transforms
> Deserts to fields and cities. He has left
> The home in which his early years were past,
> And, led by hope, and full of restless strength,
> Has plunged within the forest, there to plant
> His destiny. Beside some rapid stream
> He rears his log-built cabin."

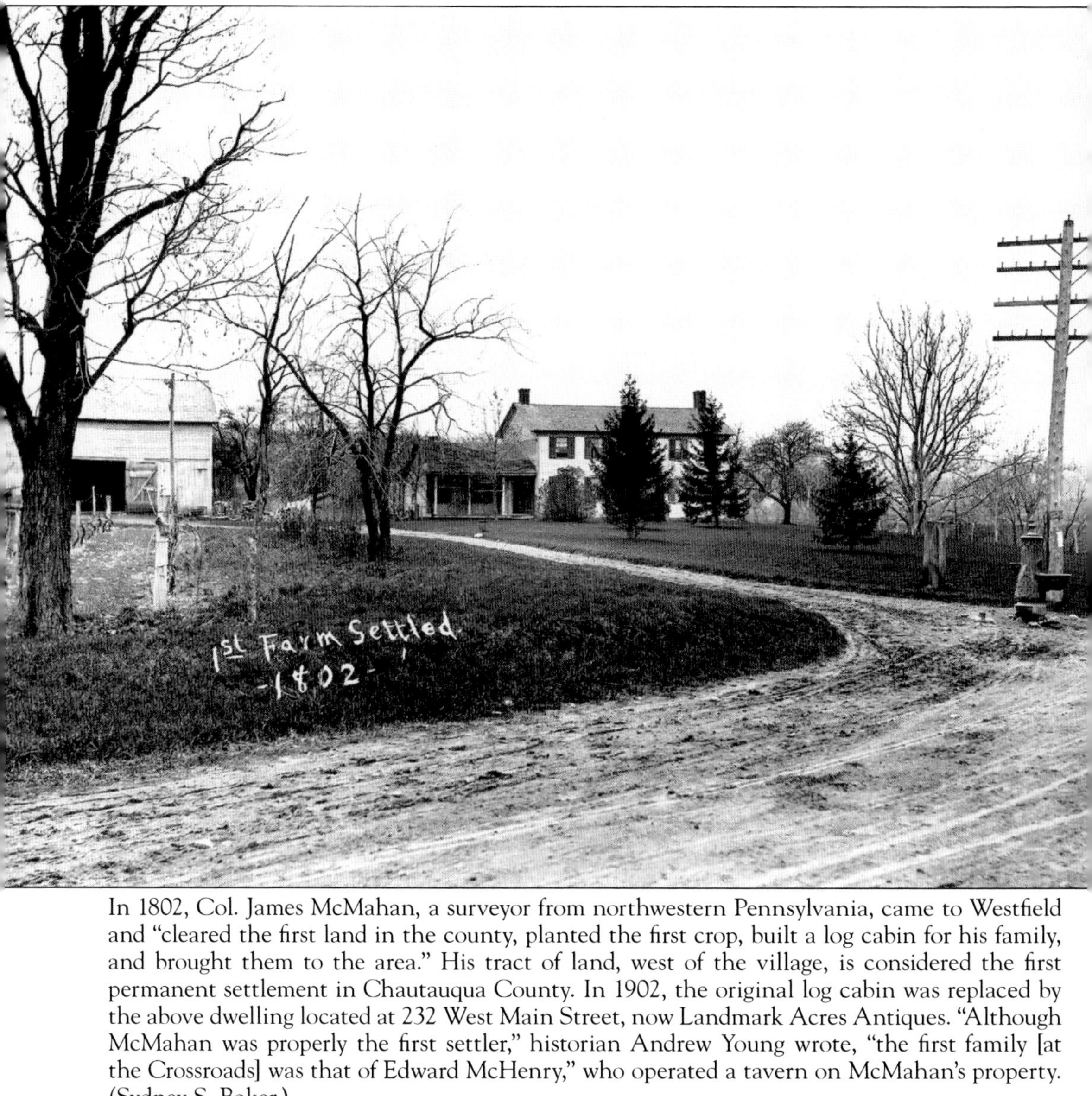

In 1802, Col. James McMahan, a surveyor from northwestern Pennsylvania, came to Westfield and "cleared the first land in the county, planted the first crop, built a log cabin for his family, and brought them to the area." His tract of land, west of the village, is considered the first permanent settlement in Chautauqua County. In 1902, the original log cabin was replaced by the above dwelling located at 232 West Main Street, now Landmark Acres Antiques. "Although McMahan was properly the first settler," historian Andrew Young wrote, "the first family [at the Crossroads] was that of Edward McHenry," who operated a tavern on McMahan's property. (Sydney S. Baker.)

John McHenry (1802–1878) is listed on the stone historic marker below located on property at Gale and West Main Streets, the Crossroads where the Erie-Buffalo Road crossed the Portage Trail. As "the first white child born in Chautauqua County," John was "paraded at county fairs and public gatherings."

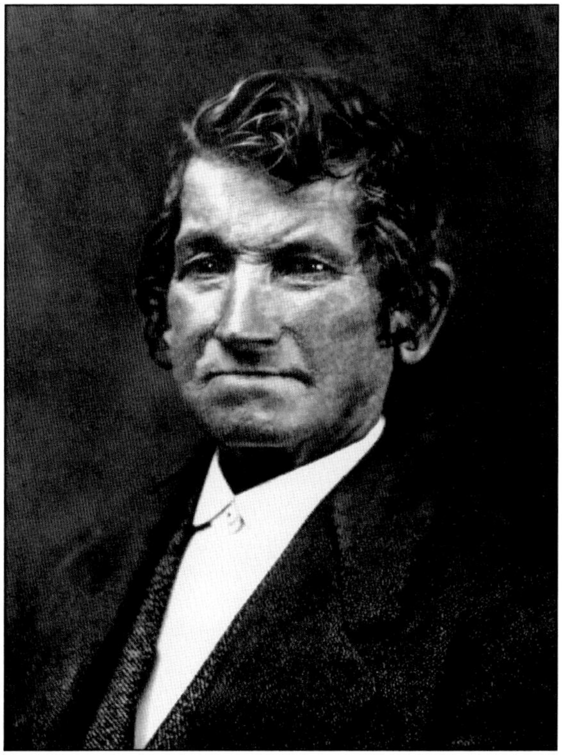

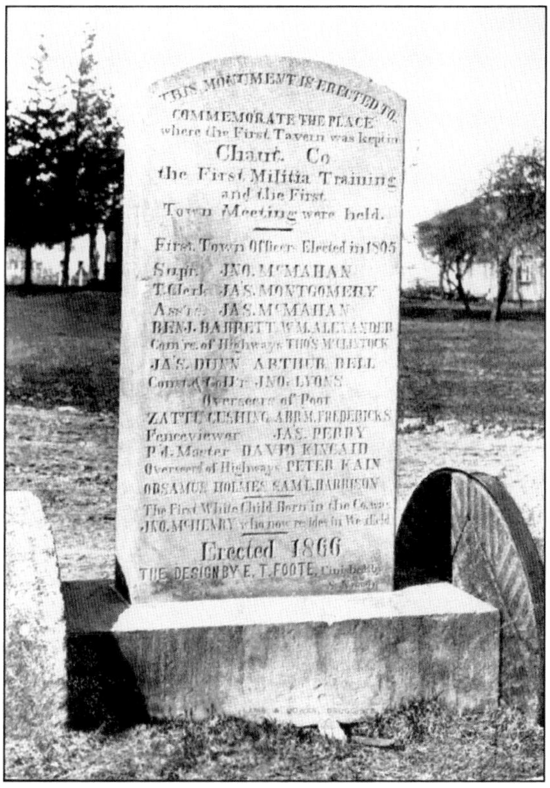

Erected in 1866, this marker commemorates the place "where the First Tavern was kept in Chaut. Co. the First Militia Training and the First Town Meeting were held." Several settlers of Westfield, Ripley, and Portland, as well as officials of the Town of Chautauqua are listed, including John McMahan and his brother James. Through their influence, many settlers emigrated from Pennsylvania to Westfield. (Ed Schaeffer.)

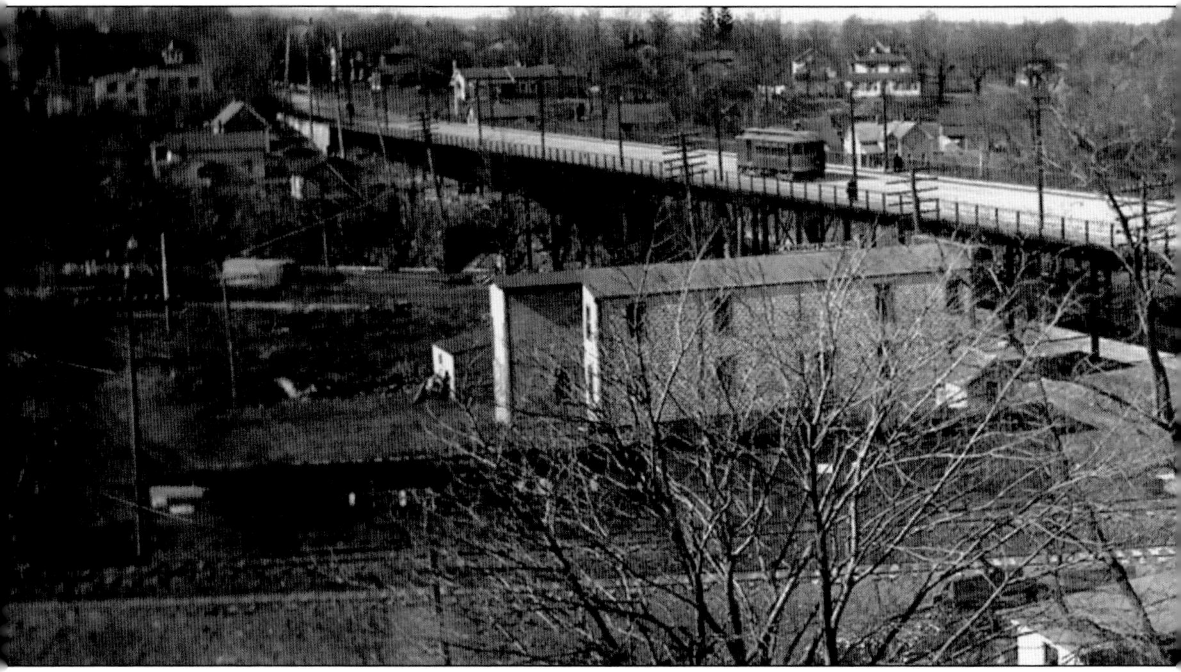

The B&LE (Buffalo and Lake Erie) Traction Company trolleys began uninterrupted travel between Buffalo and Erie in 1909, when this new viaduct over Chautauqua Creek was completed. Previously, eastbound trolleys stopped abruptly at the edge of the old iron bridge, forcing passengers to exit and walk across. When the first trolley finally crossed the Main Street Bridge on New Year's Day,

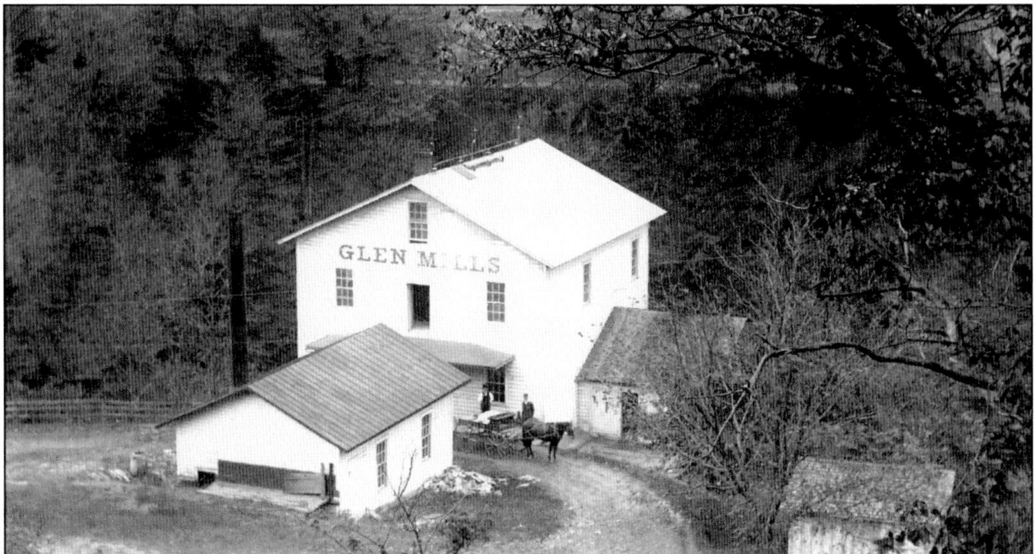

Glen Mills, located near the abutment of the Glen Mills Bridge and Falls, was a carding and cloth mill. Before it burned in 1895, it was converted into a gristmill. Two of several industries located in the same vicinity were the Westfield Paper Company, from which the first "news" paper in western New York was produced, and the Townsend Manufacturing Company that produced locks. (Chautauqua County Historical Society.)

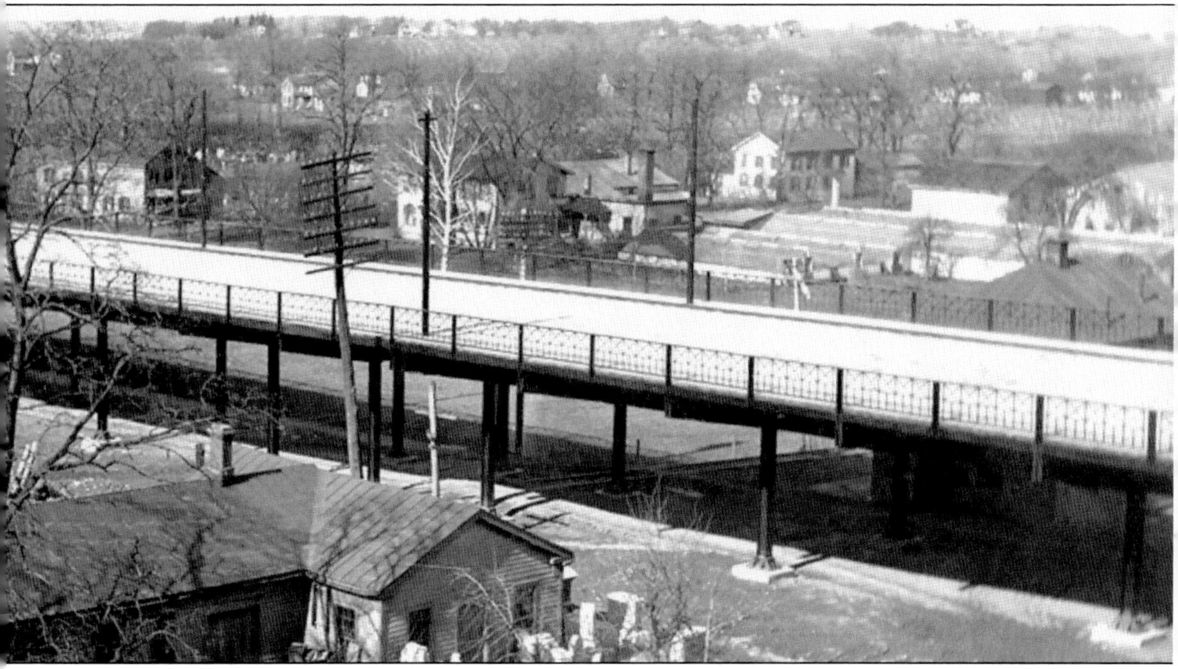

the *Westfield Republican* reported Westfield had "the Lake Shore, the Nickel Plate and Jamestown, Chautauqua & Lake Erie railroads, with trolley lines east, west, and south." In the lower right, note the Nixon Brothers Marble and Stone Works, the oldest mercantile building in the village, which the Landmark Society is currently trying to preserve. (Jack E. Ericson.)

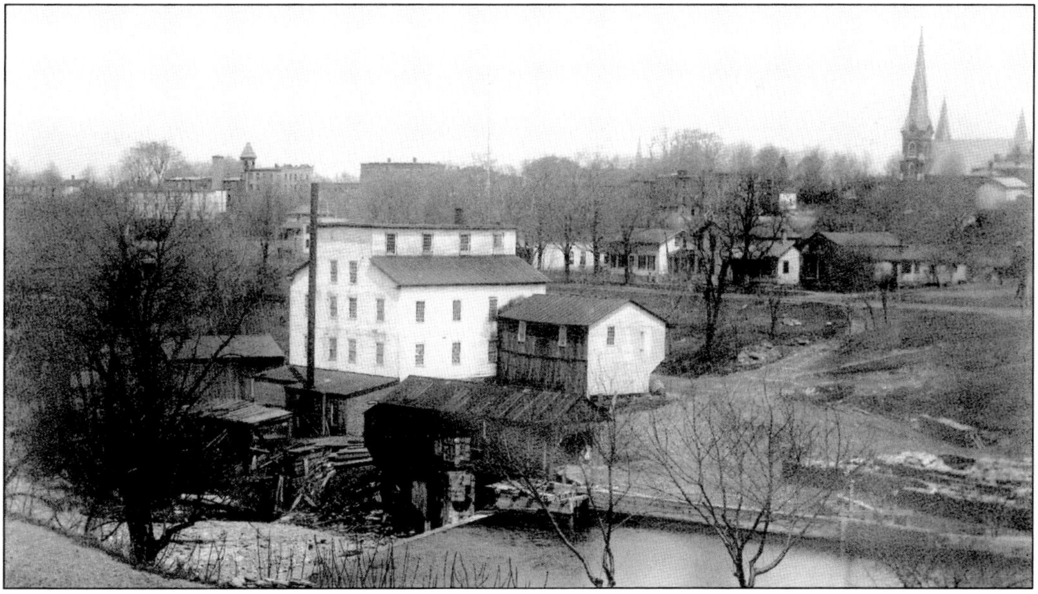

Since waterpower provided the energy for mills, James McMahan built the first gristmill around 1804 at the mouth of Chautauqua Creek, near the terminus of the Old French Road. In 1831, James McClurg partnered with Judge Thomas B. Campbell and George Hall to build the Westfield Flour and Gristmill on the same site. According to McClurg's obituary, "business was his ruling ambition . . . he availed himself of remunerative enterprises." (The Gollnitz family.)

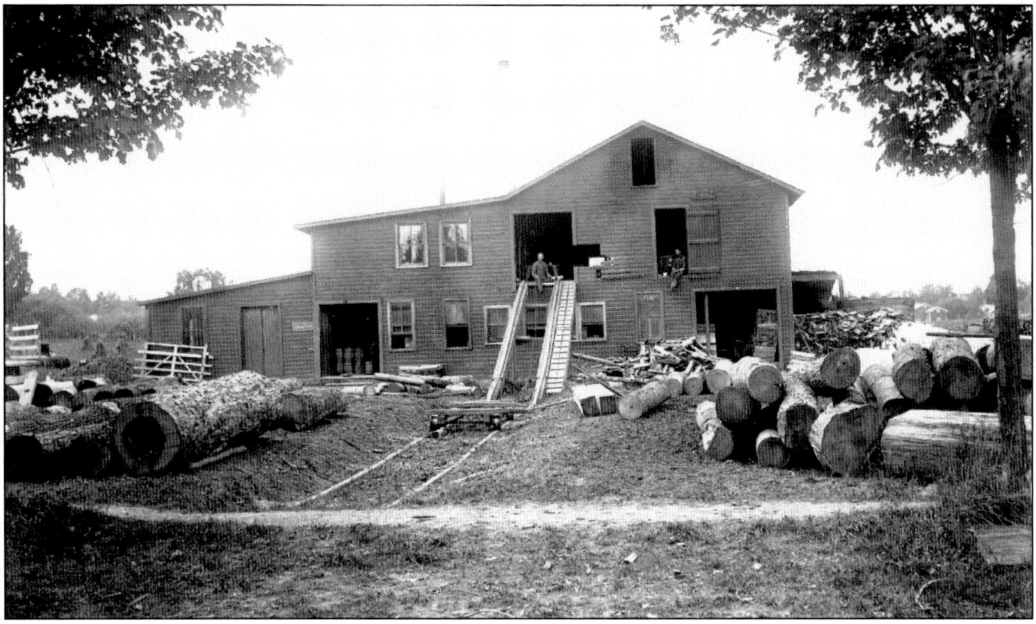

The settlers prospered with the growth of timbering, which, in addition to grape growing and farming, became one of Westfield's major industries. Dexter N. Morse's Spring Street sawmill, around 1900, which manufactured sashes, doors, and window frames, was one of many small factories owned and operated by enterprising individuals. Another was Laurence Wolfe's Cooper Shop, which made flour and apple barrels on West Main Street. (Anne Roggenbaum.)

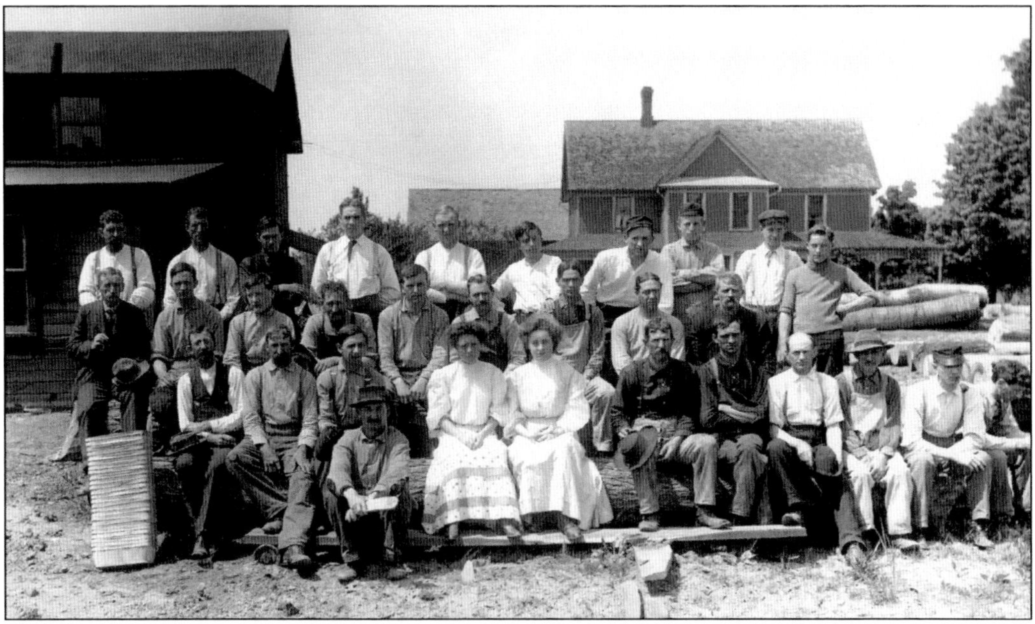

By the mid-1860s, Westfield became self-sufficient and employed settlers in a variety of businesses. They worked in general stores, taverns, paper mills, asheries, tanneries, and breweries and as blacksmiths, coopers, and potters. The first mower and reaper combination in the state was also manufactured here. Dexter Morse is seated in the front row beside the stack of baskets made in his factory in 1909 by these employees. (Anne Roggenbaum.)

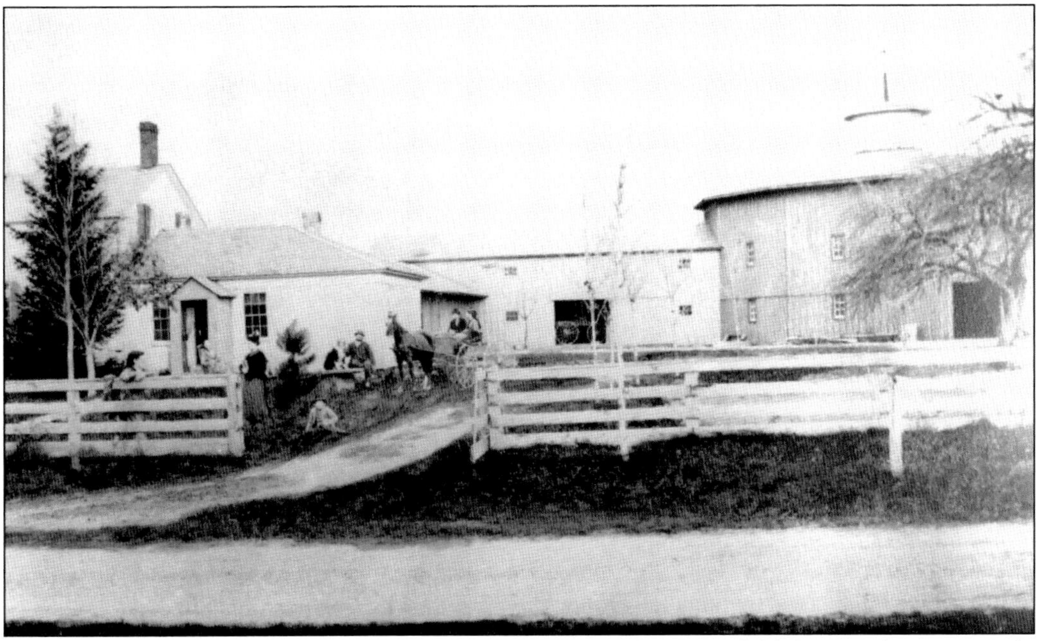

Harry A. Blowers, a nursery owner, and his family moved to Westfield from Cuba, New York, around 1860. This photograph of their property, Homedale, was taken around 1874. Located on Route 20, it was easily recognized by its 12-sided barn that housed surreys and stored hay. (Chautauqua County Historical Society.)

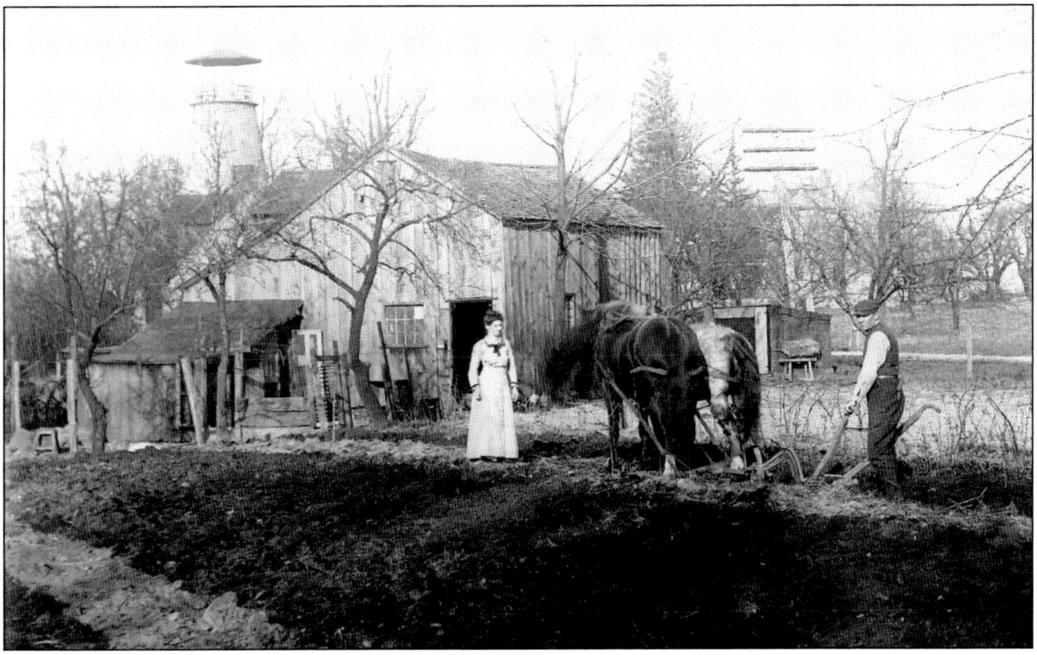

Ed Gottschalk and Gladys Miller Gottschalk owned this farm at the corner of Route 5 and Portage Street in Barcelona around 1912, which, in the 1950s, was replaced by Deo Whitwood's Red and White grocery store. His restaurant and bowling alley were popular local hangouts. Whitwood's daughter, Judy Hess, has been a lifelong resident of Barcelona.

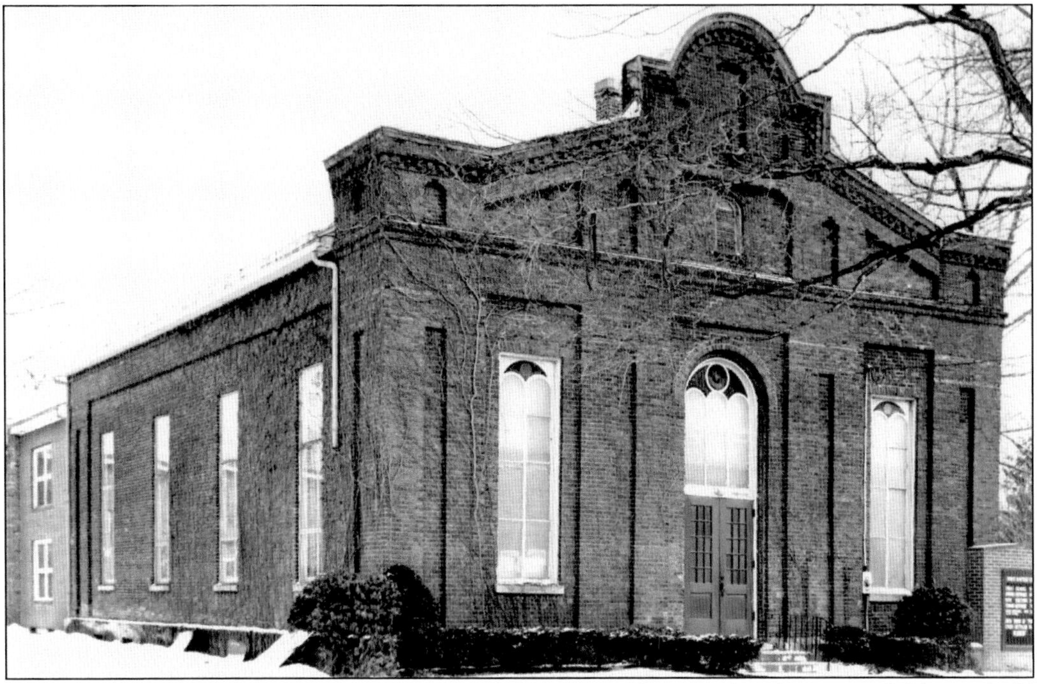

Founded around 1858, the first meetings of the German Lutheran Church in Westfield were held in private homes and in the schoolhouse on Union Street. Relocated to Chestnut Street, services, as one might expect, were conducted in German. Although the congregation disbanded, there are seven other Protestant churches in the village. (Chautauqua County Historical Society.)

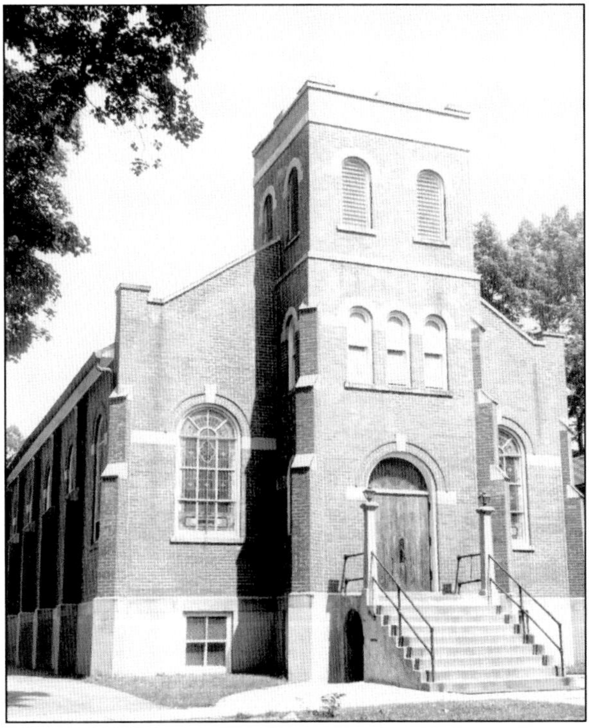

Rev. John Timon, the first bishop of the Buffalo Diocese, organized the Roman Catholic churches in Chautauqua County. In 1858, Rev. Peter Colgan dedicated the Westfield parish church to St. James Major. Until 1872, St. James Major Catholic Church was overseen by the Passionate Fathers of Dunkirk, who also served Italian, Irish, German, and Polish churches in Brocton, Ripley, French Creek, Sherman, and Mayville.

Although no building existed until 1830, itinerant preacher Lorenzo Dow helped found the Methodist church, the second one organized in Westfield. The present church was dedicated in 1872 and had designated doors and sections, segregating male and female parishioners. Through the generosity of Dr. Charles E. Welch, its handsome but unstable steeple was removed in 1908 and replaced by the two Gothic towers seen here.

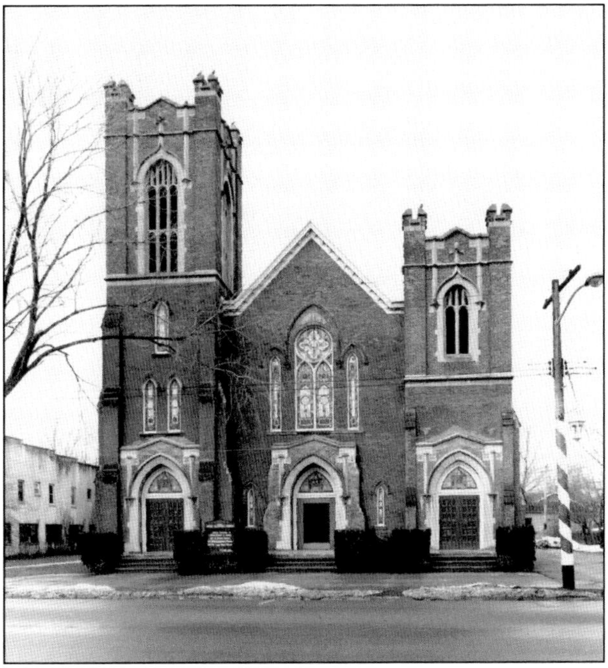

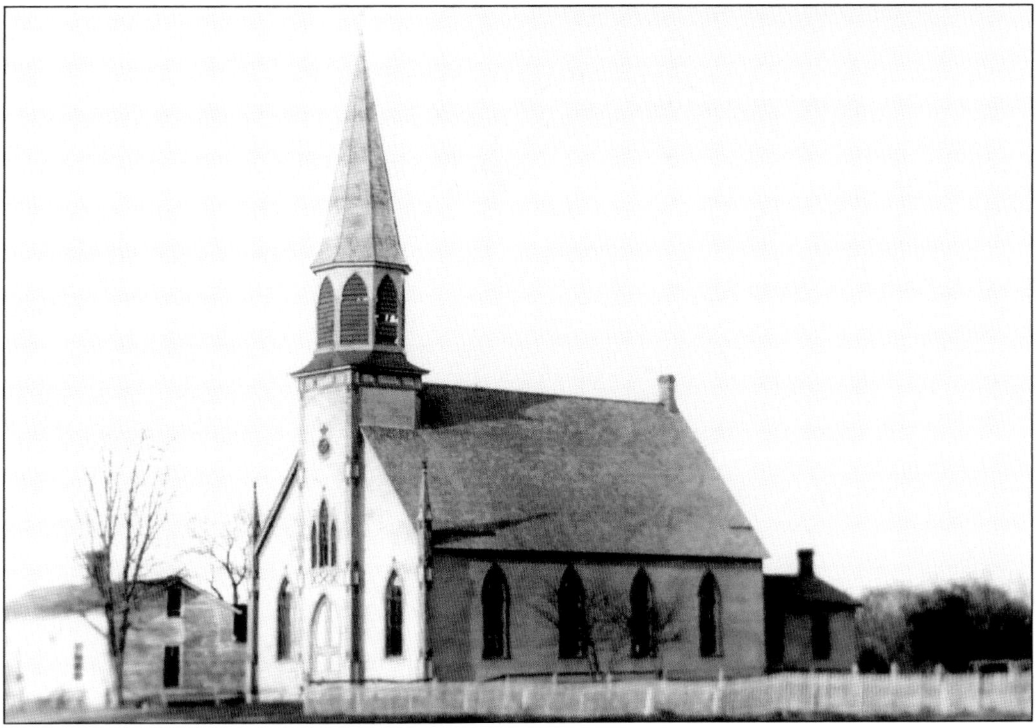

The First Baptist Church of Westfield, sister church of the Portland Baptist Church, was built in 1853. Located on the corner of Union and Kent Streets, it celebrated its 180th anniversary in 2003. The congregation supports missionaries in Spain, Costa Rica, and Romania. One of Westfield's greatest Civil War heroes, Col. Jeremiah Clinton Drake, a member of the 49th New York Infantry, was once its pastor.

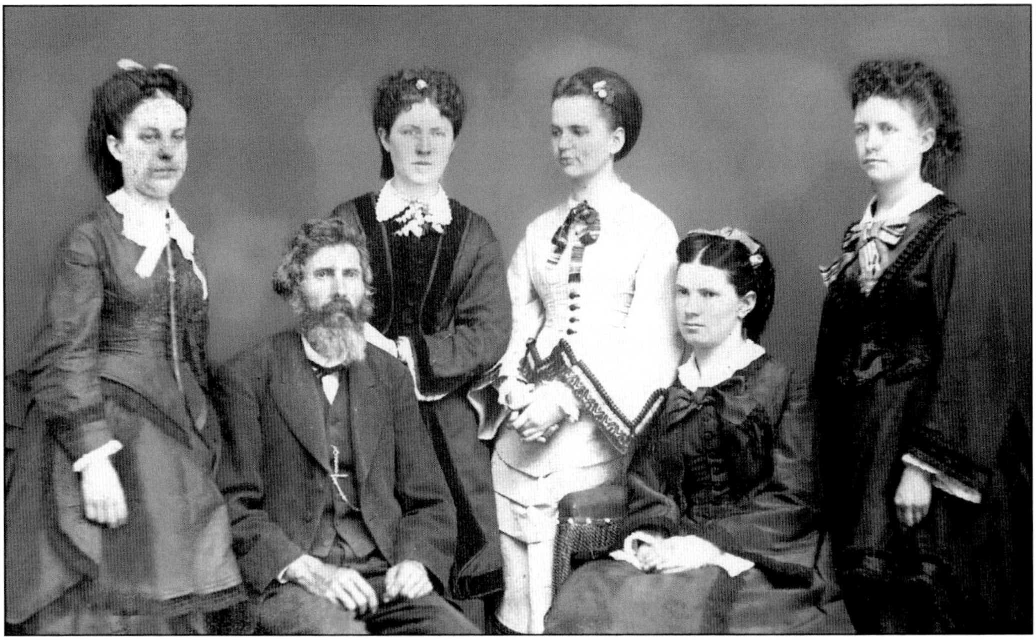

Five females constituted the class of 1872, the second graduating class from Westfield Academy. Prof. John Fosdick, a former Buffalo educator, was the principal of the Westfield Union School and Academy for nine years. He was reputed to be a stern disciplinarian, but, upon his retirement in 1878, former pupils presented him with a gold-headed ebony cane as a token of their esteem.

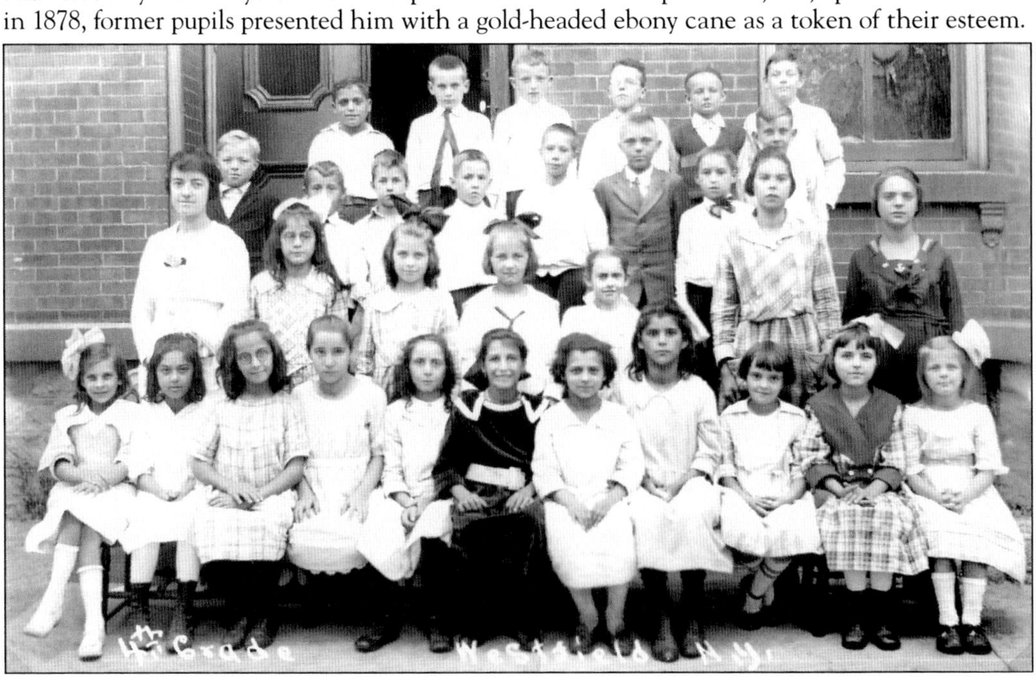

Frances Anderson, third from the left in the second row, a student in Emma Post's fourth-grade class in 1920–1921, taught in the Westfield district, as did Lovina Saigeon. During the early 1940s, Saigeon's class included approximately 16 students in eight different grades in a one-room schoolhouse. Despite her $760 salary and responsibilities of sweeping, chopping wood, cleaning windows, and starting fires, she remembers those years as the "loveliest of my life." (John Paul Wolfe.)

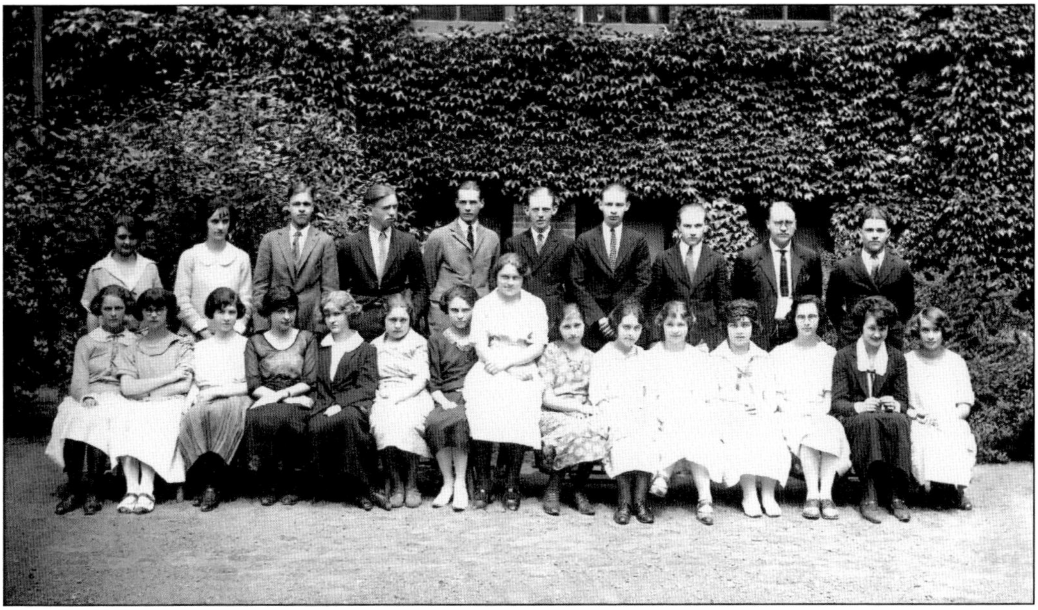

Located near today's post office, Westfield Academy was chartered in 1837 as a private institution for advanced students from western New York, Pennsylvania, and Ohio. Tuition varied according to grade level. In 1868, Westfield Union Free School District was formed. Ford Cadwell (top, far right) and classmates pose in 1920 before the high school where they received "hardy study and strict discipline spiced with a little fun and mischief." (Jane Currie.)

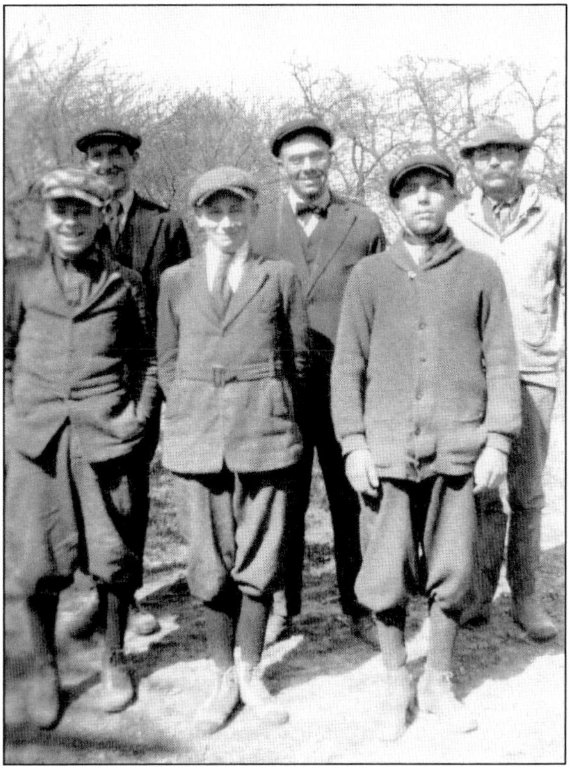

James McMahan taught school in his home in 1902. Throughout the years, district buildings were erected and consolidated, and curricula were expanded to better meet students' needs. Not surprisingly, an agriculture department was organized in 1915, as was the academy's chapter of Future Farmers of America. Ford Cadwell, coauthor Jane Currie's father, posing with members of his ag class on a field trip, became a legendary cheese maker. (Jane Currie.)

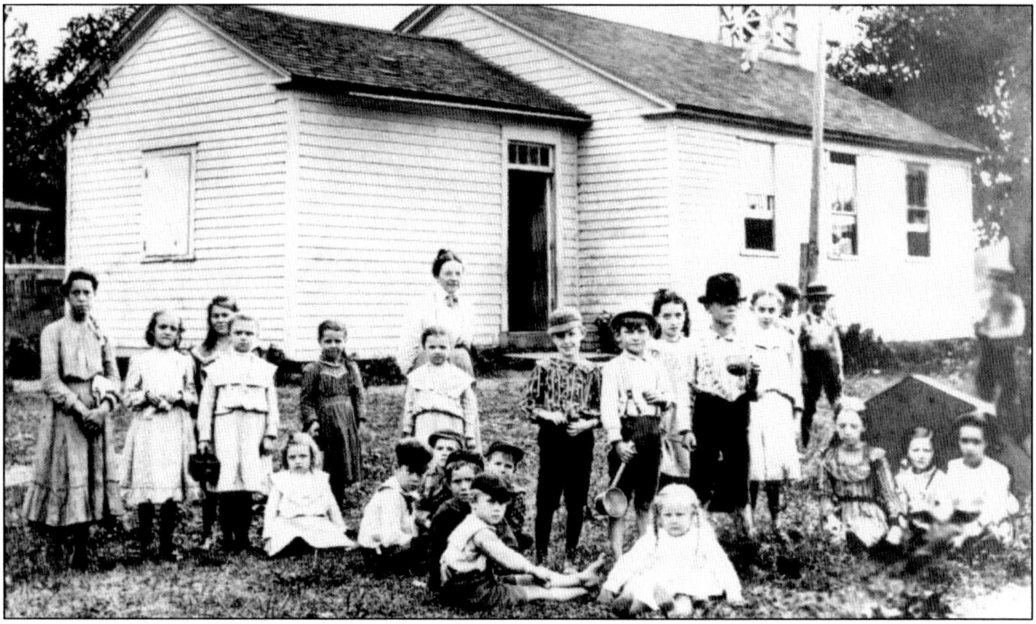

After the first one-room Westfield District No. 9 schoolhouse in Barcelona burned, elementary grades moved to this building. All students transferred "uptown" to Westfield Academy for their secondary years. Around 1855, outreach Sunday school programs were conducted in rural districts. For years, newspaper editor Hugh Willie Thompson walked from the village down to Barcelona each week to teach Sunday school. (Barcelona Commercial Fishermen's Museum.)

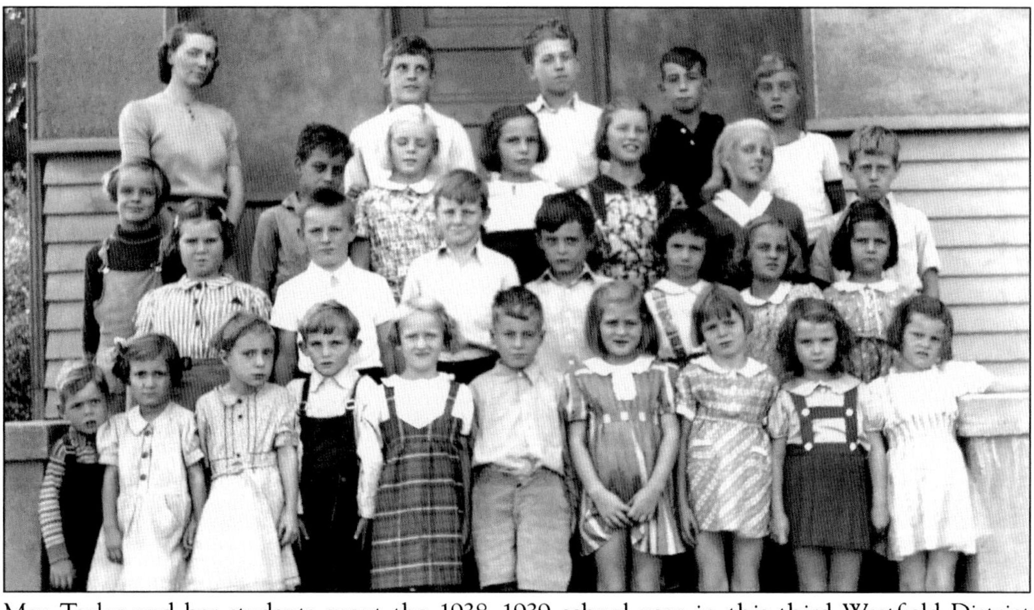

May Taylor and her students spent the 1938–1939 school year in this third Westfield District No. 9 schoolhouse on Sixth Street, now the Barcelona Commercial Fishermen's Museum. The museum's impressive collection includes class photographs, desks, yearbooks, fishing memorabilia, and Lake Erie artifacts. By taking the initiative to preserve, maintain, and share a valuable piece of Chautauqua County's history, collections manager Judy Hess has single-handedly performed a great service to her community and to posterity. (Barcelona Commercial Fishermen's Museum.)

Three

Barcelona

By the late 17th century, as mentioned, the Native Americans and the French had discovered the importance of Barcelona's location on Lake Erie. With the opening of the Erie Canal in 1825, the harbors of New York City, Buffalo, Erie, Cleveland, Detroit, and Toronto became connected. Gov. DeWitt Clinton's "ditch" opened up western New York's wilderness and fostered freight and passenger travel on the Great Lakes. Steamers en route from Buffalo, "the Queen City of the Lake," to Cleveland stopped at Portland Harbor's wharf; among these vessels were the *Walk-in-the-Water*, *Diamond*, *William Peacock*, *Waterloo*, and *Fashion*, a luxury passenger ship that made one trip one-way daily between the two ports. Stagecoaches would meet the arriving side-wheelers and deliver passengers to almost any part of Chautauqua County the same day as they left Buffalo.

On October 24, 1827, Portland Harbor opened its first post office and was designated an official U.S. government port of entry. It became a hub of activity for passengers and cargo such as furs, hides, lumber, and black salt ashes en route from Canada to Pittsburgh. Seeing "a line of farmers' wagons one fourth of a mile long, each waiting his turn to discharge his load at the docks" was commonplace. When Portland Harbor was renamed Barcelona in 1836, it was a self-sustaining community; the settlers operated their own hotels, taverns, blacksmith shops, tanneries, brickyards, gristmills, and sawmills.

Many people thought Barcelona might become a major port on Lake Erie. Obed Edson had high expectations for Barcelona's prosperity because of "its absence of competing harbors." In reality, however, the larger natural harbors of Buffalo and Erie proved him wrong. Researcher Virginia Richardson discovered "for a time [Barcelona's] future was extremely promising . . . more business was carried on there at the harbor than Westfield proper could boast."

However, that prophecy dissipated when the Buffalo and State Line Railroad was built along the Lake Erie shore. Competition from the railroad undermined the importance of Barcelona's shipping. Its status as a commercial port was irreparably changed when logs, grains, building materials, and other goods were transported by rail rather than by ship. Because of the harbor's demise, many residents felt compelled to move uptown to the village of Westfield, a more "profitable setting" and also "a sad time for Barcelona."

The fishing industry also declined dramatically for a variety of reasons. In 1985, the New York State legislature banned the use of gill nets. It also mandated fishing nets be placed in at least 55 feet of water, which meant a mile or more off Barcelona due to its lack of a natural harbor. Sadly, many fishermen were forced to uproot from Barcelona to move nearer the deeper waters off Pennsylvania and Ohio. Another cause of the industry's decline was pollution from chemicals dumped into Lake Erie by American and Canadian factories.

In 1954, the Barcelona fishing industry consisted of 100 men and 18 licensed boats with a combined catch valued at $250,000. In 1965, 145,000 pounds of fish were caught, but that dwindled to 29,000 pounds only a decade later. Like his competitors, John Monroe bemoaned the fact that "we don't catch as much fish in a year that we used to catch sometimes in one day."

Most people can only imagine the Barcelona of old, yet tales continue to be swapped by some fishermen's widows, relatives, and friends. Now enjoyed as a summer resort by tourists, boaters, and sport fishermen, only the native and extended families know Barcelona's true magic.

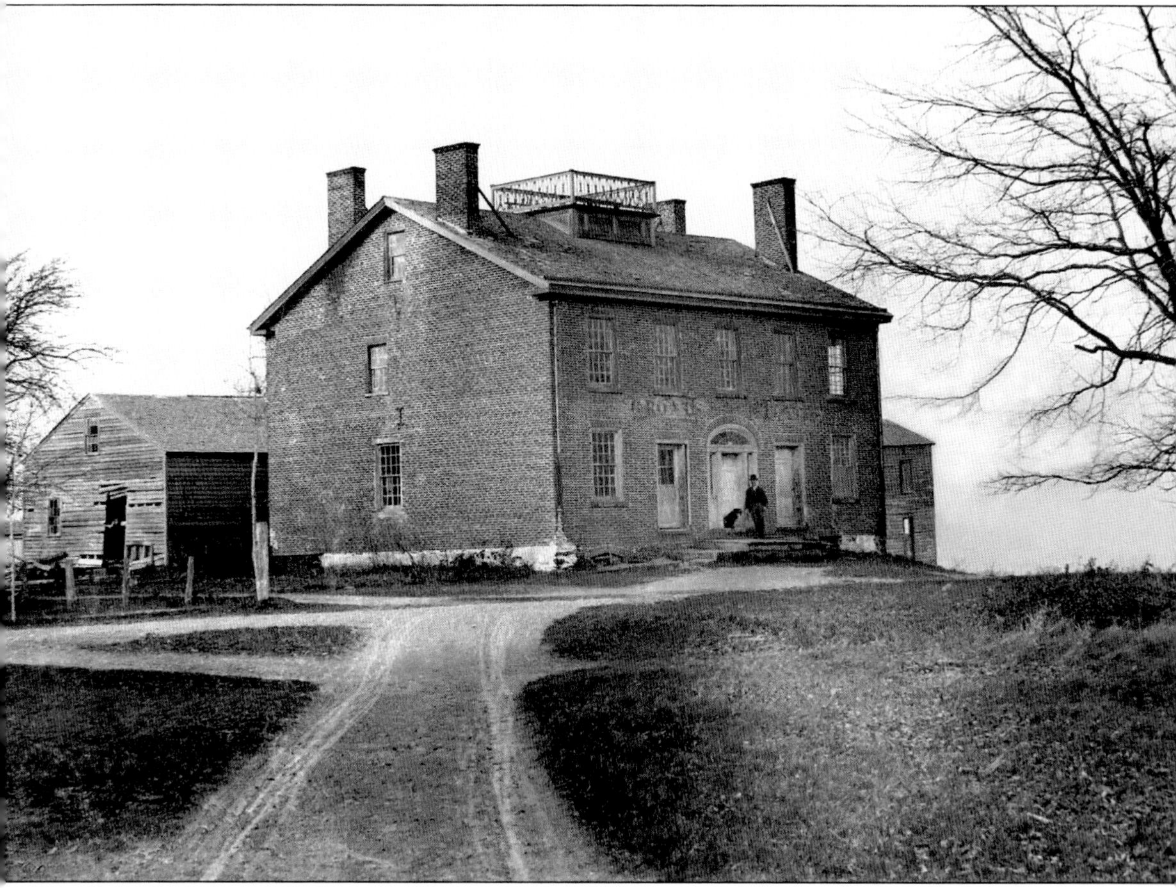

Wives prayed for the safe return of their fishermen husbands while pacing Barcelona Inn's widow's walk, overlooking Lake Erie. Built in 1827, the two-story brick hostelry, known also as Walker Inn and Groat's Inn, was in continuous operation until it was destroyed by fire in 1964. (Sydney S. Baker.)

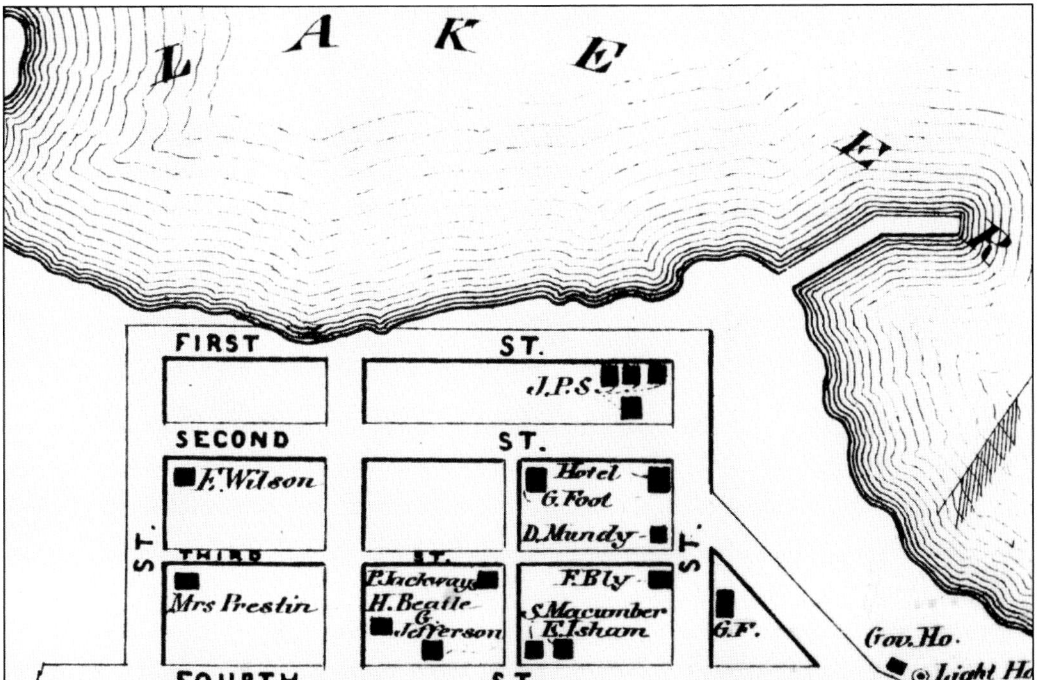

Around 1820, Joseph Ellicott of the Holland Land Company laid out the village of Portland Harbor in one-acre city lots. When Barcelona was expected to become a major commercial port, an investment group developed the properties. Among the early landowners were Hoel Beadle and Philimin Jackway. Other surnames synonymous with the heydays of the fishing industry include Gottschalk, Minnegar, Holbrook, Oakes, Grant, Lant, Walker, Monroe, Alford, Spicer, Burdick, Macomber, Perdue, McLean, and Waterman. Shared experiences resulted in a cohesive community where men and women relied upon one another, and lifelong friendships began. Today about 70 families, some descendants of the early fisherfolk listed on this 1867 map, are year-round residents. (Cristie Herbst.)

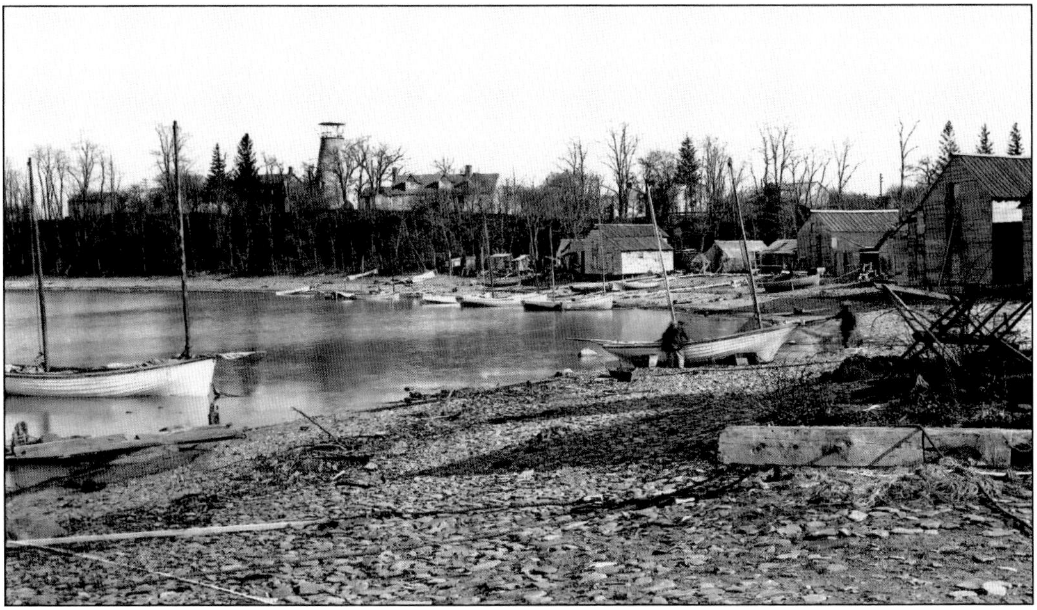

Historian Billie Dibble considers the late 1800s and the early 1900s "colorful periods in [Barcelona's] history . . . when the fishing industry was at its peak." Although this particular scene lacks activity, by 1836, when renamed from Portland Harbor, Barcelona was a vibrant port. Activities centered around the shipping docks and warehouses built by Gervis Foote, Samuel McWhorter, and David Eason.

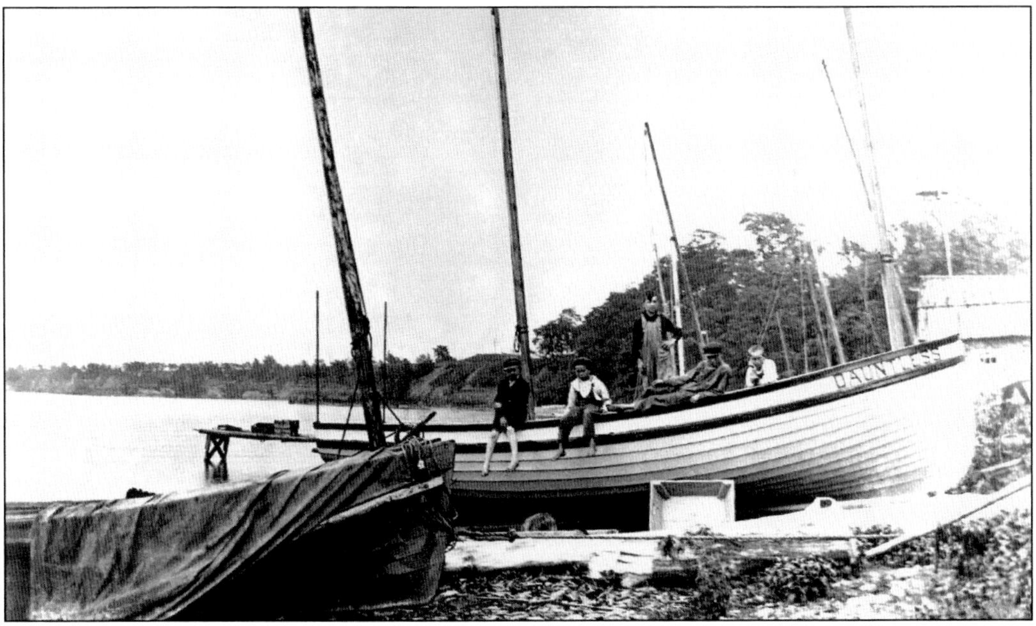

In 1900, William Jackway bought the *Black Boat*, the first sailing vessel in the area. These Tom Sawyer-looking boys are perched on the deck of the *Dauntless*, presumably owned by John Minnegar, who saw his first boat engines on exhibition at the 1901 Pan American Exposition in Buffalo. Naturally, steam-powered boats were able to reach port far faster than the old tugs and wooden boats. (Barcelona Commercial Fishermen's Museum.)

The Jackways, "a sturdy and prosperous clan," were among the earliest commercial fishermen in Barcelona. In the early 1800s, Philimin Jackway established a fish oil rendering business. At age 10, when whitefish, herring, blue pike, yellow perch, white bass, and sturgeon were in abundance, Philimin's grandson, William H. Jackway, pictured here, joined his father John's crew aboard the *Bessie Turner* and later owned his own fleet. (Martha Jackway Herbst.)

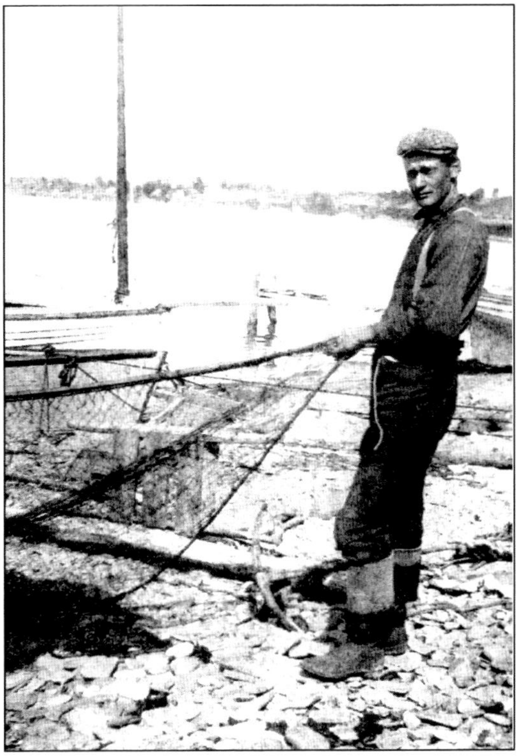

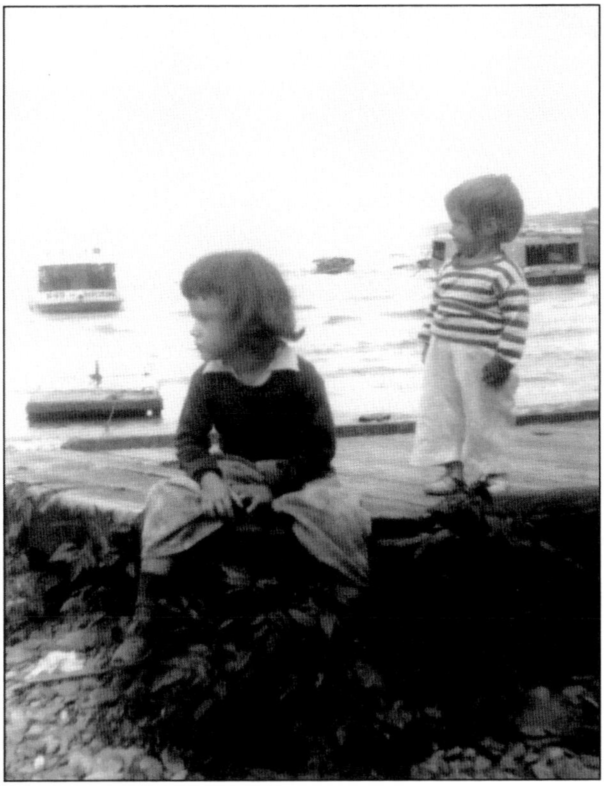

Like their neighbors who lived down the beach from the harbor, two of William's great-grandchildren, Diane Herbst Fadale (left) and her sister Cristie Herbst (right) loved being at the shore. Generations of Jackways and other Barcelona families could readily identify with William, who candidly admitted: "When I talk it seems only of fishing and Lake Erie. Well, it's been my life, so why not?" (Martha Jackway Herbst.)

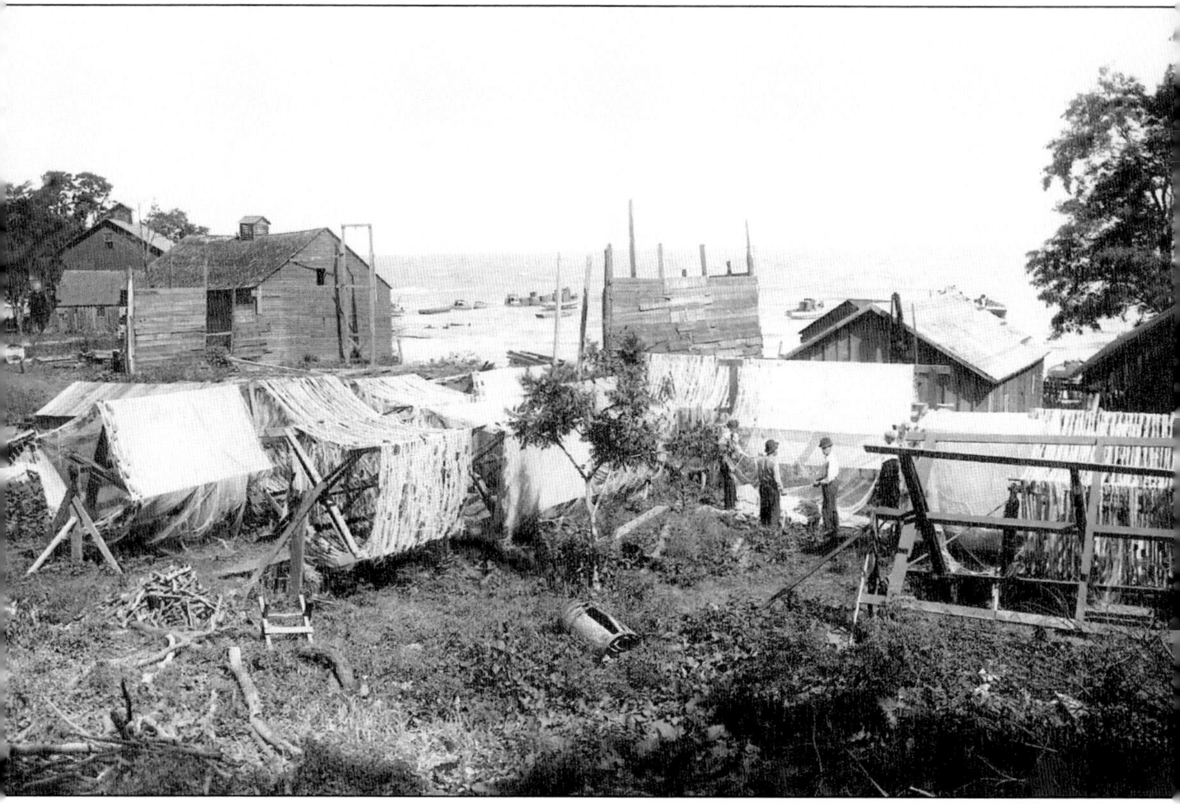

In 1857, Barcelona's residents were primarily employed in fishing, boatbuilding, and related businesses. The industrious families, whose routines seldom varied, resided in these shanties along the harbor. Fishing nets, essential to their livelihood, required constant care. The original nets were knit by hand on large hickory and oak needles, then replaced by machine-made cotton and nylon ones knit on plastic needles, which jokingly were said to "connect the holes." Daily, they were inspected, cleaned, repaired, and hung to dry as in this photograph. Knots indicated where cedar corks and leads were to be attached to help float the nets, while anchor stones were tied with string. (Sydney S. Baker.)

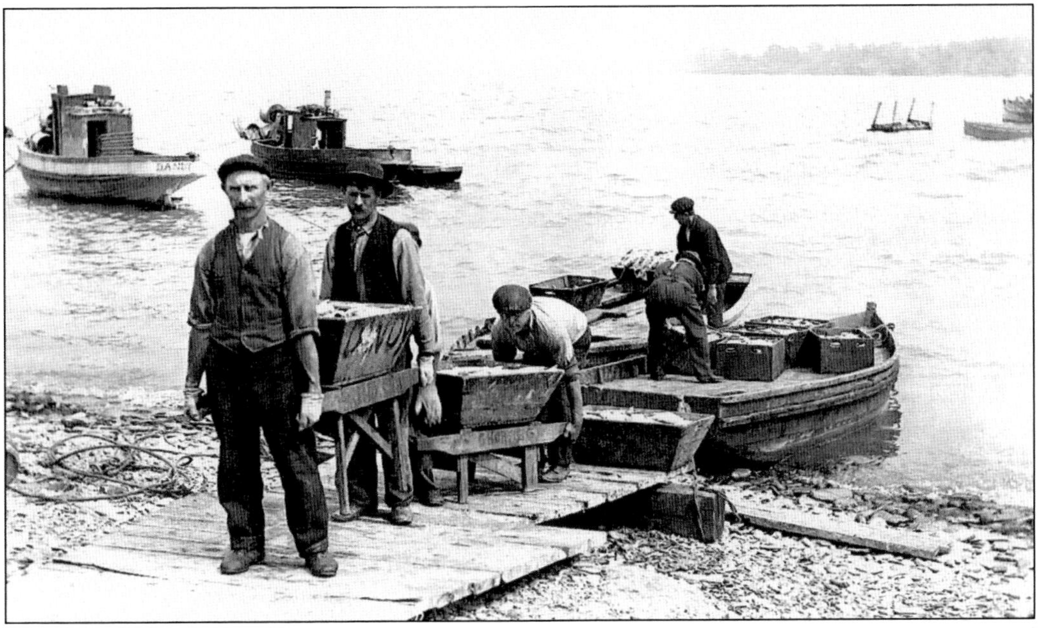

This catch might have come from the *Dandy* seen over the heads of Dick McLean, left, and Fred Oakes, right. Trucked to the fish house, the haul would then be cleaned, completely scaled, filleted, packed in boxes of ice, and delivered locally or to markets as far away as Buffalo, Cleveland, and Sandusky, Ohio. Peddlers went uptown to hawk fish from their horse-drawn carts. (Barcelona Commercial Fishermen's Museum.)

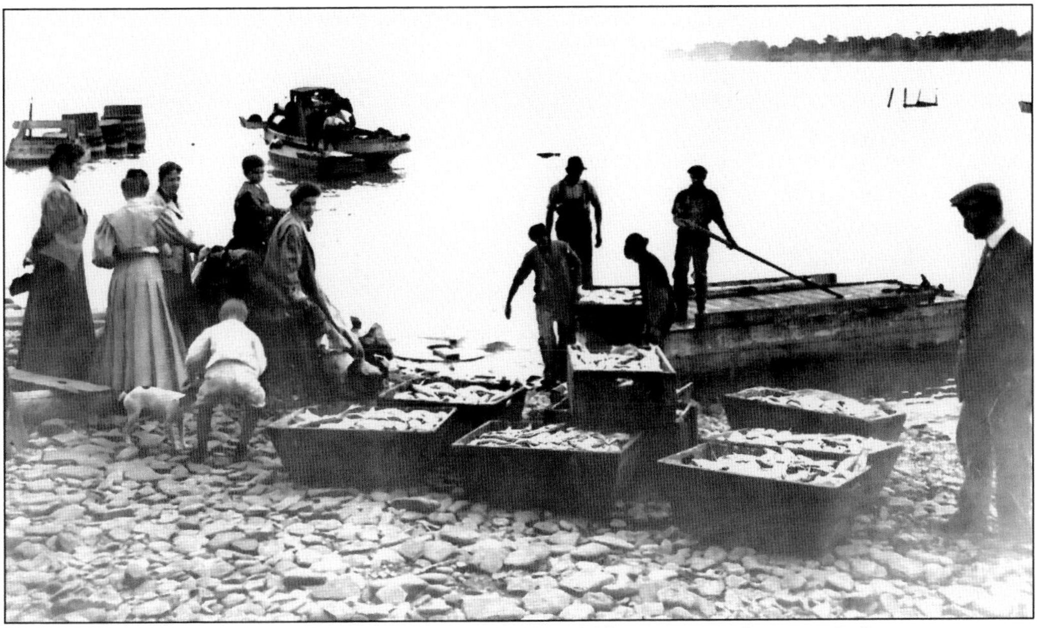

At dawn, crews headed for their moored boats in raftlike scows and proceeded to open waters to nets already set and marked by buoys. William Jackway recalled that, like other fishermen, his fleet "usually went out about 10 miles, and we never figured on being out after dark." Upon their return, women and children often helped the crew unload the fish boxes, ever grateful for fair weather.

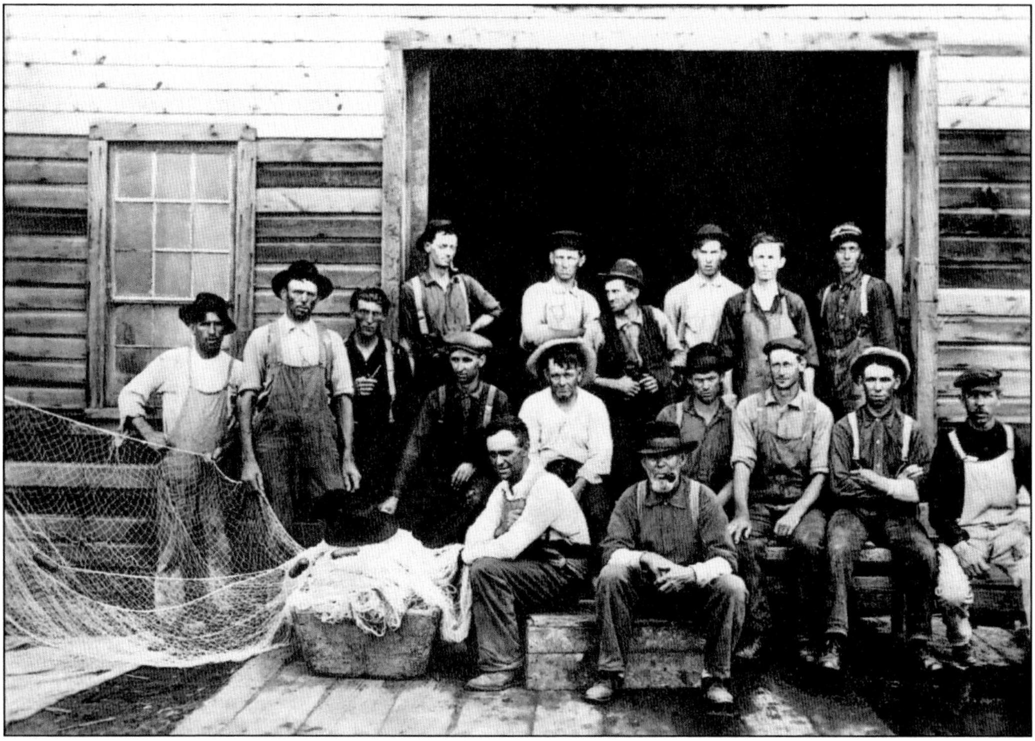

This photograph of notable Barcelona fishermen was saved for posterity. Bearded Tony Gottschalk is sitting in the front with an unidentified gentleman to his left. In the middle row, from left to right, are unidentified, Henry Kolpien, unidentified, Herm Lant, Bones Teasel, Art May, William Jackway, Bert Wakely, and Ernie Wakely; (back row) Bill Lant, unidentified, Wells Brooks, John Gottschalk, and two more unidentified men. (Barcelona Commercial Fishermen's Museum.)

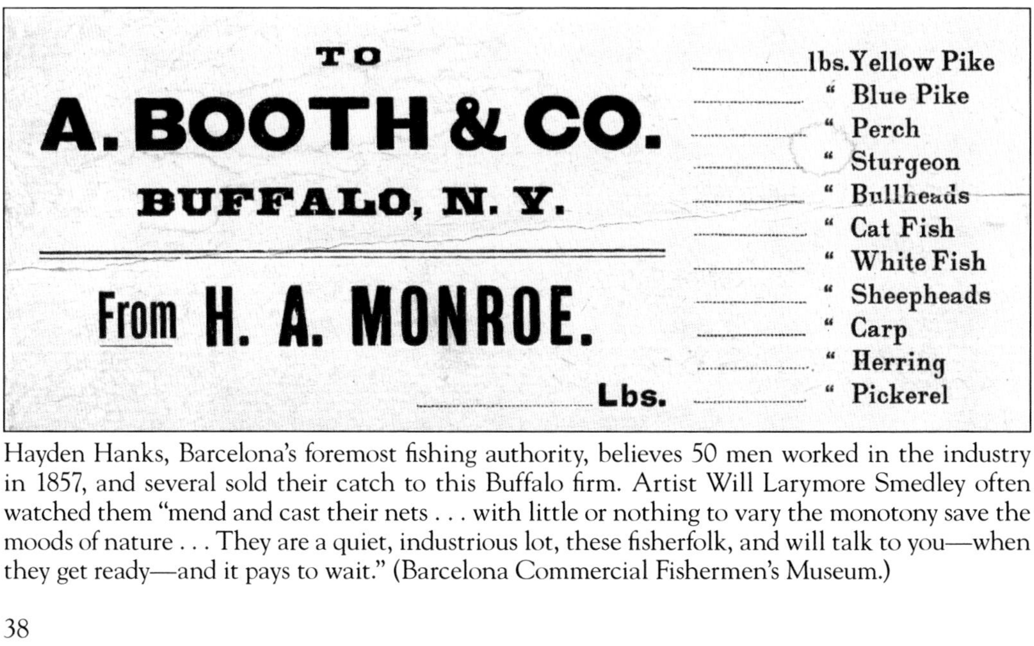

TO
A. BOOTH & CO.
BUFFALO, N. Y.
From H. A. MONROE.
__________ Lbs.

__________ lbs. Yellow Pike
__________ " Blue Pike
__________ " Perch
__________ " Sturgeon
__________ " Bullheads
__________ " Cat Fish
__________ " White Fish
__________ " Sheepheads
__________ " Carp
__________ " Herring
__________ " Pickerel

Hayden Hanks, Barcelona's foremost fishing authority, believes 50 men worked in the industry in 1857, and several sold their catch to this Buffalo firm. Artist Will Larymore Smedley often watched them "mend and cast their nets . . . with little or nothing to vary the monotony save the moods of nature . . . They are a quiet, industrious lot, these fisherfolk, and will talk to you—when they get ready—and it pays to wait." (Barcelona Commercial Fishermen's Museum.)

Judy Hess, collections manager of the Barcelona Fishermen's Museum and Schoolhouse No. 9 on Sixth Street, identified the white-bearded fisherman as Tony Gottschalk, who took "his catches to town with a tin horn in hand [to announce] he had fresh fish for sale." A widower with two children, Gottschalk married the widow Lena Lant. Daughter Edith is helping to repair this net. (Ed Schaeffer.)

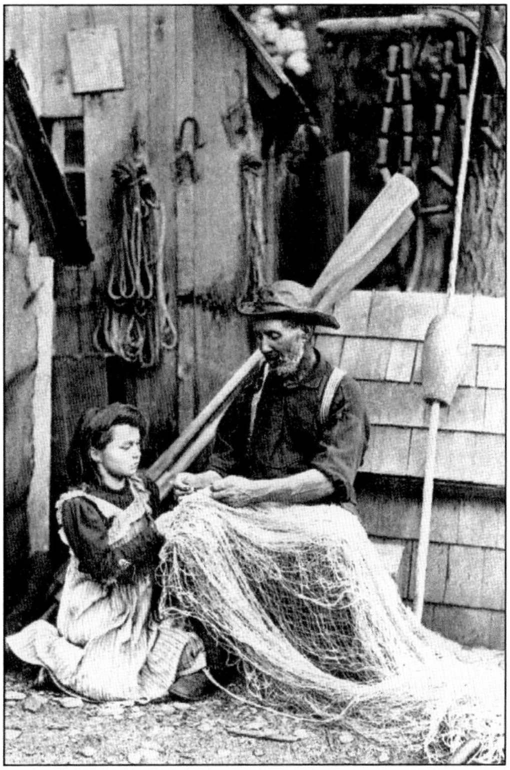

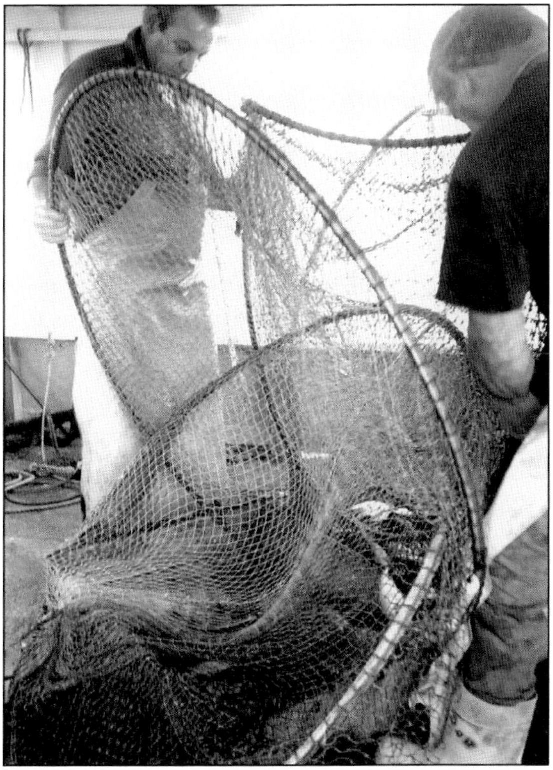

The banning of gill nets in the 1985 made fishing far less lucrative. Whitefish, caught in those nets, because of their soft mouths, were virtually off-limits. George Alford, left, and Tim Perdue are handling hoop nets designed to trap fish swimming into them. Unfortunately, the second method yielded only about one-eighth of the fish ensnared by gill nets. (Barcelona Commercial Fishermen's Museum.)

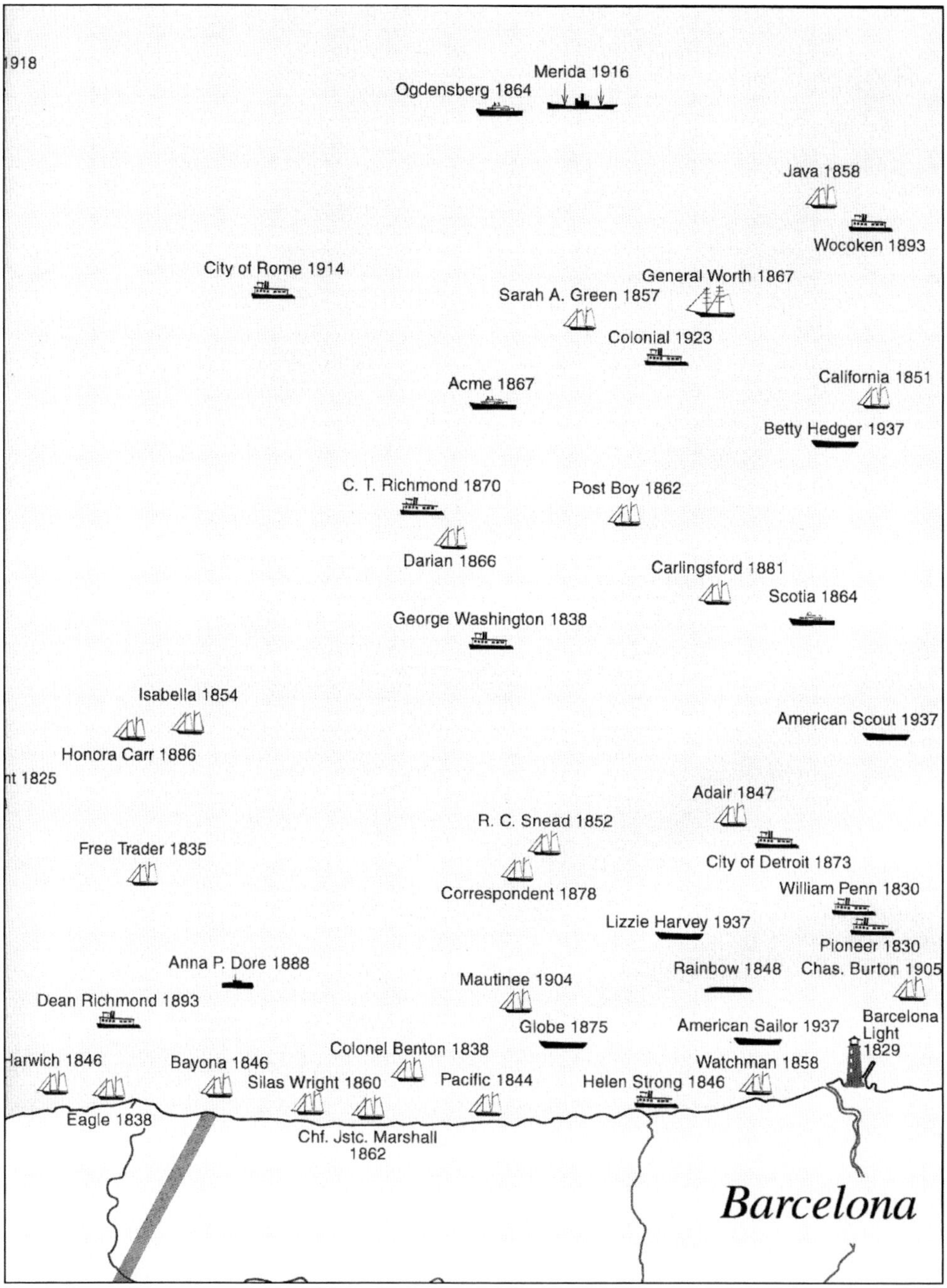

Barcelona's fishermen braved the unpredictable waters of Lake Erie in wooden boats without the luxury of modern navigational systems. A reporter once noted that experienced mariners considered the fishing industry "no job for tenderfeet . . . either on boats braving the sullenly tossing wastes of old Erie's waters, or in handling the catch—just a job to be done, and done." Other vessels sailed the same waters, with over 162 watercraft sighted off this shore in 1863 alone. Frequent and sudden lake storms engendered hundreds of shipwrecks, many indicated on this map. Incredibly, in October 2005, divers located the remains of the *George J. Whelan*, a steamboat that sank off Barcelona in 1930. ("Graveyards of the Great Lakes" map.)

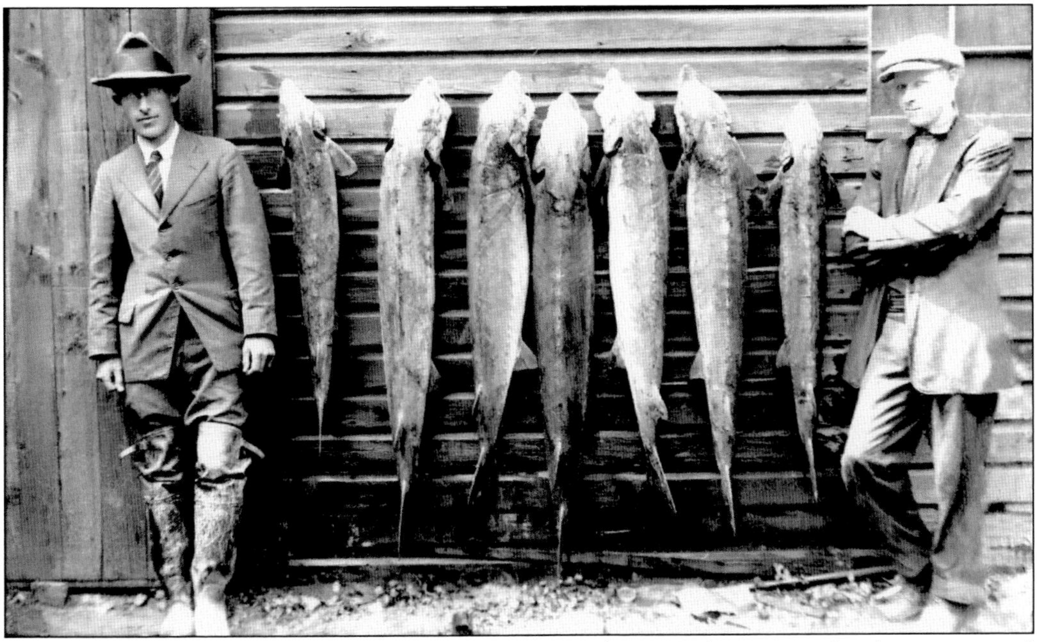

Railroads proved a boon to the commercial fishing industry. Fishermen and sailors patronized local hotels and businesses, and the Barcelona Fish Company and Lant Fish House prospered. Also, catch like this shown with Clarence Shore (left) and Pike Monroe was packed in ice, loaded onto trains, and transported with little chance of spoilage.

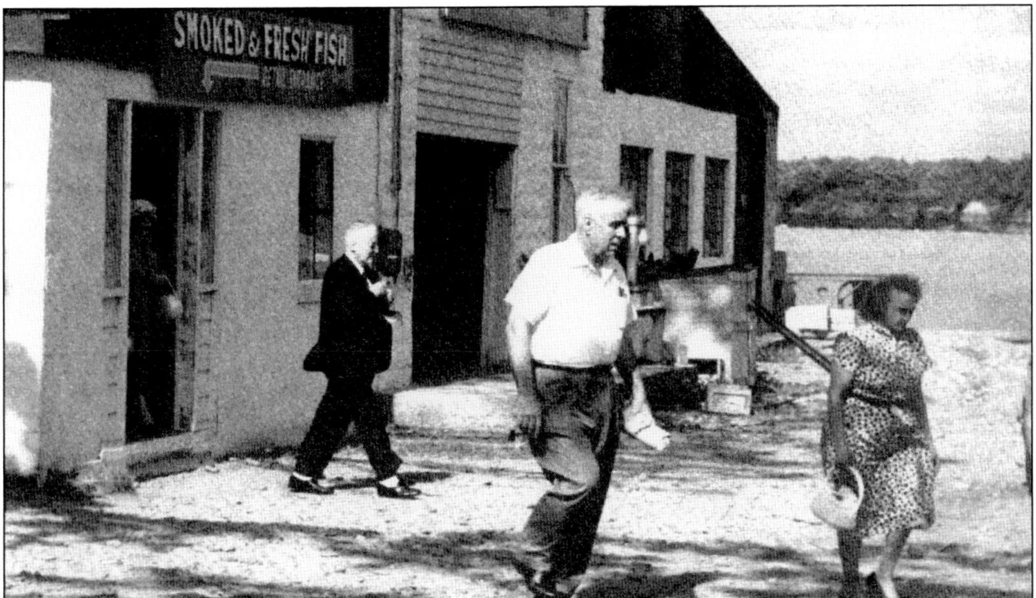

The concrete block smokehouse at Barcelona was a "must stop" for visitors like this man carrying home the well-wrapped smoked Lake Erie whitefish. A renowned delicacy, the Monroe brothers' signature ingredient was the flavoring from corncob fires. By the 1980s, however, Hank Monroe admitted "fresh fish doesn't sell nearly as well as the smoked whitefish we [import from] the inland lakes of Canada." (Dan Chapman.)

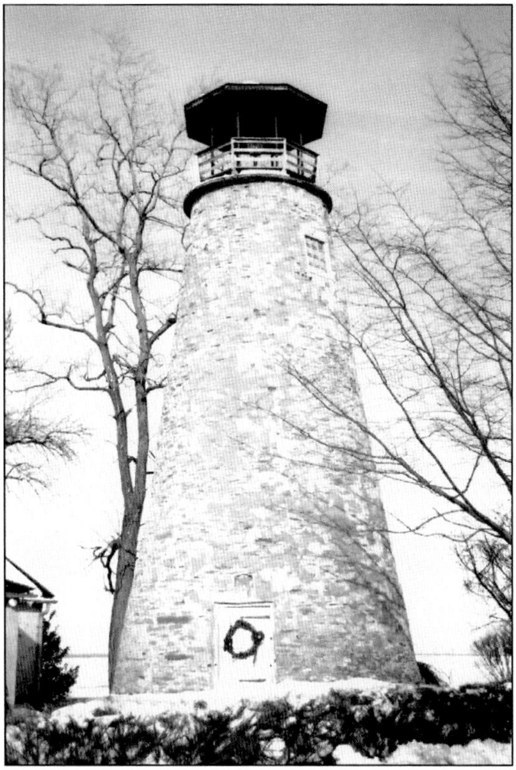

In the late 19th century, lighthouses were commonplace throughout the world. One of the oldest on the Great Lakes, the Barcelona Lighthouse, was added to the National Register of Historic Places in 1972. The 40-foot fieldstone tower's beacon was visible from Long Point, Ontario, 29 miles across Lake Erie. (Jane Currie.)

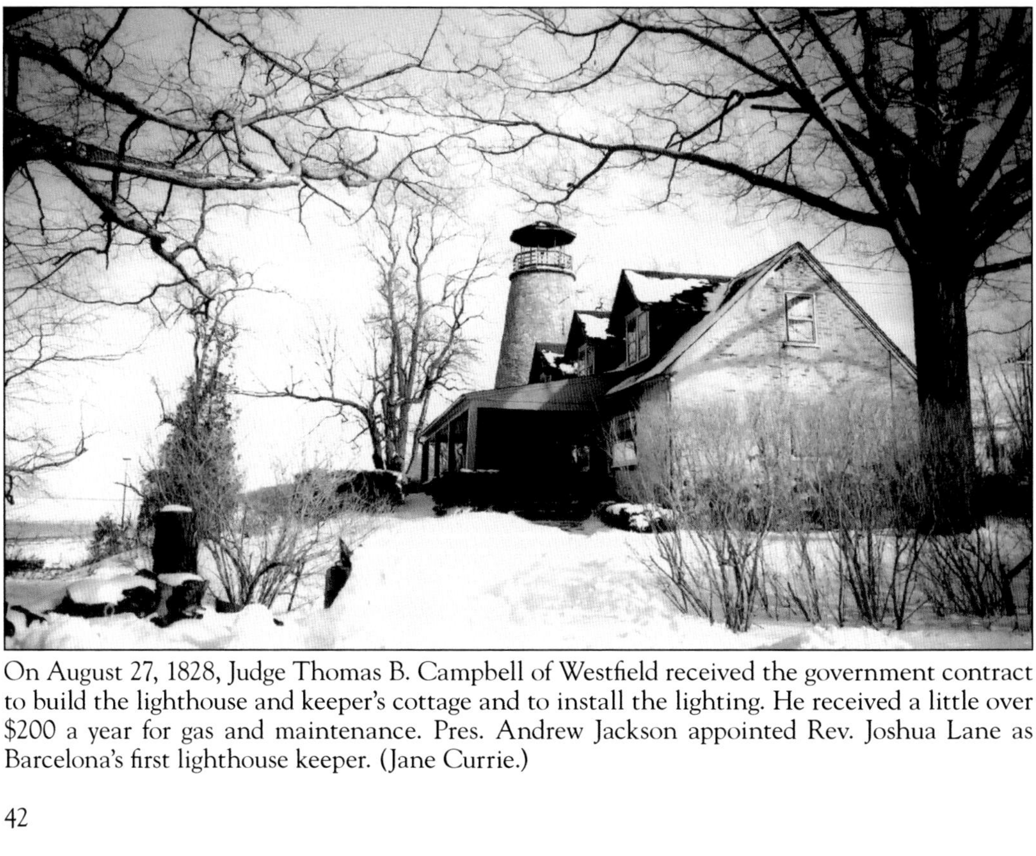

On August 27, 1828, Judge Thomas B. Campbell of Westfield received the government contract to build the lighthouse and keeper's cottage and to install the lighting. He received a little over $200 a year for gas and maintenance. Pres. Andrew Jackson appointed Rev. Joshua Lane as Barcelona's first lighthouse keeper. (Jane Currie.)

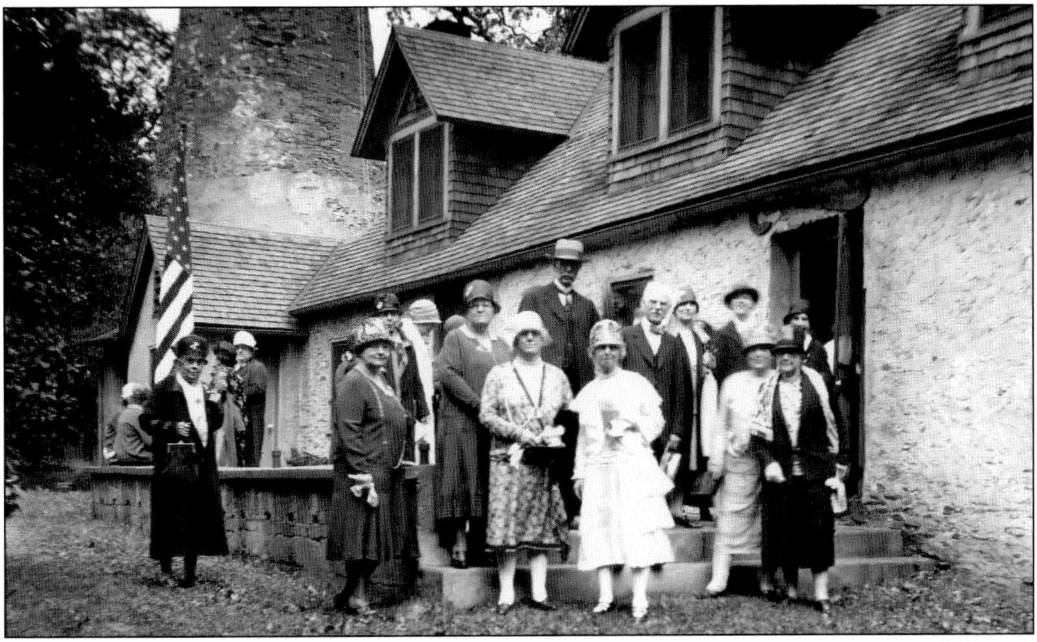

On June 14, 1929, some 200 guests celebrated the 100th anniversary of the Barcelona Lighthouse. The Daughters of the American Revolution, Patterson chapter, presented a bronze tablet to owner Catherine Patterson Crandall, whose daughters Prudence and Faith raised Old Glory to unveil it above the door. Crandall believed the tower would long stand to link the past with the present and arouse interest in history. (Chautauqua County Historical Society.)

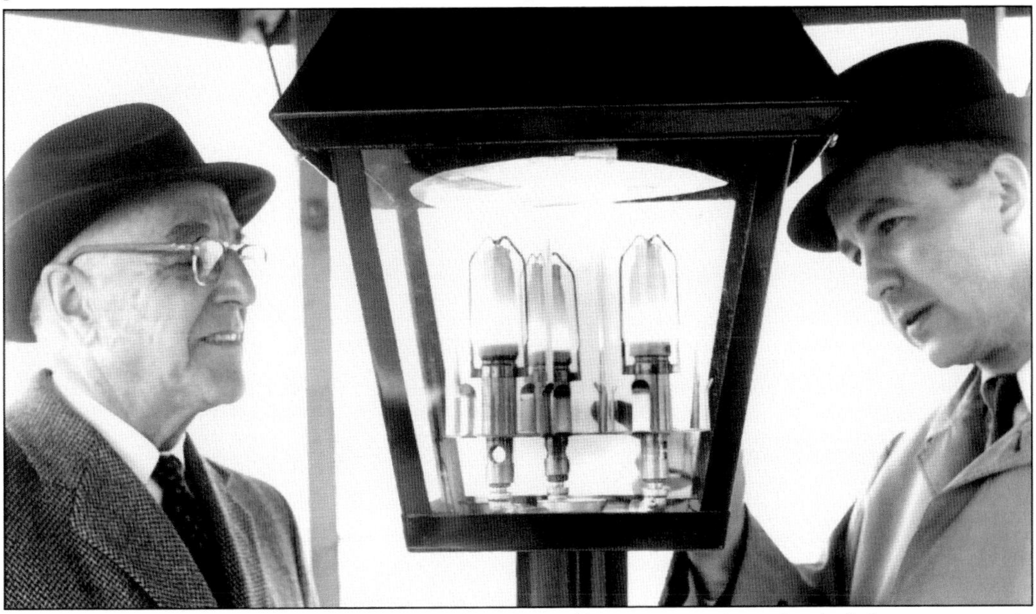

Prior to the use of natural gas, whale oil and candles were used in the lighthouse to guide mariners home. Conveyed through wooden logs or pipes from the burning springs located about a mile away, natural gas illuminated the lamp for nearly three decades. George Patterson Crandall (left) and Louis R. Rief of the Iroquois Gas Company inspect the perpetual gaslight installed in 1962.

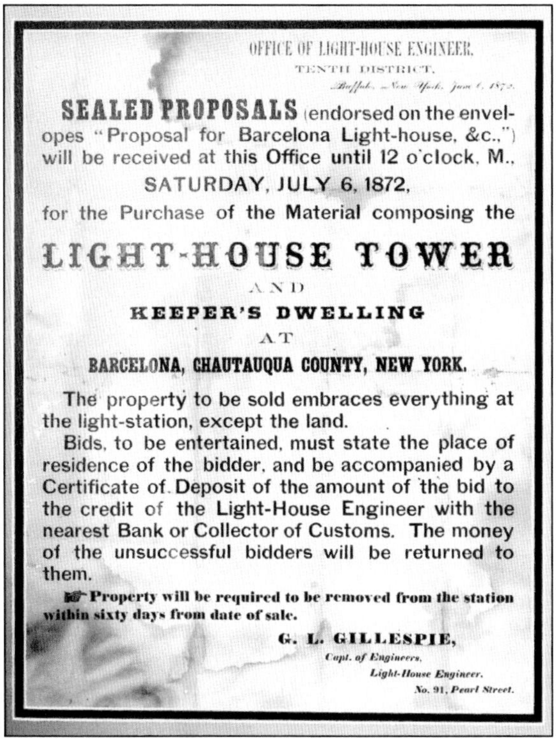

OFFICE OF LIGHT-HOUSE ENGINEER,
TENTH DISTRICT,
Buffalo, New York, June 6, 1872.

SEALED PROPOSALS (endorsed on the envelopes "Proposal for Barcelona Light-house, &c.,") will be received at this Office until 12 o'clock, M., SATURDAY, JULY 6, 1872, for the Purchase of the Material composing the

LIGHT-HOUSE TOWER
AND
KEEPER'S DWELLING
AT
BARCELONA, CHAUTAUQUA COUNTY, NEW YORK.

The property to be sold embraces everything at the light-station, except the land.

Bids, to be entertained, must state the place of residence of the bidder, and be accompanied by a Certificate of Deposit of the amount of the bid to the credit of the Light-House Engineer with the nearest Bank or Collector of Customs. The money of the unsuccessful bidders will be returned to them.

☞ **Property will be required to be removed from the station within sixty days from date of sale.**

G. L. GILLESPIE,
Capt. of Engineers,
Light-House Engineer.
No. 91, Pearl Street.

In 1872, the auctioned lighthouse property was purchased by Lt. Gov. George W. Patterson. Under family ownership ever since, Nellie B. and George Patterson Crandall converted the keeper's house into their summer residence in 1972. In 2005, the more recent owners placed the lighthouse, cottage, and garage, purchased originally for $3,400, on the eBay Web site for $999,000. (Bruce and Ann Mulkin.)

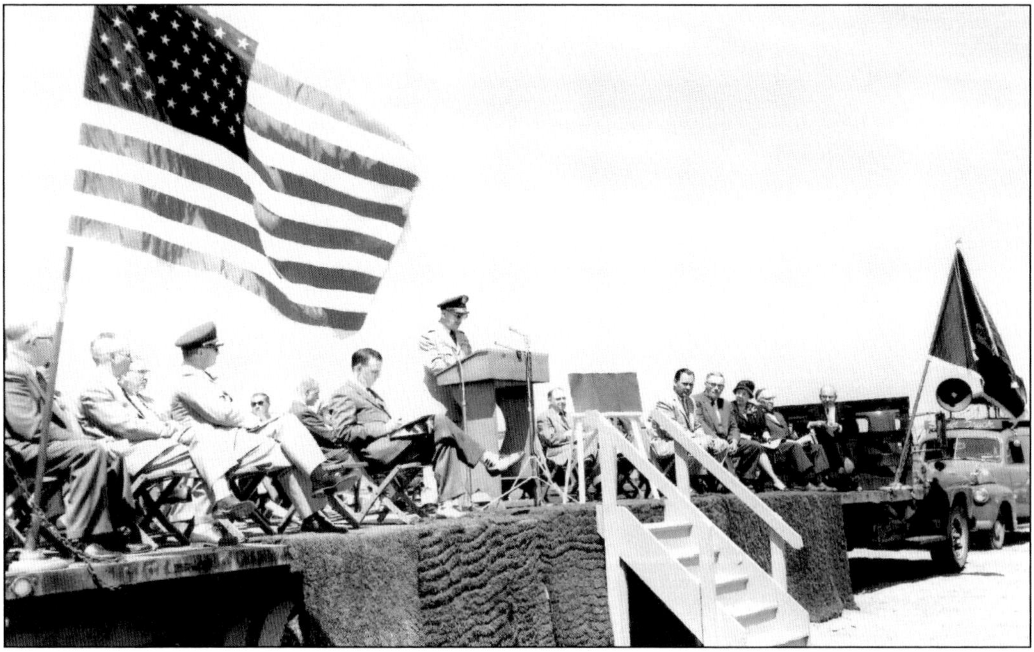

Five-year-old Anne Nixon was chosen to cut the ribbon at the dedication ceremonies for the Daniel A. Reed Memorial Pier on July 21, 1960. Longtime congressman Reed, a Dunkirk resident, solicited funds from the federal government to improve Barcelona harbor in order to make it a haven for small craft, a vacation spot for sportsmen, and a mooring place for commercial fishermen. (Chautauqua County Historical Society.)

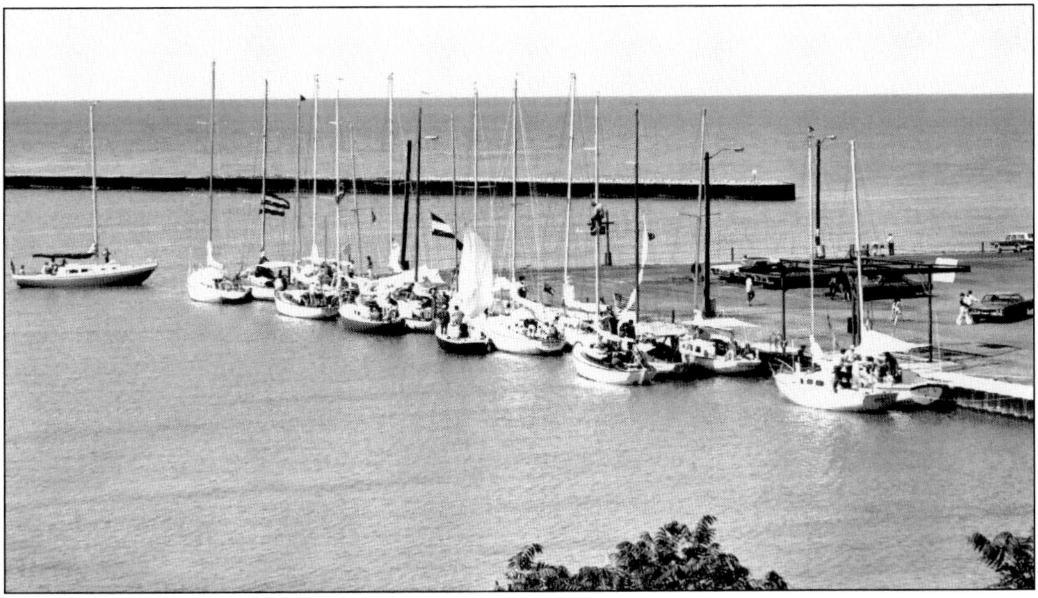

In the late 19th century, a Ripley resident noted a picturesque Barcelona harbor: "clusters of a dozen or even a score of vessels all close together, their white sails glistening in the sun, and others dotting the blue waters of the lake as far as the eye could see." The memorable gray tugboats were replaced by more luxurious pleasure craft.

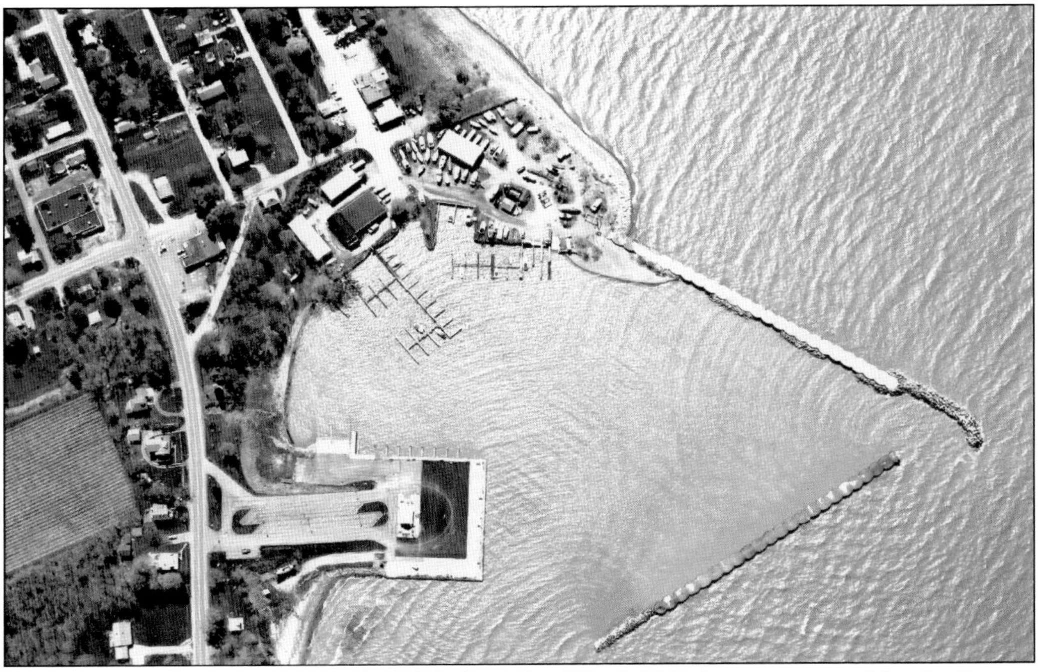

Although caught elsewhere, smoked fish from the Westfield Fisheries, operated by the Irwins, continues to be a treat during the summer season. Barcelona harbor also offers a small marina run by the Monroe family, a few restaurants, and a charter boat whose captains, Jim Herbert and Sam Genco, promise passengers "to explore some of the best-kept secrets on Lake Erie." (Pamela Berndt Arnold and pilot Jim Nohlquist.)

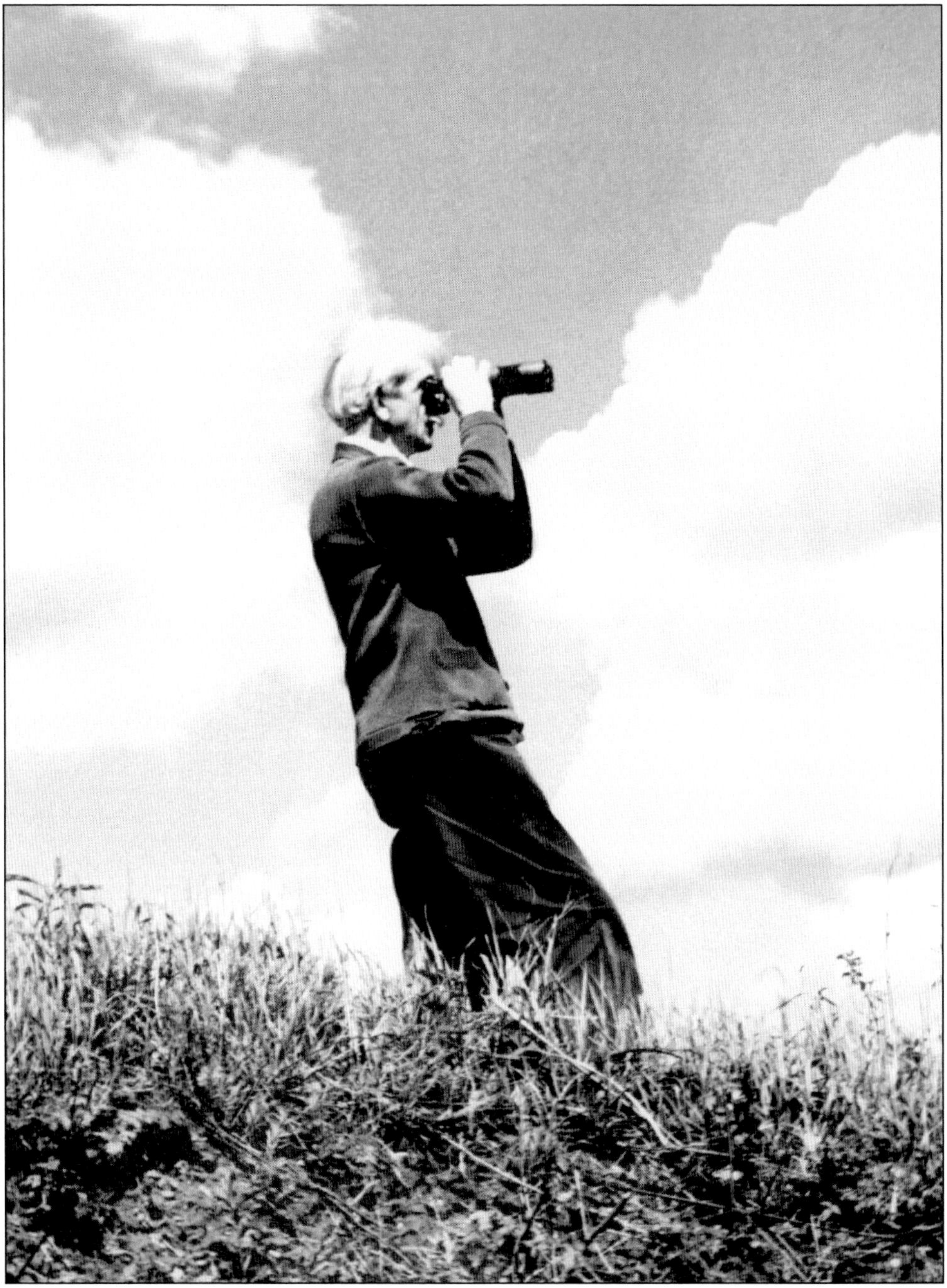

Like his student Roger Tory Peterson, Will Larymore Smedley was a photographer and artist with a passion for the natural world. An 1896 graduate of Cleveland's Case School of Applied Design, he attained national prominence as a landscape and portrait artist, exhibiting in major American galleries and locally at the Chautauqua Institution and the Patterson Library in Westfield. After marrying Adelaide Wilson, he maintained his New York City studio but established another in their home on the Chautauqua grounds. Considered a Renaissance man by family friend Mary Ellen Sheridan, Smedley has immortalized Barcelona and the neighboring countryside in his landscapes. (Mary Ellen Sheridan.)

Four

National Connections

In 2002, Chautauqua County celebrated its bicentennial in grand style, proud of the role that Westfield and other small towns in the county have played locally and nationally. Nestled in the far western corner of New York State, Westfield has shared the spotlight with several national events and prominent Americans.

The earliest settlers defended their country. When British troops controlled Lake Erie and the bordering 40-mile Chautauqua County coastline around 1812, Capt. James McMahan and his militia, mostly men from the Crossroads, were posted at Barcelona to protect the nation from attacks by British craft. During the War of 1812, Adm. Oliver Hazard Perry's defeat of the British in the Battle of Lake Erie gave the United States control of the Great Lakes.

Wagonloads of volunteers from neighboring communities met in Westfield to join the Union Army in the War Between the States. In 1861, the 9th New York Volunteer, or Stoneman's Cavalry Regiment, was based at Camp Seward off Spring Street. These men from Chautauqua, Cattaraugus, Wyoming, and St. Lawrence Counties in New York, and from Warren, Pennsylvania, participated in the Battle of Bull Run, the Siege of Richmond, and the Battle of Gettysburg, where a monument commemorates their heroism. William Barker Cushing and his brothers were one of the most famous Chautauqua County families to serve in the Civil War. Cushing became a naval hero when, with a single torpedo, he and his men sank the Confederate ironclad *Albemarle* in the Roanoke River.

The majority of the Chautauqua County enlistees who served in the Civil War survived and received assistance from the Grand Army of the Republic (GAR), founded in 1866 for that purpose. From 1945 to 1956, its national headquarters was located at the Fenton Mansion in nearby Jamestown. The Women's Relief Corps, its companion society, was founded "to assist members of the GAR and to perpetuate the memory of their heroic deeds." At the 45th annual GAR encampment held at Niagara Falls, a Relief Corps member compassionately addressed the aging veterans: "Your paths are winding over the hill to the sunset but you have known the glory and the honor of the noon-day sun and its sheen will follow you to the eventide at the end of your journey."

During World Wars I and II, civilian patriotism heightened. Similar to the turnout for the Red Cross auction in 1917, a crowd of nearly 10,000 townspeople assembled in Moore Park on July 24, 1942, to attend a rollicking war rally. Speeches, bands, and community floats featured Gov. George Patterson's 1825 carriage, the Red Cross auxiliary, Civilian Defense, canteen groups, Westfield Hospital, Welch Grape Juice Company, and the Growers Co-Op Grape Juice Company.

Fishermen John Jackway and Dudley Beadle served in the Civil War, and 25 men, a large percentage of the male population of Barcelona, were on active duty during World War II. Sons of these families are listed on a World War II Honor Roll plaque: Baideme, Holbrook, Jackway, Henry, Beadle, Perdue, Alford, Fickle, Irwin, Monroe, Brown, Wicks, Whitwood, Brownell, Thomas, Lyons, and Tunison. The Veterans of Foreign Wars Post in uptown Westfield is named in honor of William P. Jackway.

During World War II, additional manpower was needed to harvest crops and help with scrap metal collections. Local men, women, and children were joined by German prisoners of war brought into a camp on Nichols Avenue and by Italian prisoners of war sequestered in Eason Hall. Their work on farms and in the food-processing plants "helped save valuable crops to be packed for later use for our own fighting men throughout the world and our civilian population."

This chapter also includes a smattering of prominent Americans with Westfield ties. Imagine witnessing President Lincoln's funeral train pass through Westfield. Imagine Teddy Roosevelt's son commenting after his father's visit here: "On election night . . . at Oyster Bay, we were always glad to get the returns from Chautauqua County; and they were not only among the first returns to be received, but among the most encouraging . . . father used to be especially eager to hear from Chautauqua." Imagine the meeting in Mayville in 1855 of New York State senator William H. Seward, former lieutenant governor George W. Patterson, and *New York Tribune* editor Horace Greeley that gave birth to the Republican Party in New York State and their subsequent meeting with Martin C. Rice to found the *Westfield Republican*, "the mouthpiece of the new movement."

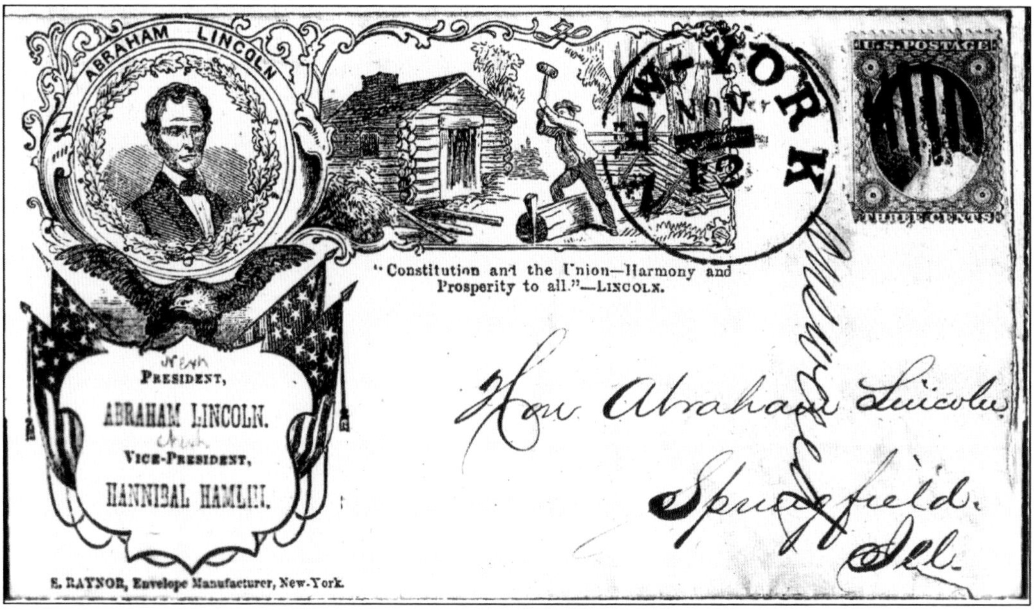

Pres. Abraham Lincoln stopped in Chautauqua County in March 1861 to meet Grace Bedell, with whom he had corresponded. (Chautauqua County Historical Society.)

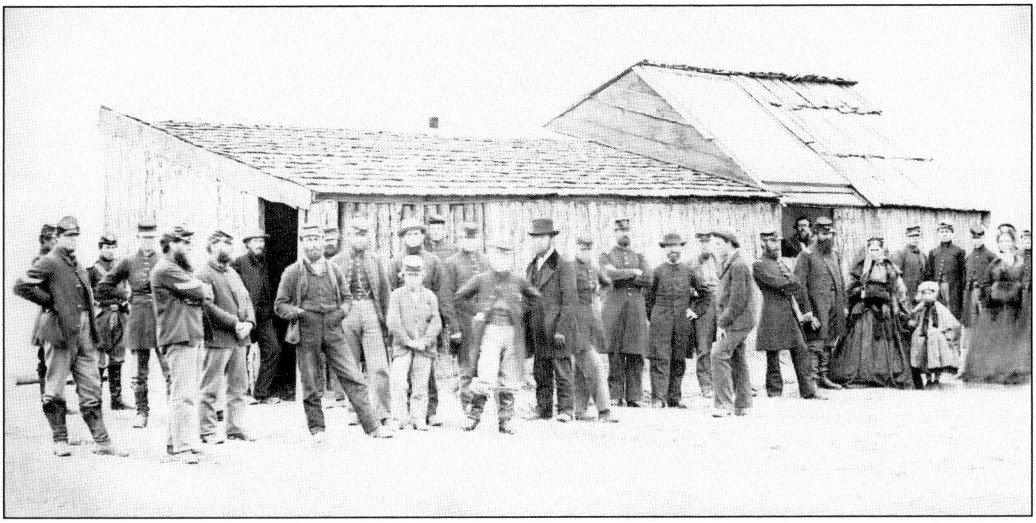

These men and women of the 112th New York Volunteer Infantry from Westfield served at Camp Suffolk, Virginia, during the winter of 1862–1863. (Chautauqua County Historical Society.)

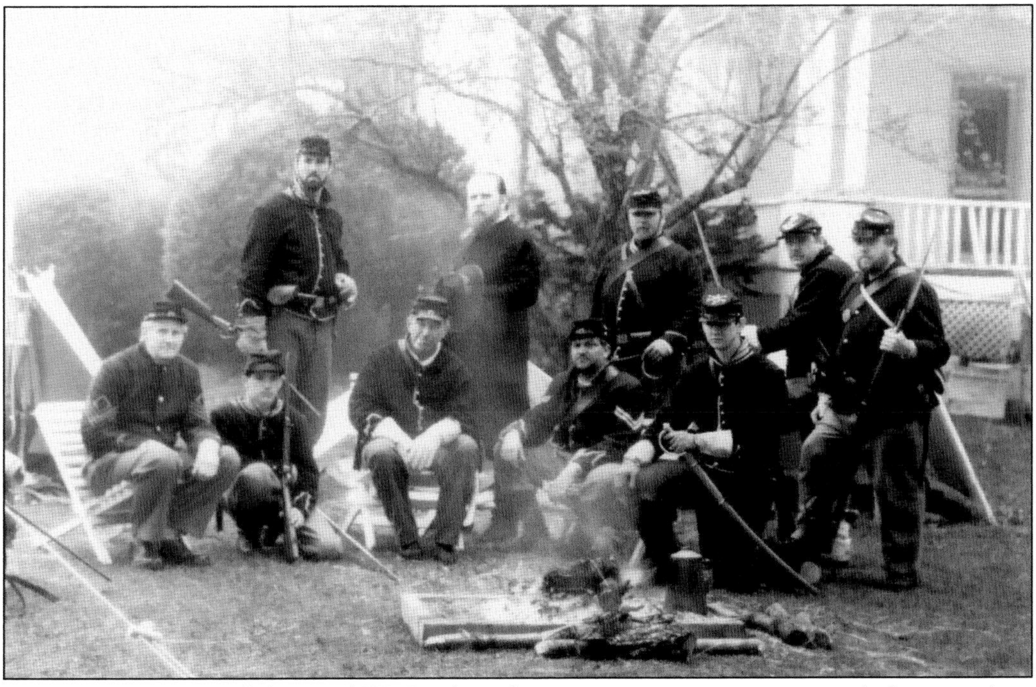

To create awareness of the Civil War's role in history, reenactment groups, including members of the 8th New York Cavalry Civil War Re-enactors make classroom presentations to local middle school students prior to their annual trip to Gettysburg, Pennsylvania. In parades and at cemetery dedications, soldiers wearing period clothing participate in staged skirmishes between the Union and Confederates. Many skirmishes occur in Moore Park. (Roy Newman.)

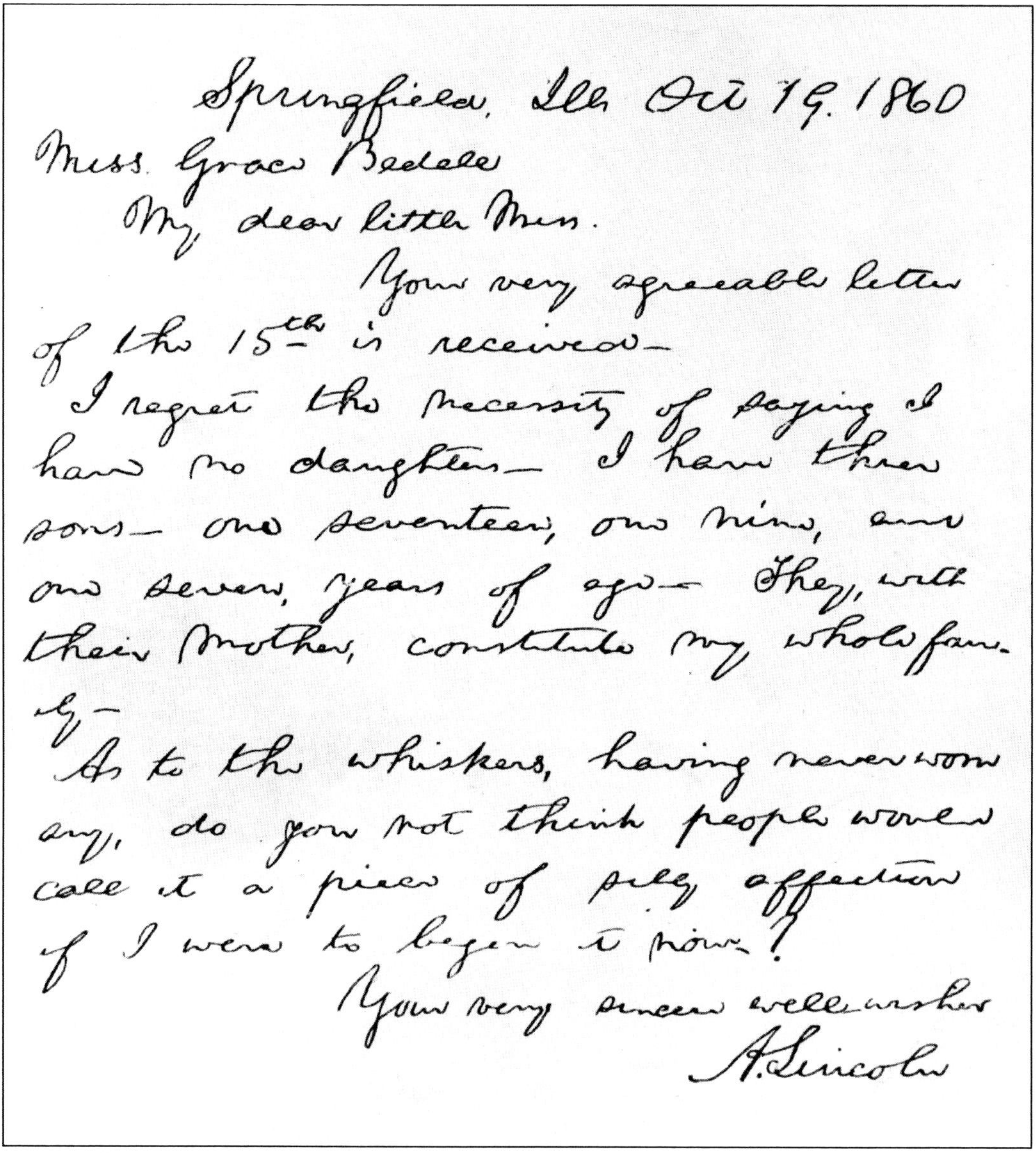

Springfield, Ills. Oct 19. 1860
Miss. Grace Bedell
My dear little Miss.
Your very agreeable letter of the 15th. is received—
I regret the necessity of saying I have no daughters— I have three sons— one seventeen, one nine, and one seven, years of age— They, with their mother, constitute my whole family—
As to the whiskers, having never worn any, do you not think people would call it a piece of silly affection if I were to begin it now?
Your very sincere well-wisher
A. Lincoln

On October 15, 1860, 11-year-old Grace Bedell of Westfield wrote a naïve letter to Abraham Lincoln: "I have got 4 brothers and part of them will vote for you any way, and if you will let your whiskers grow I will try and get the rest of them to vote for you you would look a great deal better for your face is so thin. All the ladies like whiskers and they would tease their husbands to vote for you and then you would be President." Lincoln's response is above. The bronze statues of Lincoln and Bedell, sculpted by Don Sottle, were placed at the corner of Portage and Main Streets on July 10, 1999. (Chautauqua County Historical Society.)

On March 3, 1861, en route to Washington, D. C., for Lincoln's inauguration as the 16th president of the United States, his train made a stop in Westfield to thank Grace Bedell. Dr. Kent Brown chaired the Lincoln-Bedell Statue Project to raise funds to "perpetuate this peculiar and unduplicated incident" in bronze. Lincoln's outstretched hand towards the young girl symbolizes his humility and compassion for all Americans. (Jane Currie.)

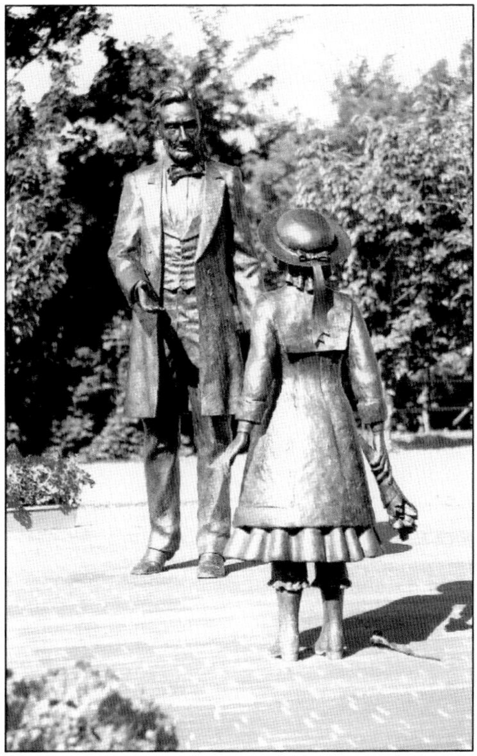

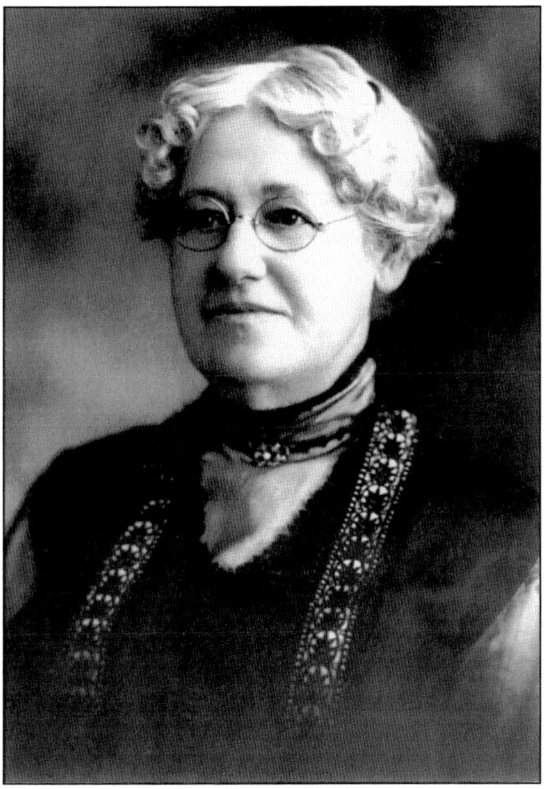

In her later years, Grace Bedell, recognized as "Lincoln's little girl," was invited to lay a wreath on President Lincoln's tomb. She was also permitted to rock in Lincoln's rocking chair at his restored home in Springfield, Illinois, "the only person so privileged." (Chautauqua County Historical Society.)

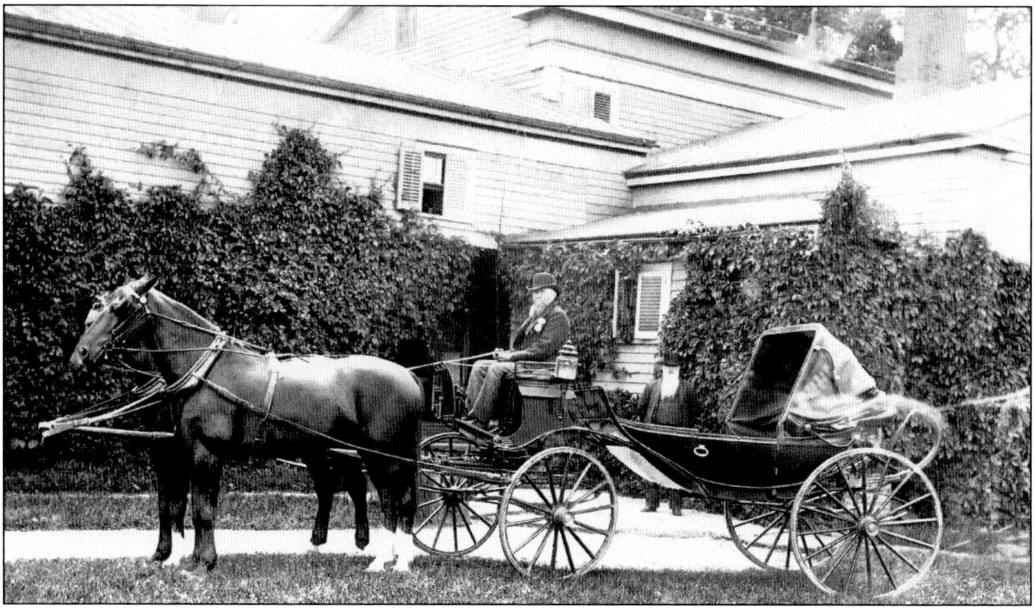

Long before Col. Jeremiah Clinton Drake drilled his historic well in 1859, the Brewer family of Titusville, Pennsylvania, used oil from a well on their property as an illuminant and a lubricant. Dr. Francis Beattie Brewer, a pioneer in the field of petroleum production, moved to Westfield in 1861. William Farrell appears to be waiting for Brewer to enter President Lincoln's carriage, owned by Brewer. (Chautauqua County Historical Society.)

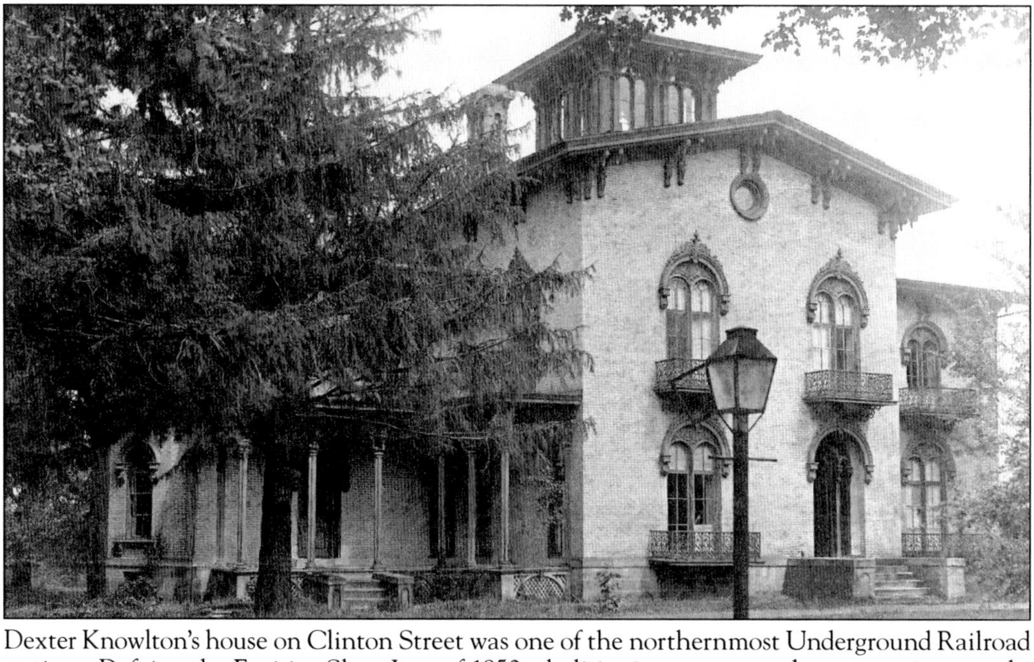

Dexter Knowlton's house on Clinton Street was one of the northernmost Underground Railroad stations. Defying the Fugitive Slave Law of 1850, abolitionists sequestered runaways in tunnels, barns, attics, and water wells. Sympathizers helped them flee from Westfield to waiting boats in Barcelona or Buffalo for the final leg to Canada. This property became the Holt House and then the site of the high school. (Chautauqua County Historical Society.)

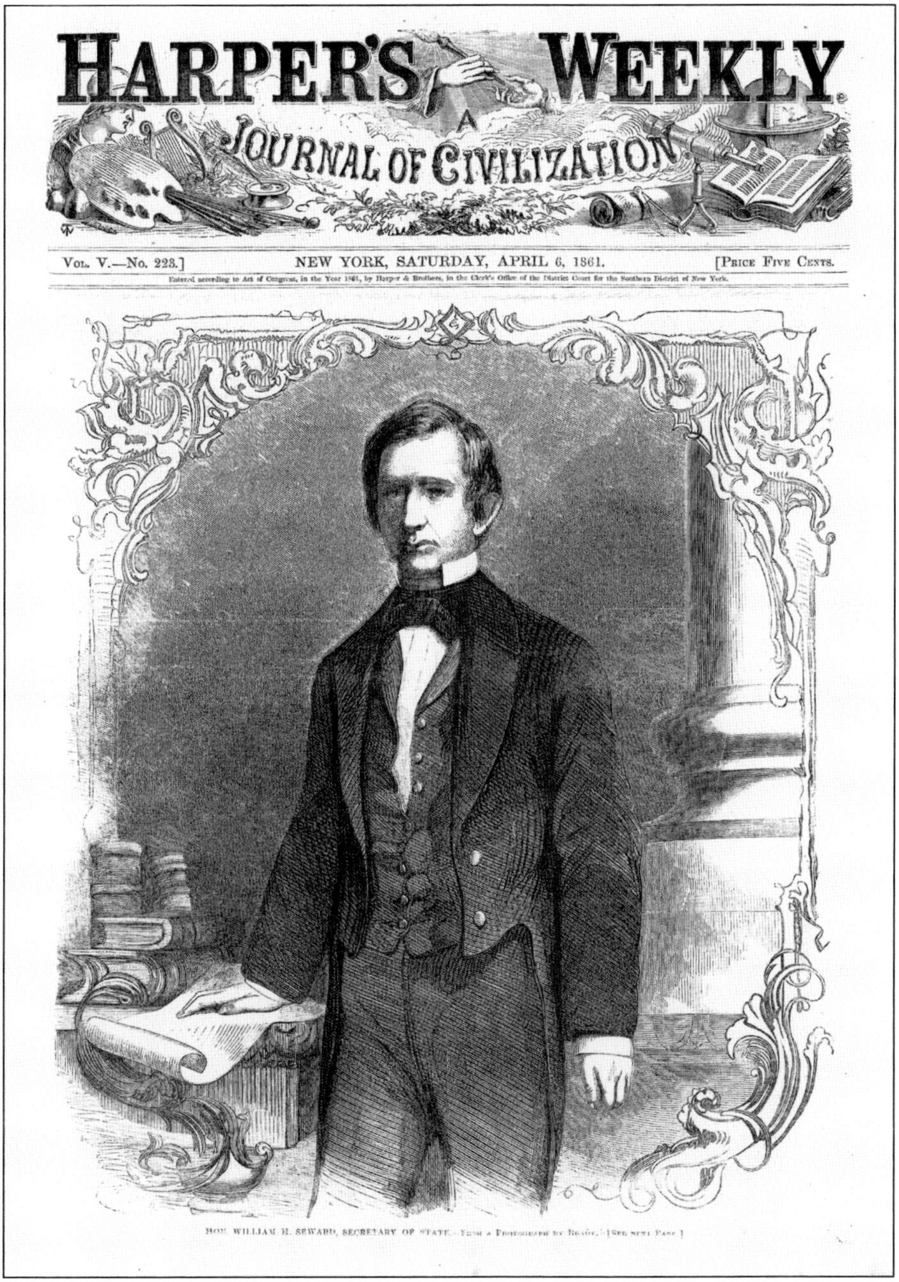

After the attack on the Holland Land Company office, William Peacock was replaced by attorney William H. Seward (1801–1872) to improve relations with county settlers. Seward became governor of New York and subsequently served as secretary of state in the cabinets of Pres. Abraham Lincoln and Pres. Andrew Johnson. Speaking at the Westfield House, Seward told his neighbors, "I don't wish to come to you in the capacity of Governor . . . I desire only to remember that I have been your neighbor and fellow citizen . . . be assured that wherever my future lot shall be cast, I shall cherish unfailing gratitude for your friendship and an ardent desire for your prosperity and happiness." (Jim and Debbie Dahlberg, innkeepers, the William Seward Inn.)

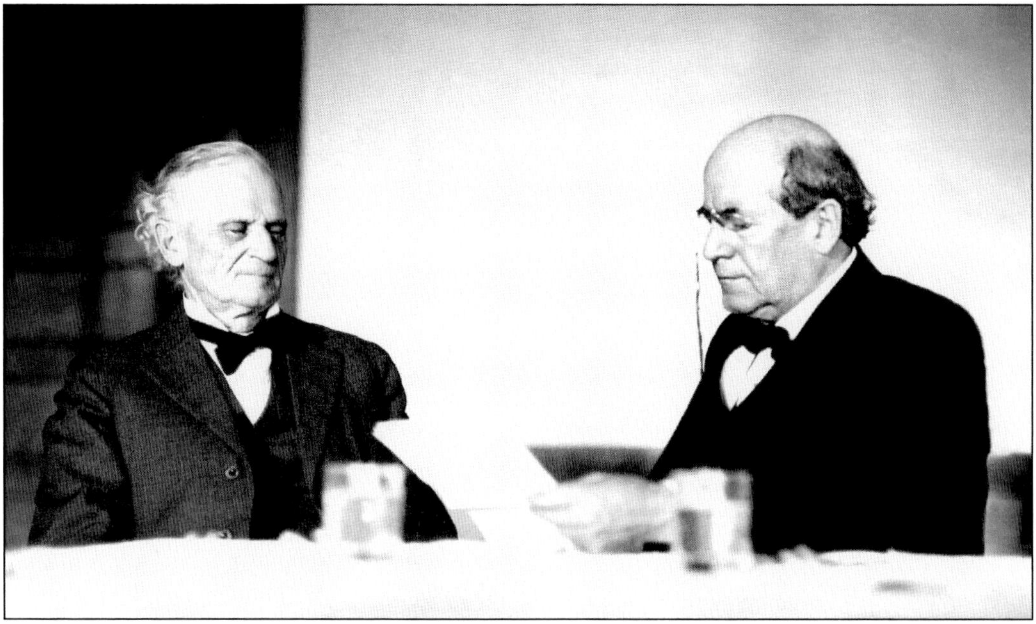

Desirous of finding a substitute for alcohol for church communions, Thomas B. Welch's experiments resulted in pasteurized grape juice. His like-minded son, Dr. Charles E. Welch, left, was even the 1916 nominee for governor of New York on the Prohibition ticket. The "grape juice controversy" originated at a diplomatic dinner when Secretary of State William Jennings Bryan, right, served Welch's Grape Juice rather than the usual libations. (The Welch family.)

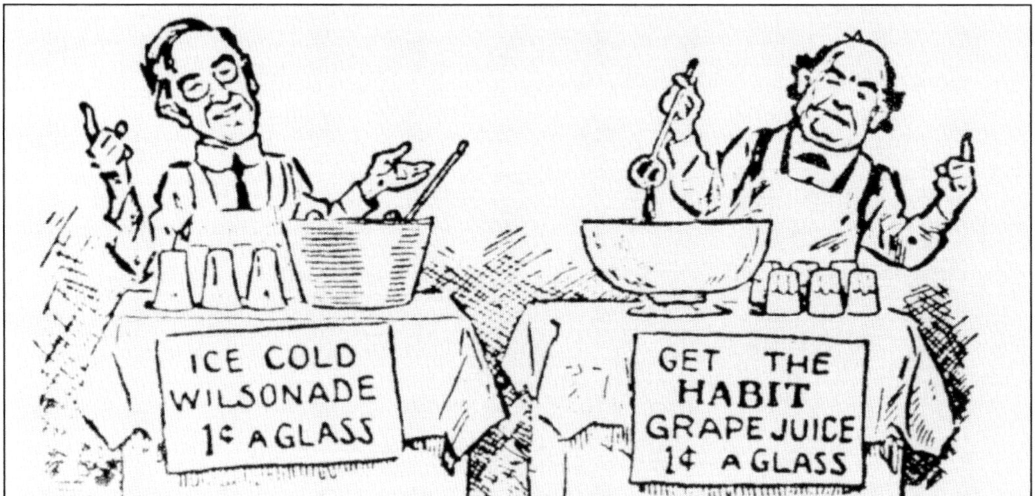

Similarly, Josephus Daniels, secretary of the navy, substituted Welch's nonalcoholic grape juice for traditional rum grogs. National publicity regarding the controversy increased during Pres. Woodrow Wilson's tenure as evidenced in this cartoon. Intentional or not, these massive advertising campaigns created by political cartoonists and columnists boosted sales and made Welch's a household word. (From *This Is Welch's Own Story*.)

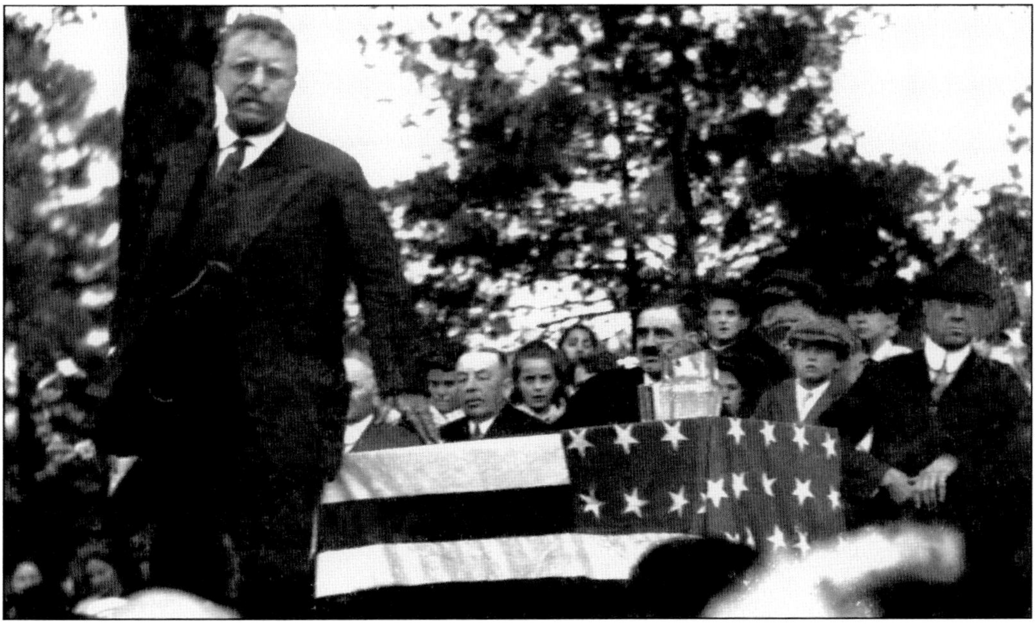

In October 1914, former president Theodore Roosevelt visited Westfield, Jamestown, and the Chautauqua Institution to campaign for Progressive Party candidates. Twelve-year-old Jesse Hulbert Tibbits's diary reads, "In his Rough Rider outfit, swinging a cane, [Roosevelt] marched into the park and gave an address. I don't remember the topic, but I was greatly impressed. I had read about him and seen his pictures in a book at home."

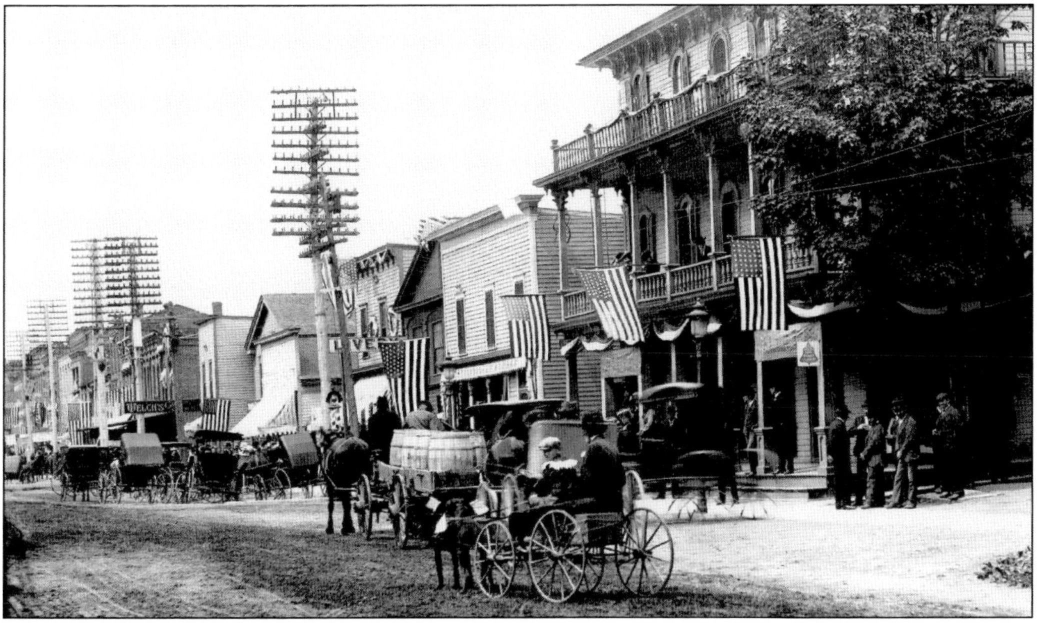

The Minton House at 91 East Main Street was a popular spot until the block burned in 1909. James V. Minton, seated center in the top photograph, was related to George M. Pullman, inventor of the railroad sleeping and dining cars. When he visited family in Westfield, Pullman, a county native, left his fully staffed private cars on the railroad siding and stayed with his relatives. (Sydney S. Baker.)

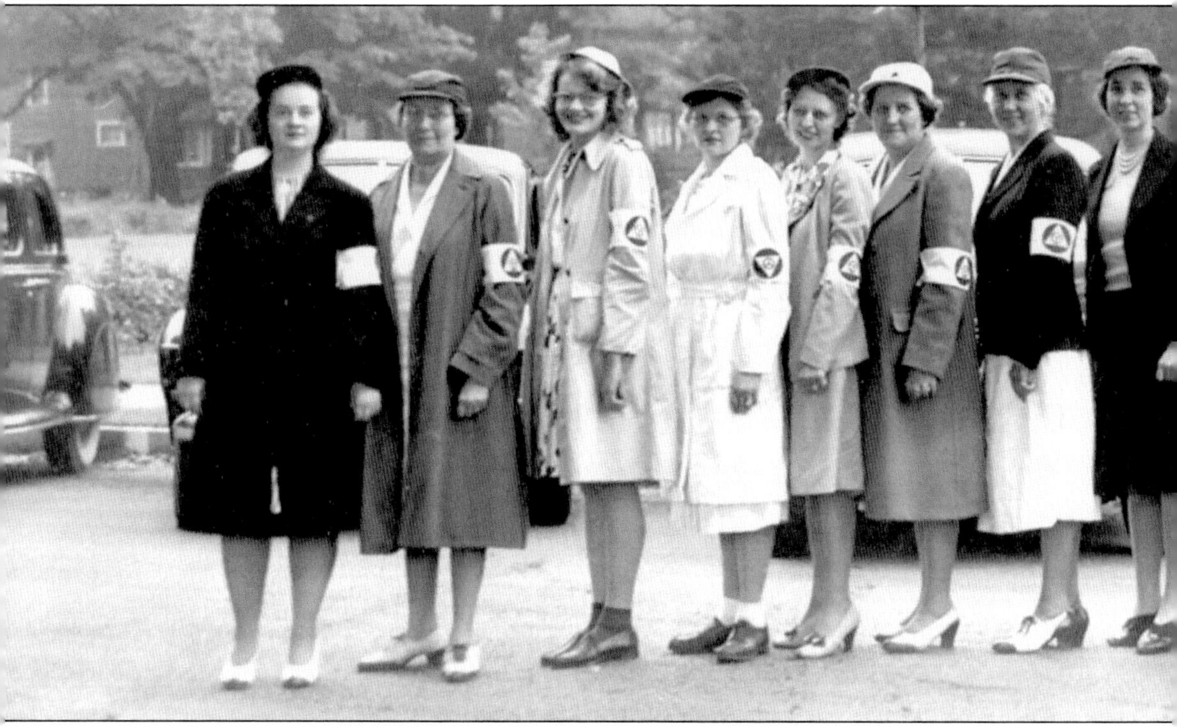

During World War II, à la "Rosie the Riveter," women worked in factories producing war materials, manned airplane spotter stations, and assumed other civilian defense roles. In 1943, this cadre of Westfield women served in the Motor Corps, meeting special transportation needs. From left to

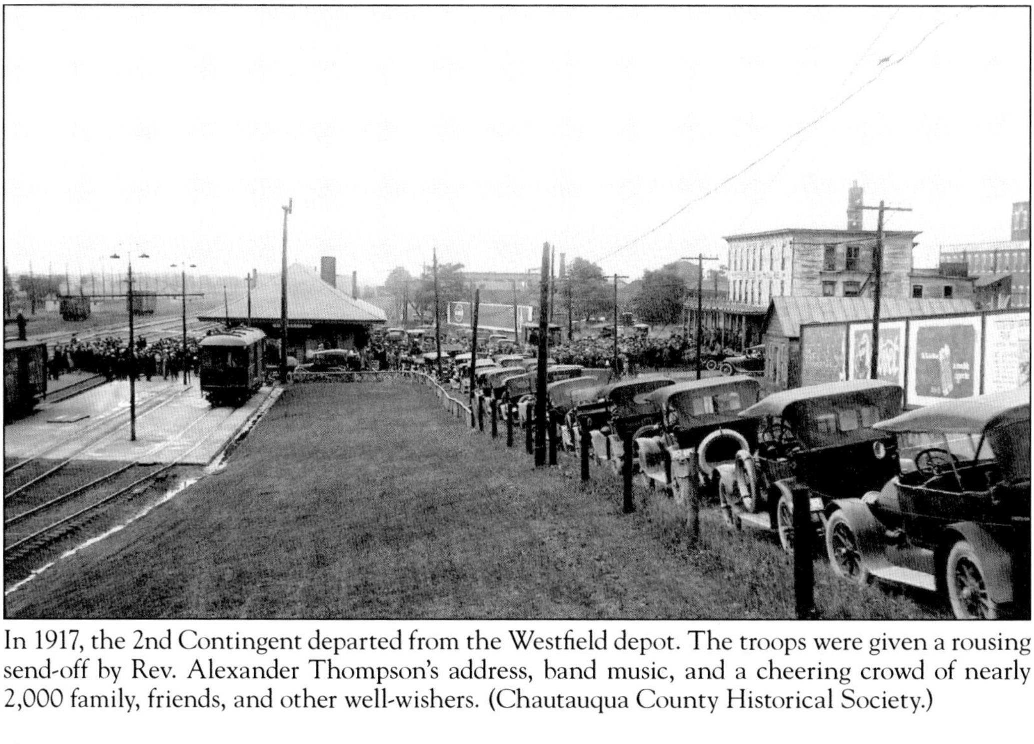

In 1917, the 2nd Contingent departed from the Westfield depot. The troops were given a rousing send-off by Rev. Alexander Thompson's address, band music, and a cheering crowd of nearly 2,000 family, friends, and other well-wishers. (Chautauqua County Historical Society.)

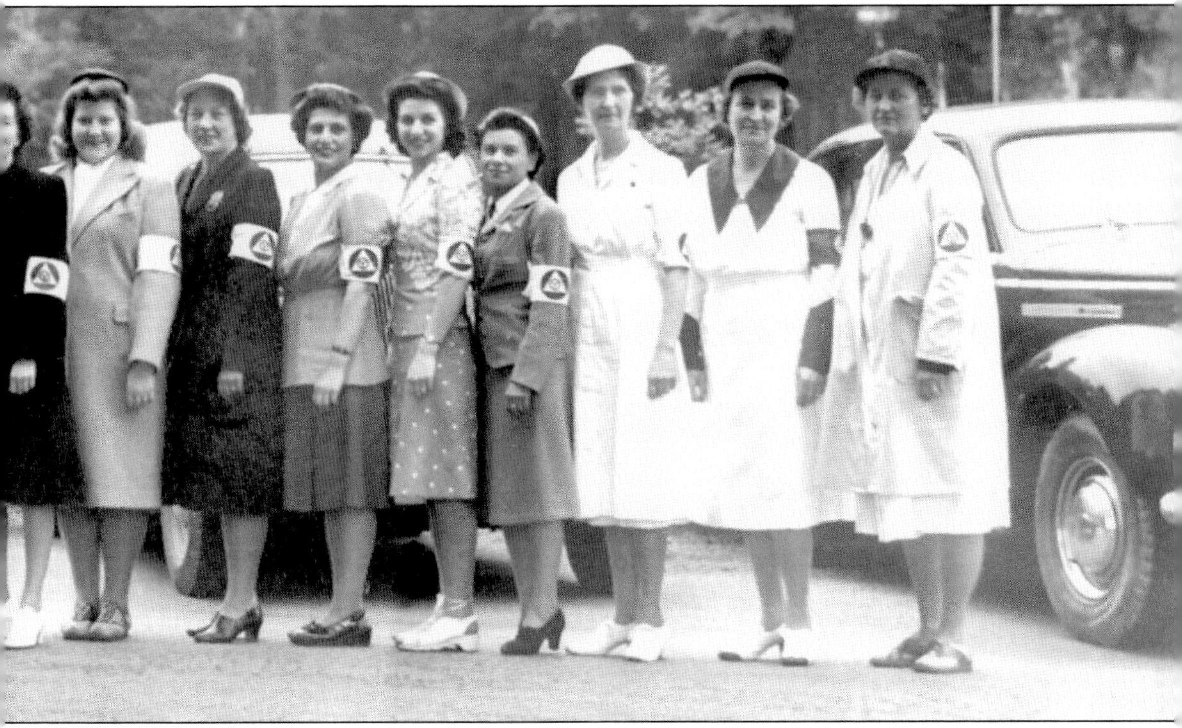

right are Helen Kerns, Nan Johnson, Katherine Alexander, Wyllian King, Jennie Smith, Marion Mitchell, Eva Axman, Kay Jones, Mary Dinsbier, Harriet Blanding, Charlotte Guest, Marguerite Breads, three unidentified women, Clara Douglas, Margaret Rood, and Marion Nixon.

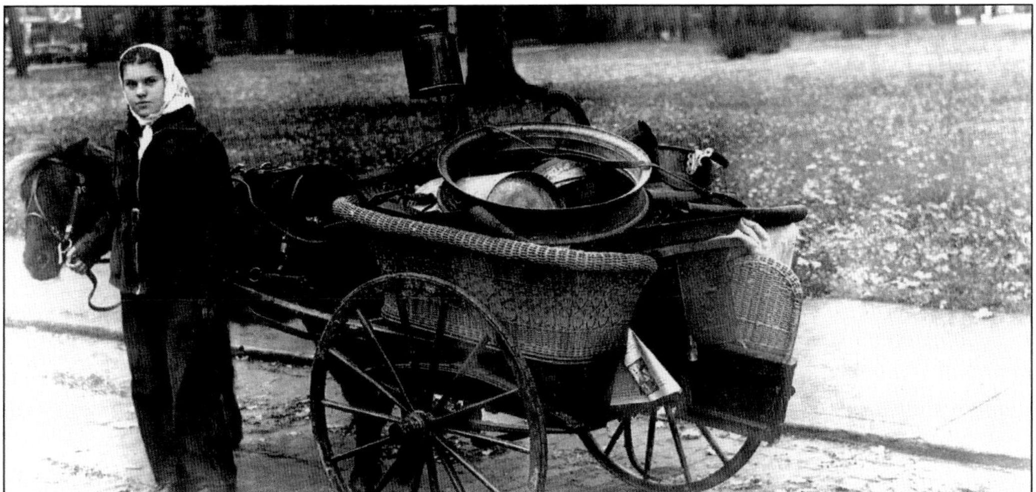

During both World War I and World War II, Westfield citizens were encouraged to aid the war effort by saving scrap. Materials including rubber, tinfoil, and metal were saved and collected by adults and children. On October 28, 1942, the *Westfield Republican* captured this photograph of young Virginia Hopson (Griffin) contributing by loading up her Timothy. Today Griffin vividly recalls that her dear pony became increasingly annoyed as she heaped more and more scrap onto the rig as she did her duty for the war effort. (Virginia Hopson Griffin.)

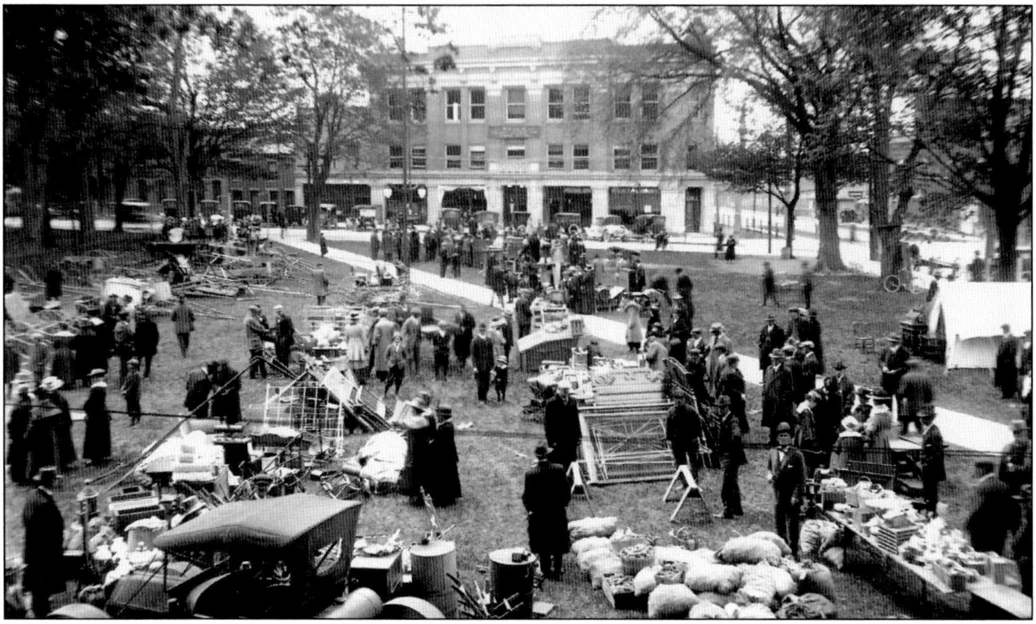

Droves of townsfolk helped raise $2,700 to benefit the Red Cross and "our boys" on the battlefront. Farm implements and animals, carriages, buggies, professional services of physicians and attorneys, lumber, fruits, and vegetables were donated for the community auction in Moore Park on May 11, 1918. Harry M. Hopson had witnessed a similar event while purchasing horses in the Midwest and introduced the idea in Westfield. (Sydney S. Baker.)

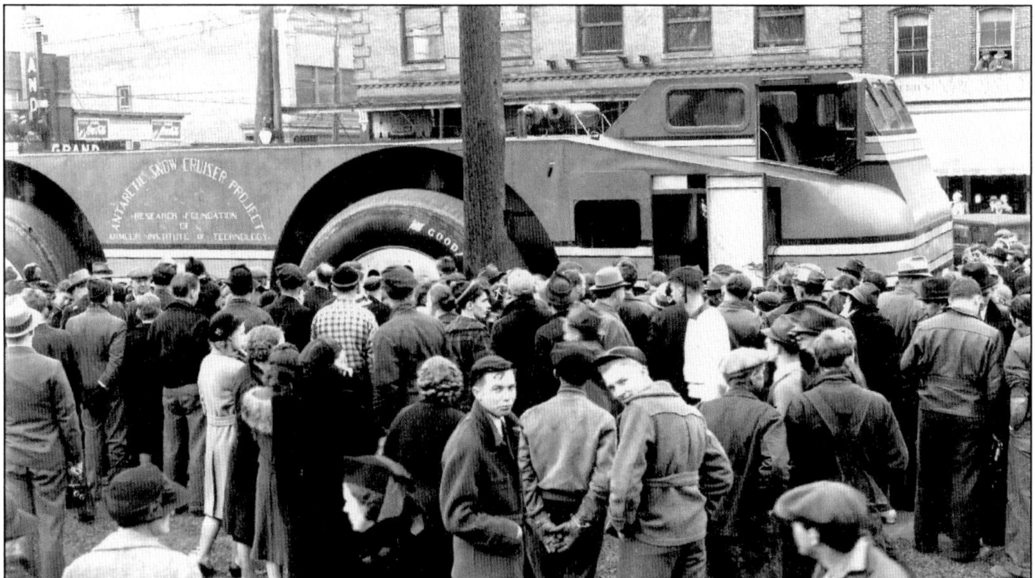

While traveling from Chicago to Boston in 1939, Adm. Richard E. Byrd's Snow Cruiser stopped in Westfield. Curious citizens viewed the giant "snowmobile," which cost $150,000, was 55 feet long, 15 feet high, and 20 feet wide. Chicago-based Armour Institute of Technology donated it to the U.S. Antarctic Service for use in the second Deep Freeze Expedition's exploration of Antarctica and the South Pole. (Alice Chapman.)

Five

The Grape Belt

Since the mid-1860s, Chautauqua County's major industry has been agriculture. Although dairying remains prevalent, quality loam soil and a moderate climate have helped make the four-mile strip between the hills and Lake Erie uniquely suited to the growing of grapes and other fruits whose production has undeniably brought great prosperity to the county. The Chautauqua and Lake Erie Grape Belt is comprised of nearly 70 miles along the Lake Erie shoreline. Its approximately 20,000 acres of vineyard are home to the oldest and largest Concord grape–growing region in the world.

After years of frustrated experimentation to create a grape hardy enough to withstand frosts, Ephraim Bull developed the Concord grape from a strain of wild grapes on his farm near Concord, Massachusetts. In 1853, he received a silver medal from the Horticultural Society of Massachusetts for perfecting the Concord grape. Grown from May until the October harvest, this large, aromatic purple grape produces fine table grapes and wine.

Elijah Fay of Brocton, the pioneer of grape growing in Chautauqua County's Grape Belt region, harvested Bull's invention around the same time as Dr. Thomas B. Welch, communion steward for the Methodist church in Vineland, New Jersey, and his son Charles were experimenting with unfermented grape juice.

Influenced by John Heyl Vincent, his host at the Chautauqua Assembly, Dr. Charles E. Welch first relocated his family from Vineland to the vineyards near Watkins Glen, New York. In 1897, Charles settled in Westfield, where he founded the Welch Grape Juice Company that, in turn, made Westfield synonymous with the Concord grape industry. Today the grapes are not only a healthy food but also important to the wine industry in the United States.

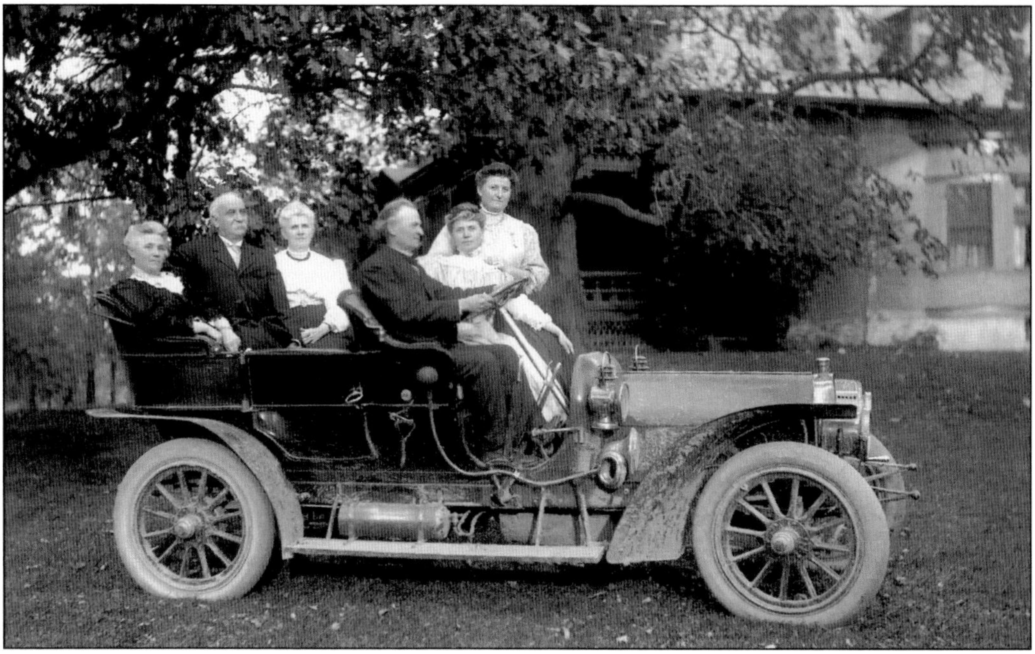

Although he stored his car in the barn during the winter, Dr. Charles E. Welch found one of the first Fords delivered to Buffalo in 1903 very attractive. One of the first automobile owners in Westfield, he chauffeured his siblings, left to right, Clara, George, Emma, Villa, and May in a later model still lacking a windshield, headlights, or overhead covering. (Ed Schaeffer.)

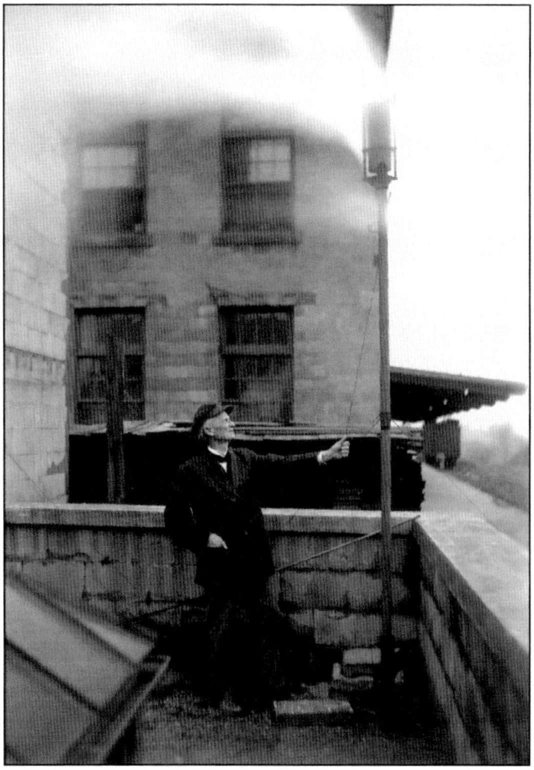

Dr. Welch's annual whistle blast signaled the pressing of grapes. Apparently, this was his way to tell his workers "Thanks for another year. Here we go again." Welch insisted upon quality grapes, often inspecting them himself. Growers knew that he paid more for Concord grapes than his competitors and, thus, sought Welch's favor. Although grapes were perishable, Welch's operation shut down on the Sabbath. (Peter Flagg.)

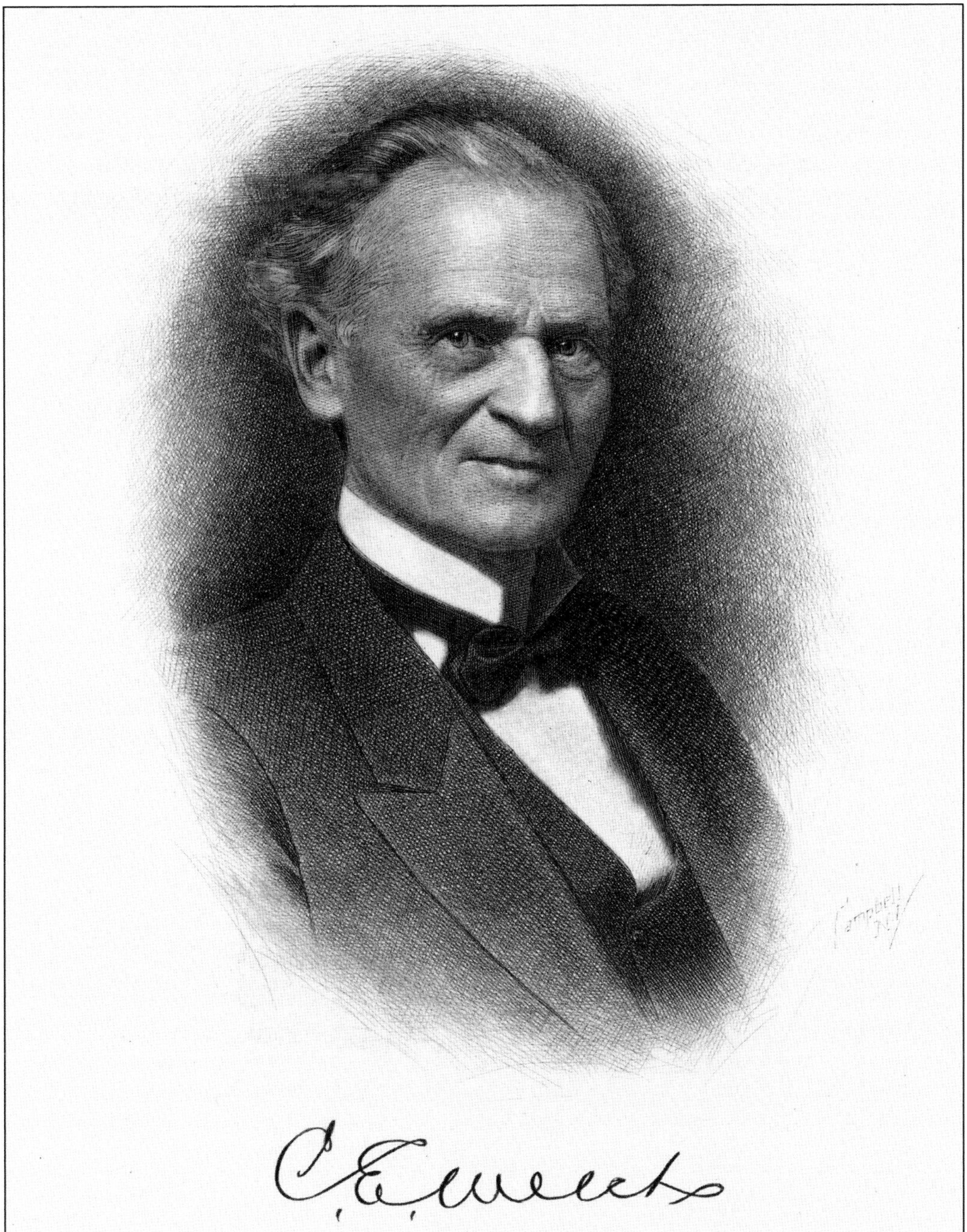

Unlike today's corporate moguls, Dr. Charles E. Welch (1852–1926) maintained his humility. His son John Welch explains: "When Charlie Welch gave grape juice a new start . . . he felt he was continuing his father's [Thomas B.'s] dedicated effort. . . . My father added another purpose—to make money for the Lord. And it was not his intention to accumulate money for himself. As he pushed and steered the new business up that long hill, from the communion 'wine,' to medicinal use and finally to a popular beverage, with profits appearing, he never departed from that purpose—to create money for benevolent gifts." (Chautauqua County Historical Society.)

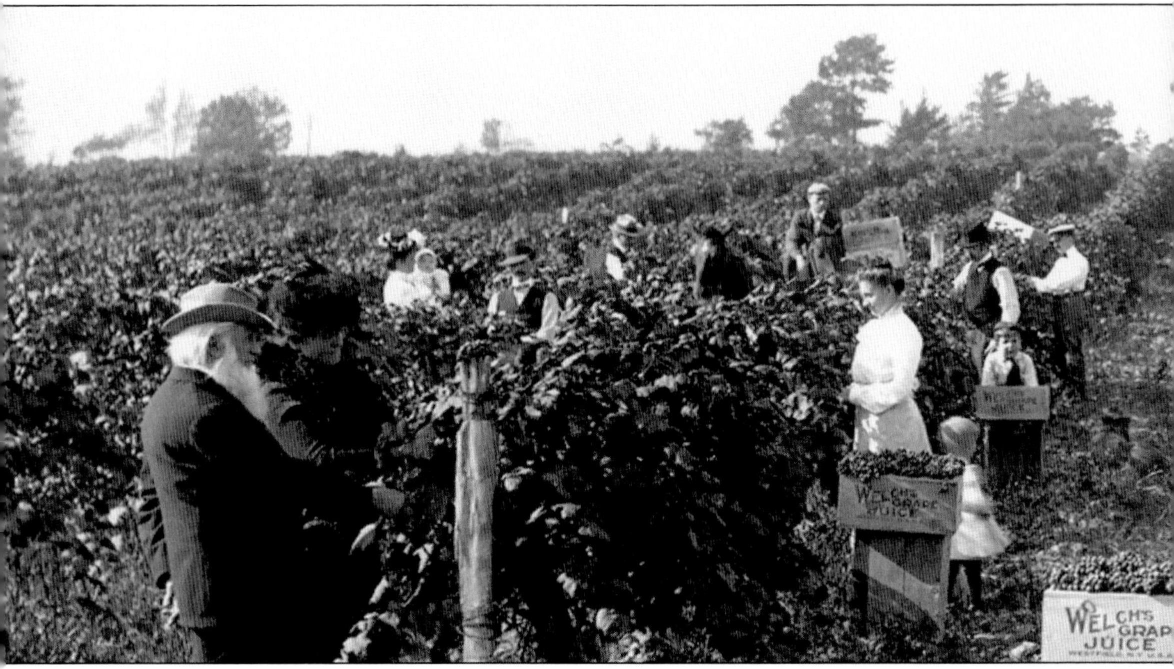

Parallel rows of Concord grapes tied to two- or three-foot-high wires were visible for miles. Handpicked by the grower's family members, neighbors, and migrant workers, the grape clusters, cut at the stem by hand shears, were dropped into wooden crates that rested on stools. Pickers carried the crates and stools from one vine to another. The white-bearded Thomas Bramwell

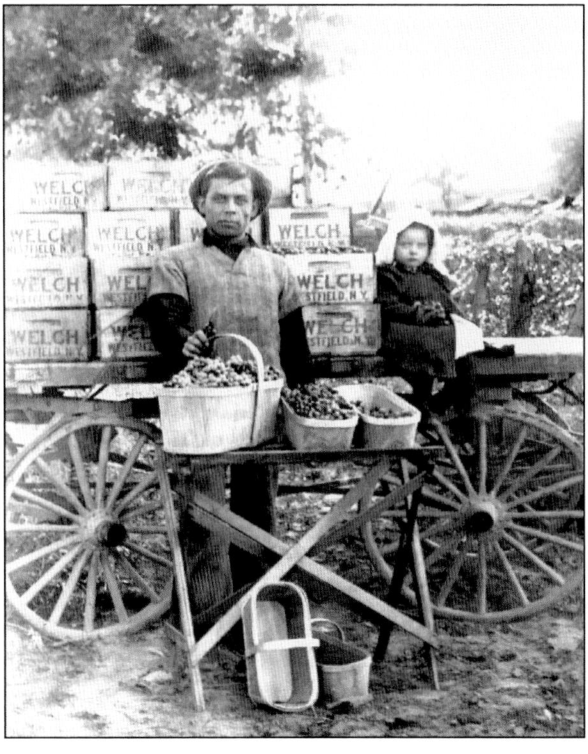

In 1900, most of the grape crop was packed into small baskets for local consumption. This photograph was taken in 1908 at Jay Anderson's fruit farm on Route 20. Three-year-old Caroline Anderson Morgan scowls as Walter, the hired hand, displays his grapes destined for the empty Welch baskets and boxes in the background. (John Paul Wolfe.)

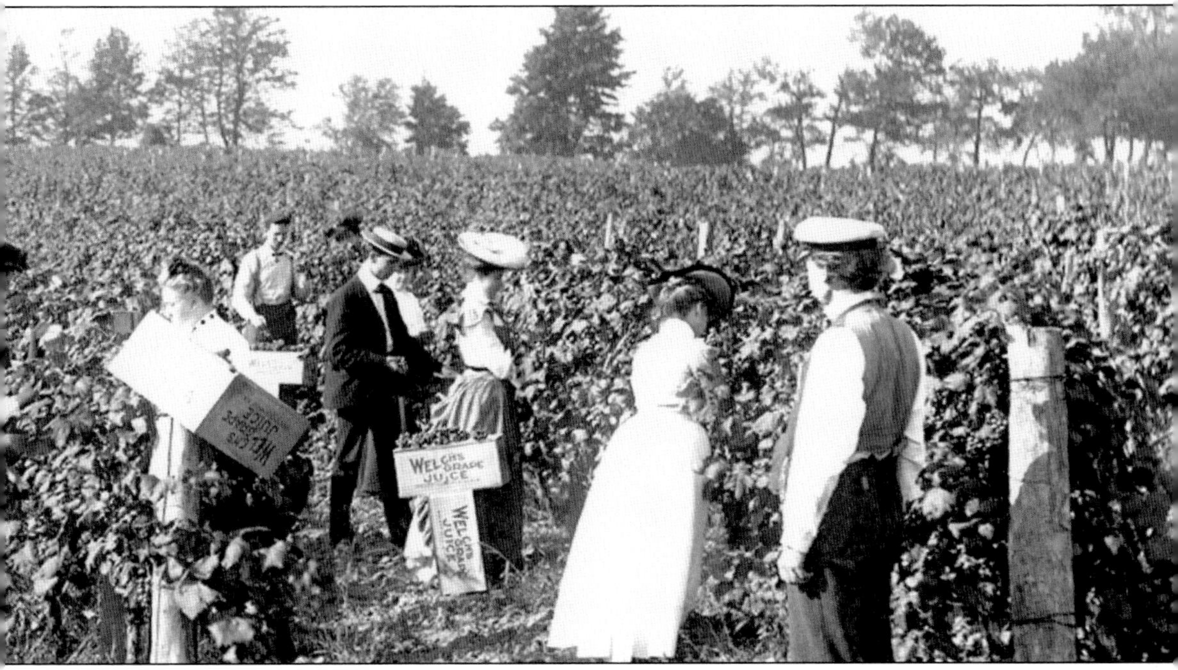

Welch, on the left, and his son Charles E. Welch, far right, visited this vineyard in 1902, overseeing the harvesting process. In 1923, the Chautauqua and Erie Grape Company sought to create a market for table wines. Nearly 60 women were hired to sort grapes, pack them into four-quart baskets, and ship them to southern states for that purpose. (Ed Schaeffer.)

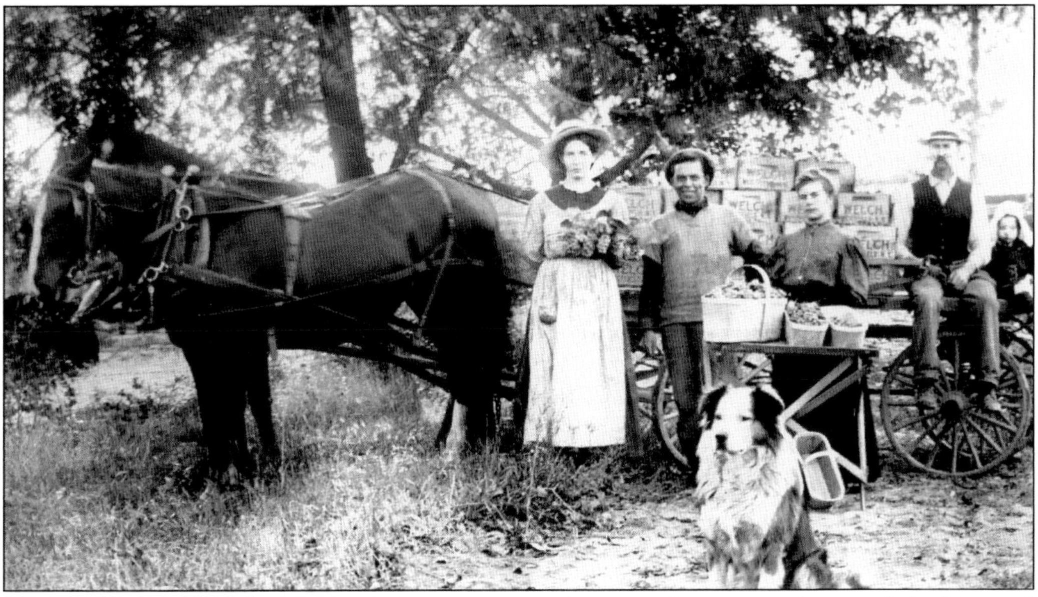

When additional hands were needed, everyone on the grape farms turned out to help. Pictured on the same day as the opposite page, Walter smiles while the others appear rather somber. Since the task was physically grueling, perhaps he was pleased not to be working alone. Dr. Welch, far more gleeful than these pickers for obvious reasons, proudly proclaimed, "Everywhere is hustle and bustle during the Chautauqua grape harvest." (John Paul Wolfe.)

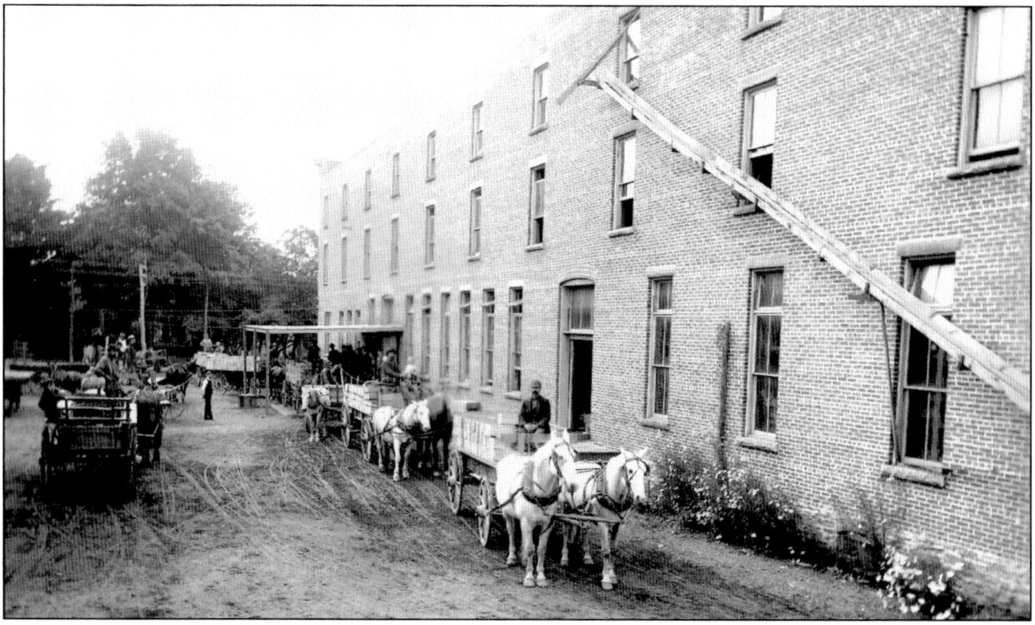

Horse-drawn wagons queued up and proceeded slowly down North Portage Street, delivering grapes from the growers to the processing plant. Once the grapes were unloaded, empty crates were procured to repeat the process. Westfield's proximity to the railroad greatly influenced Dr. Charles E. Welch's decision to build his factory there, but, by 1927, when farmers owned their own trucks, railroad loading stations were abandoned. (Peter Flagg.)

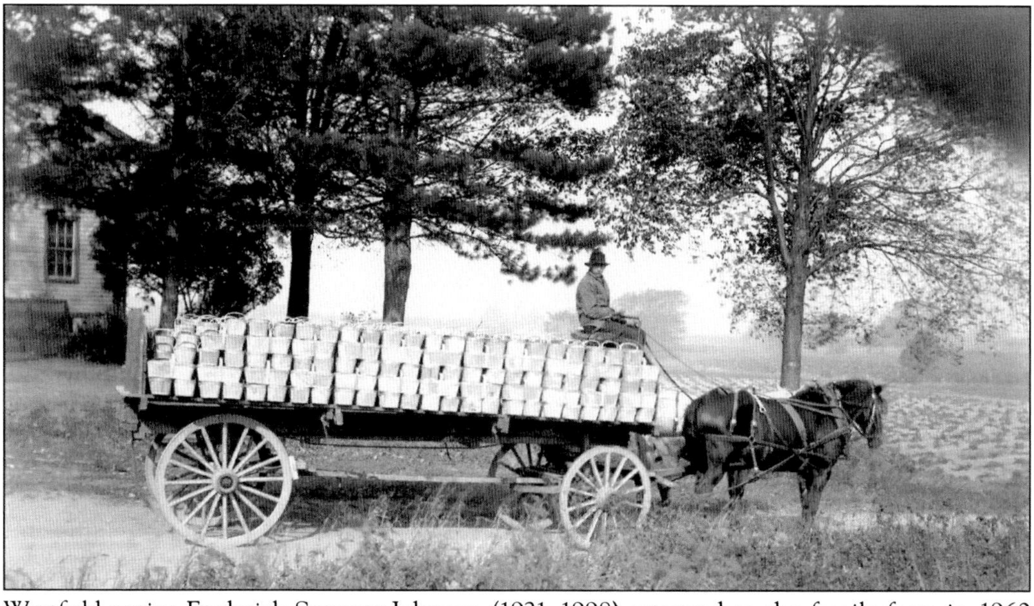

Westfield native Frederick Spencer Johnson (1921–1998) returned to the family farm in 1960 following college, military service, and stints at Dole Pineapple in Hawaii and on Nelson Rockefeller's Venezuela farm. The following year, he founded Frederick S. Johnson Vineyards in Westfield, the oldest estate winery in New York State. Ever innovative, Johnson's three business-savvy children have successfully expanded upon their father's vision at the Route 20 establishment. (Johnson Estate Wineries.)

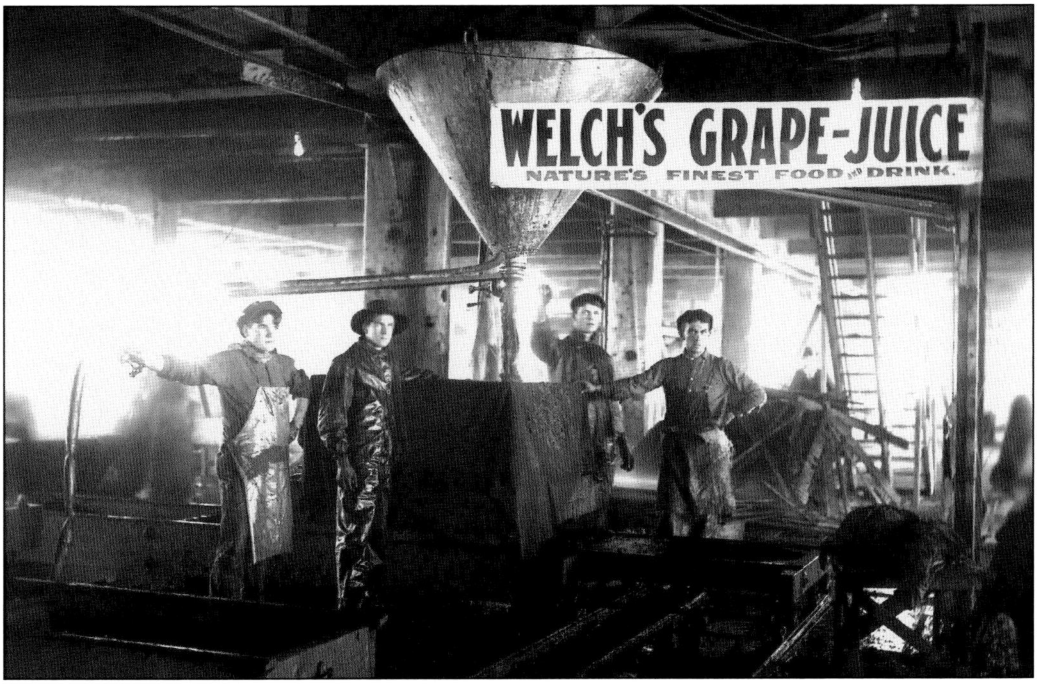

Welch's first grapes were pressed in October 1897, and by mid-November, 288 tons were processed. At grape-pressing time, every available person in the Westfield environs was recruited to crate, weigh, and inspect the harvest. These workmen, like other employees at the Welch Grape Juice Plant, worked around the clock during harvesting time. (Peter Flagg.)

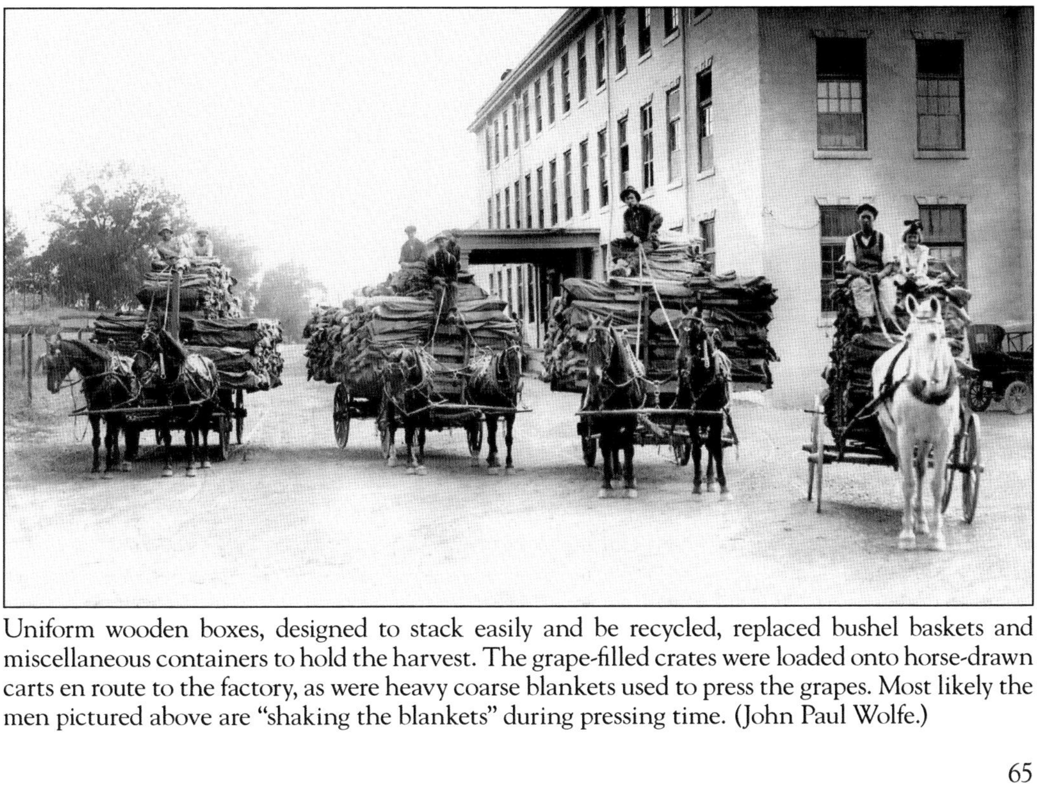

Uniform wooden boxes, designed to stack easily and be recycled, replaced bushel baskets and miscellaneous containers to hold the harvest. The grape-filled crates were loaded onto horse-drawn carts en route to the factory, as were heavy coarse blankets used to press the grapes. Most likely the men pictured above are "shaking the blankets" during pressing time. (John Paul Wolfe.)

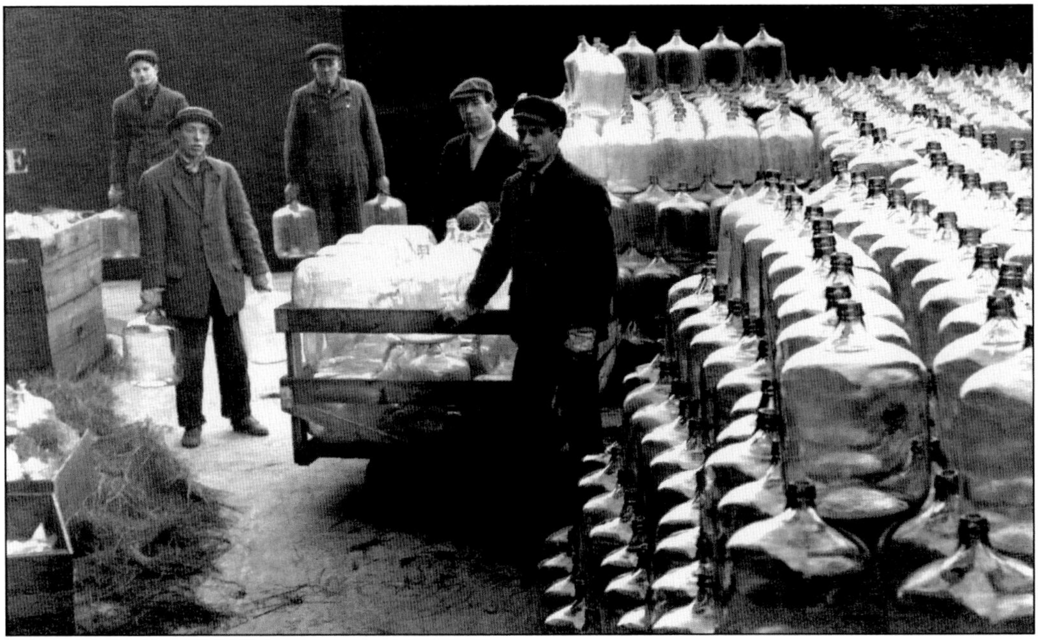

In the 1920s, juice pressed from the grapes was stored indefinitely in these five-gallon carboys at the Welch Grape Juice Company and other plants. These large glass casks were filled with hot, processed grape juice and stacked by hand to settle the sediment. Today amateur winemakers follow a similar process but find the task far less backbreaking. (Jack E. Ericson.)

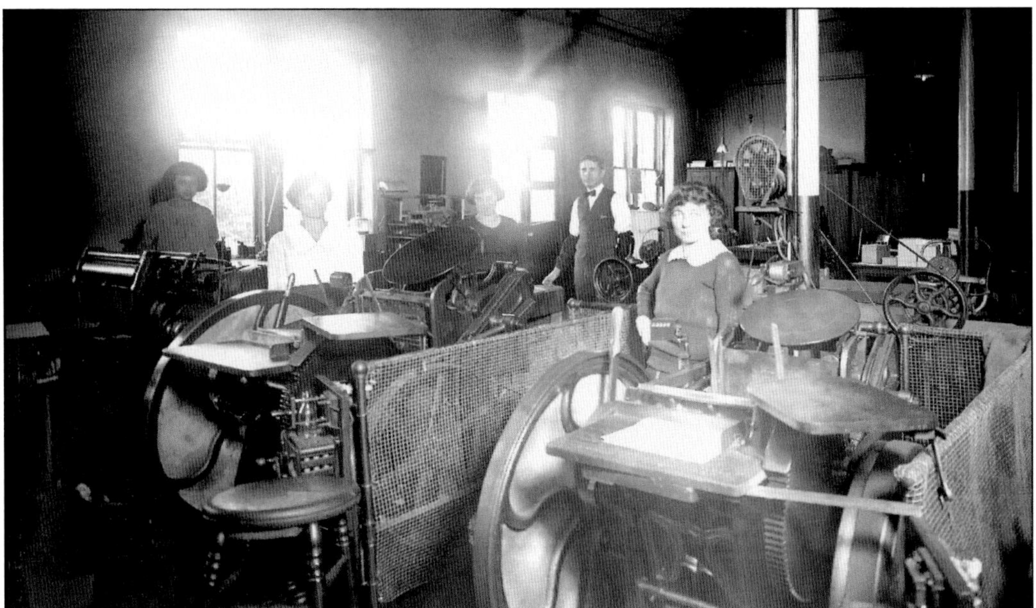

In 1908, Welch placed the following advertisement in a religious publication: "Printer Wanted: We have a complete job in booklet printery, and are needing a complete printer. Good place for somebody who can make good. No tobacco or drink. Methodist preferred." After Factory No. 1 was converted into a print shop, these women were mass producing labels for the Welch Grape Juice Company in the 1920s. (John Paul Wolfe.)

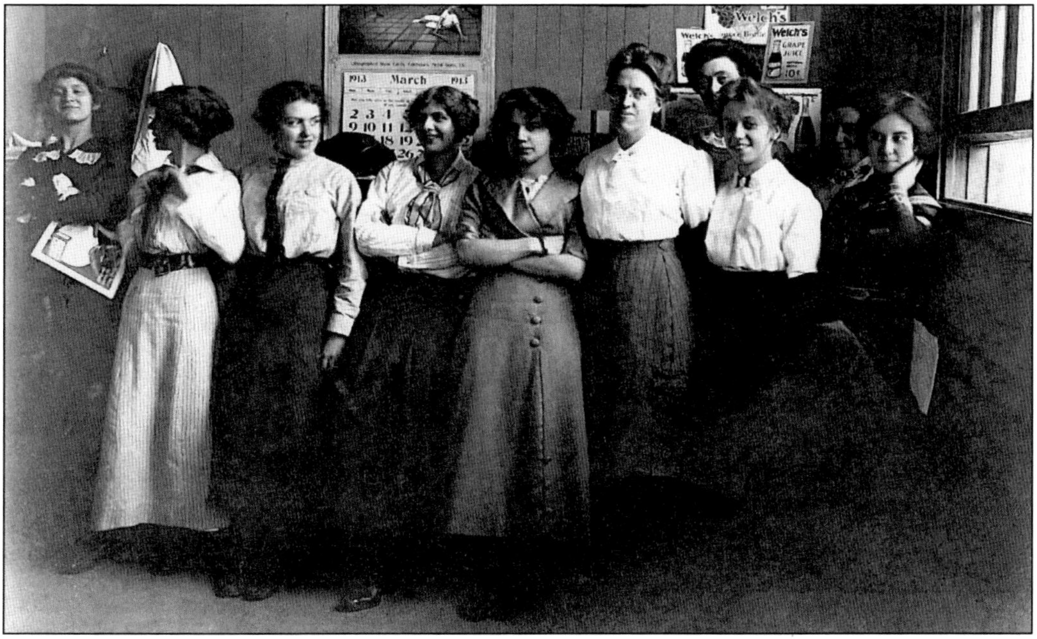

This 1913 photograph captures 10 office workers in the Welch Grape Juice Company office. Mary Hill, Alice Chapman's mother, is on the far right. Did these ladies know the art of eating Welch's Concord grape—"the job of slipping the skins and swallowing the juicy insides"? Or were they "the rare breed that just eats the skins"? (Alice Chapman.)

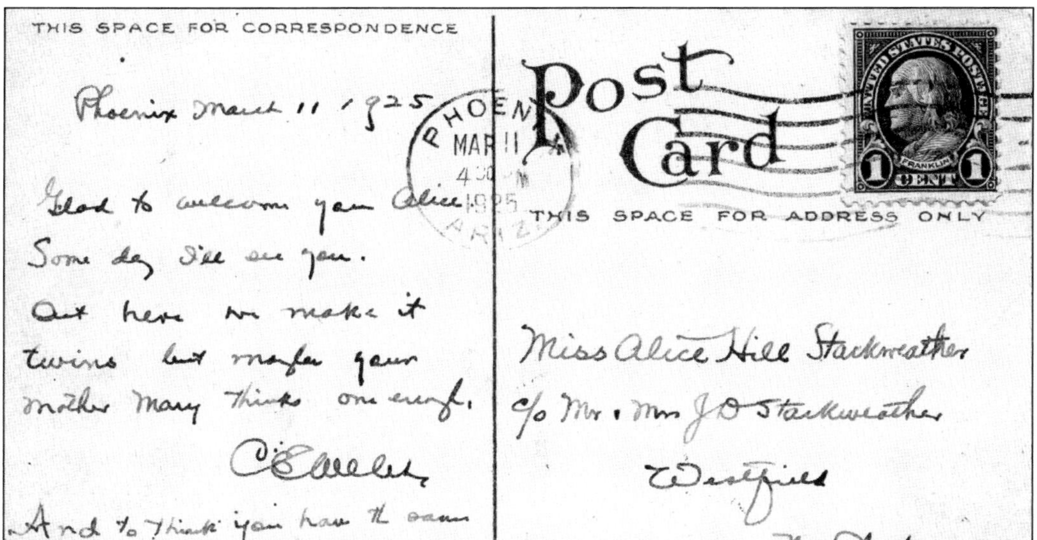

Dr. Charles E. Welch, who loved children, took the time to send this postcard, dated March 11, 1925, to his employee Mary Hill on her daughter's birth. This cherished handwritten card, addressed to Miss Alice Hill Starkweather of Westfield, New York, ended, "And to think you have the same birthday as I have. We'll celebrate." A noble gesture from a noble man! (Alice Chapman.)

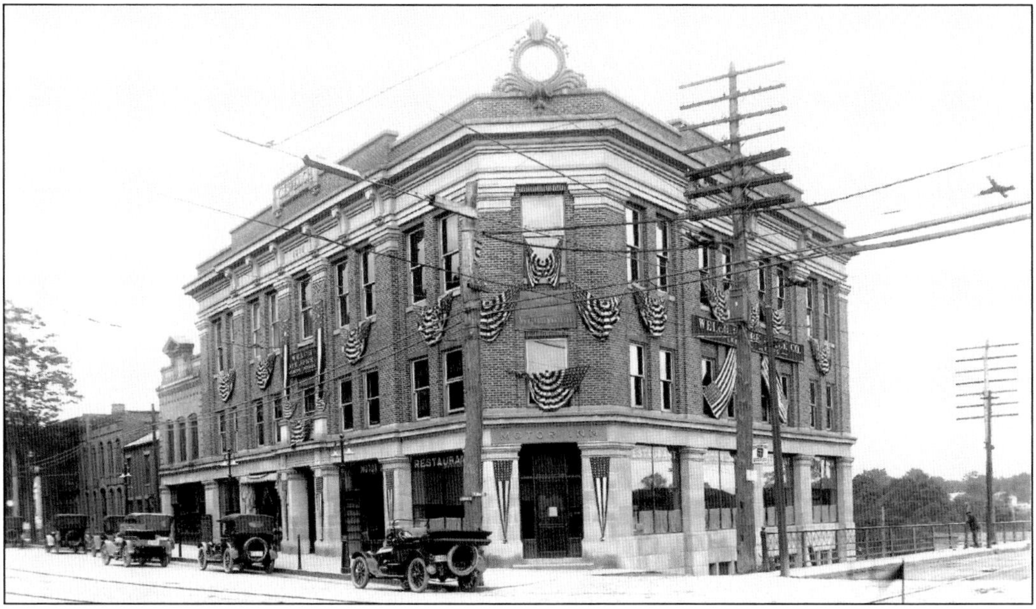

The Welch Building in the Welch Block, at the southwest corner of Main and Portage Streets, has housed stores and the Motor Inn restaurant as well as the offices of the Welch Grape Juice Company and, in recent years, those of the National Grape Cooperative, its parent company. In 2005, Northington Holdings of Buffalo purchased the 1909 structure for redevelopment. (Sydney S. Baker.)

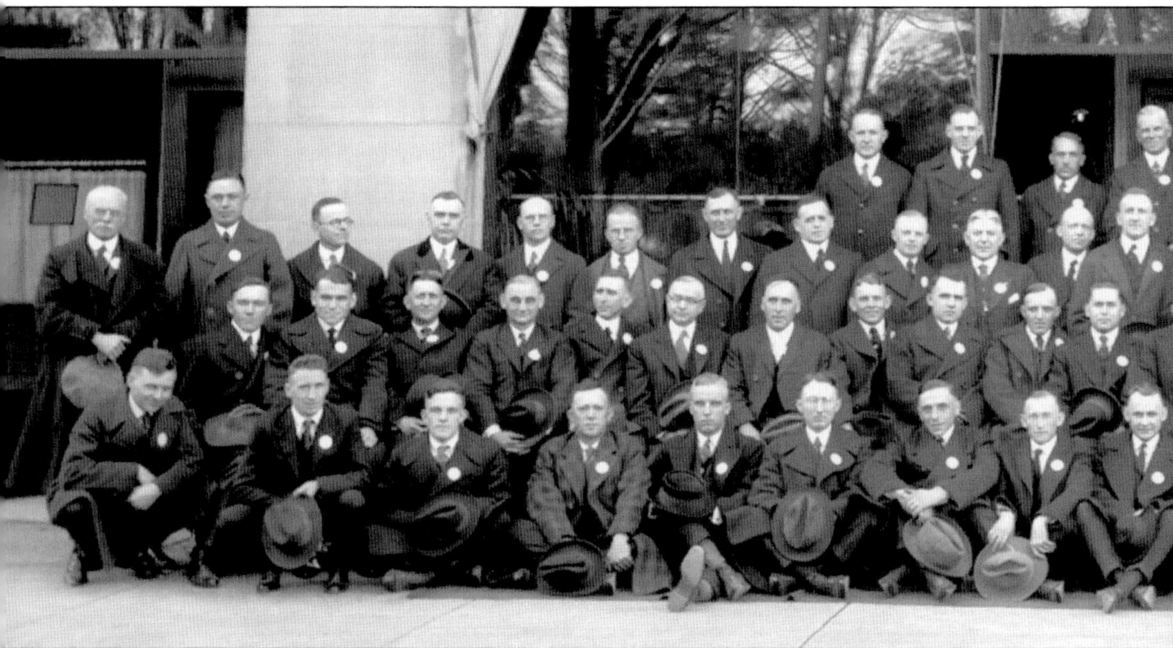

"Welch business booms because of this live bunch on the road." The annual fall sales convention of the Welch Grape Juice Company was held at its headquarters in Westfield. In addition to the perfunctory meetings, president Dr. Charles E. Welch, second row right, organized trips to Niagara Falls and picnics at Chedwell, his summer home on Chautauqua Lake. As might be

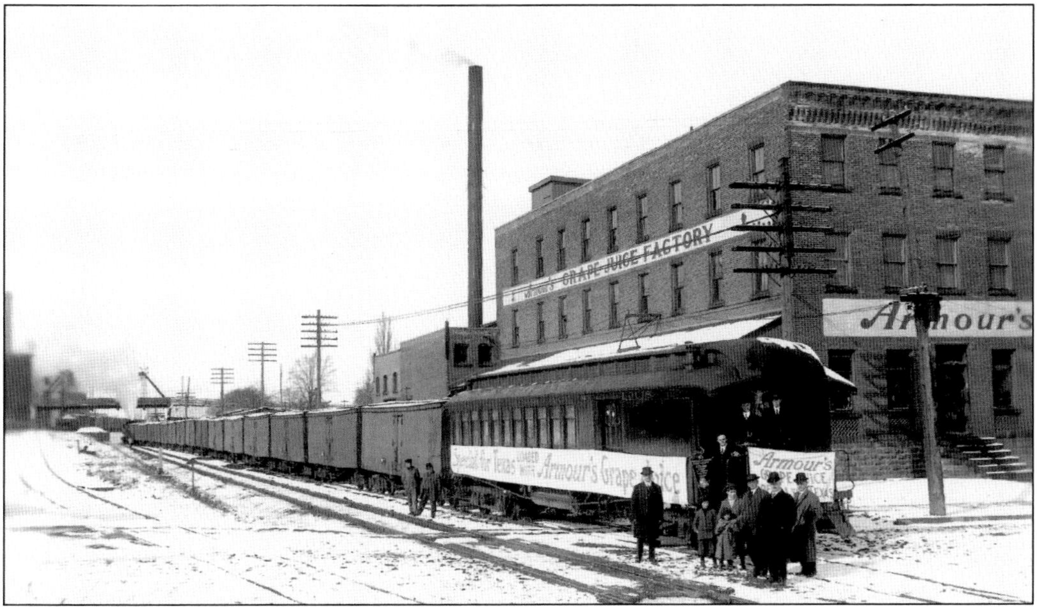

The Fenner Grape Juice Company on Franklin Street was built in 1898 by pharmacist Byron Fenner and sold to Armour and Company, meat packers of Chicago, in 1912. Because the plant's devastating 1918 fire occurred during pressing season, nearly 400 tons of grapes used for bottled juice were destroyed. In 1935, the company was sold to the Westfield Planter's Cooperative Association. (Peter Flagg.)

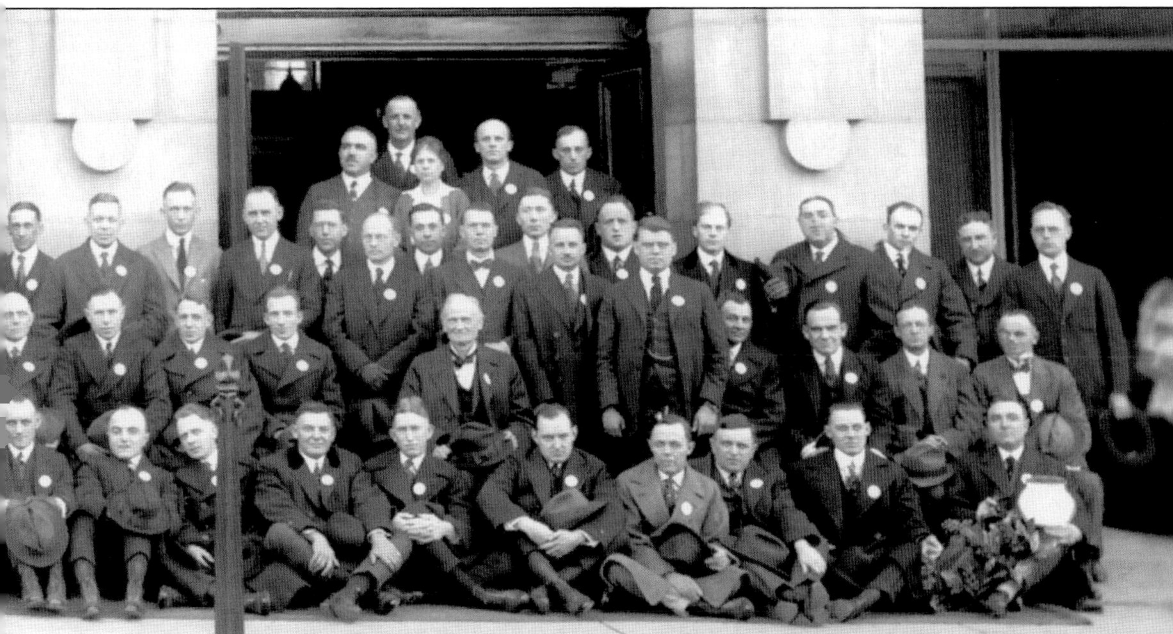

expected, they all attended worship services on the Sabbath. Chautauquans might be interested to learn that W. B. Lindsey, grandfather of the institution's former president Daniel L. Bratton, was an official of this Welch Grape Juice Company for more than 40 years, a member of the Westfield Methodist Church, and president of the YMCA. (Peter Flagg.)

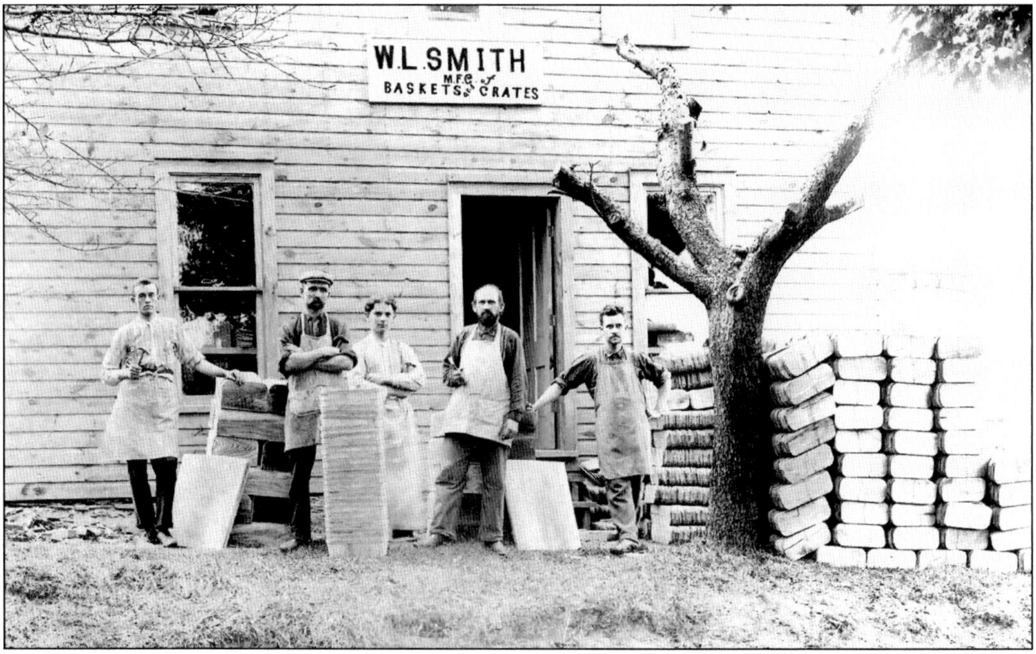

Grape basket making was a busy industry in Westfield, employing many workers such as these men standing in front of W. L. Smith's basket and crate factory and the women at the Morse basket factory on Spring Street, shown on page 24. Although first made from pasteboard, wooden baskets and crates were needed for shipping. The Dean Brothers Company was one of several grape-packaging operations in Westfield. (Alice Chapman.)

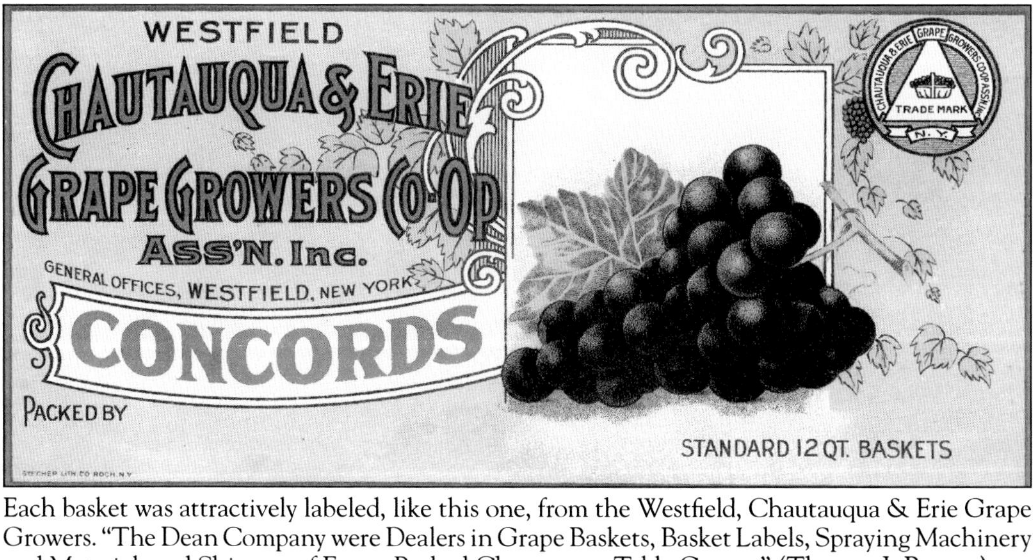

Each basket was attractively labeled, like this one, from the Westfield, Chautauqua & Erie Grape Growers. "The Dean Company were Dealers in Grape Baskets, Basket Labels, Spraying Machinery and Material, and Shippers of Fancy Packed Chautauqua Table Grapes." (Thomas J. Brown.)

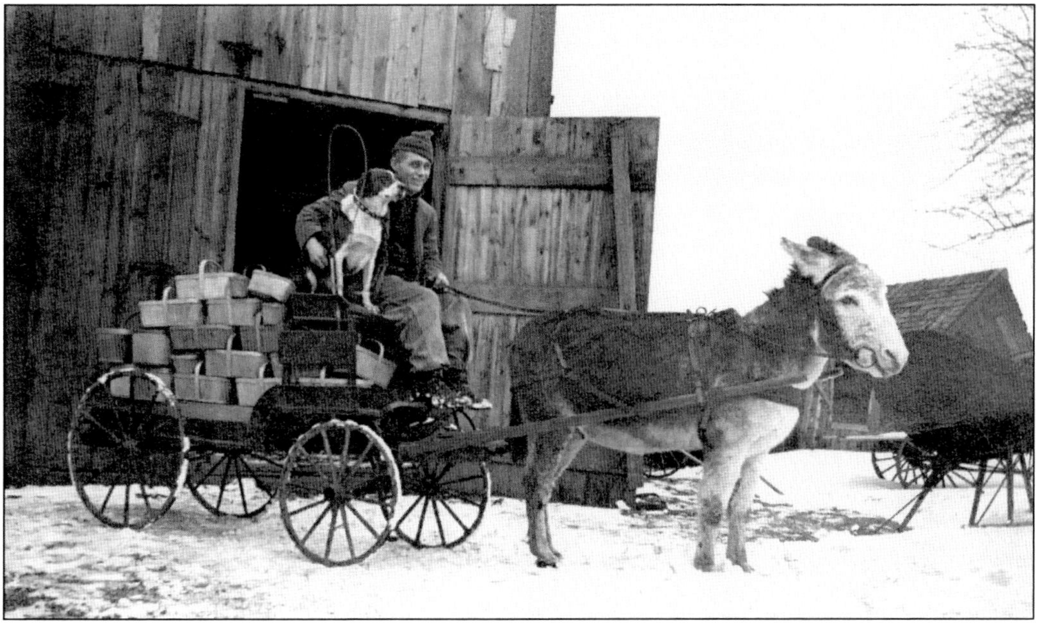

Charles C. Lewis, above, might have joined a grape cooperative. National Grape Cooperative's Jack Kaplan reminded associates: "We dreamed of a company . . . paying good wages to all who worked for it; and earning satisfactory profits for the benefit of all who owned it. . . . We dreamed of a company whose owners would be the grape farmers themselves . . . beholden to no one but their families, their consciences, and the general public." (Thomas J. Brown.)

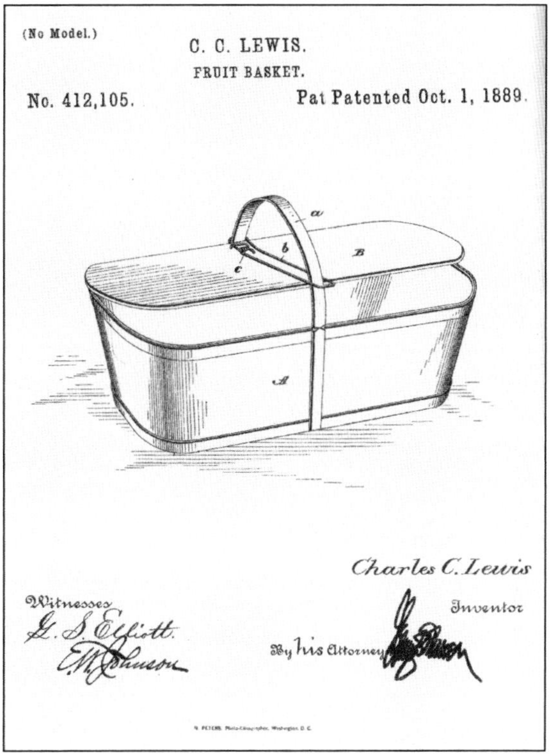

Lewis, of Westfield, was granted Patent No. 412,105 from the U.S. Patent Office on October 1, 1889, for this invention. His unique fruit basket was designed with a fastening device that firmly and securely covered the contents but prevented the sides "from spreading under the weight and pressure sustained under transportation." Lewis claimed his invention was simple and inexpensive. (Thomas J. Brown.)

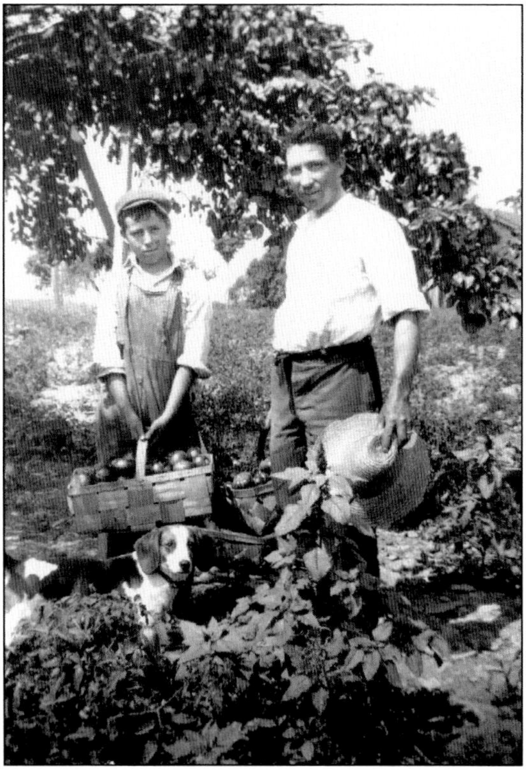

An abundance of other fruits and vegetables were also produced in the Grape Belt region. Tomatoes grown on small farms were sold to local canning factories located near the train depot. Westfield Food Products, Inc. (one of the largest plants) processed, packed, and shipped tomato products, berries, cherries, currants, and beans. By 1950, concentrated frozen grape juice was available in addition to jellies and jams. (Alice Chapman.)

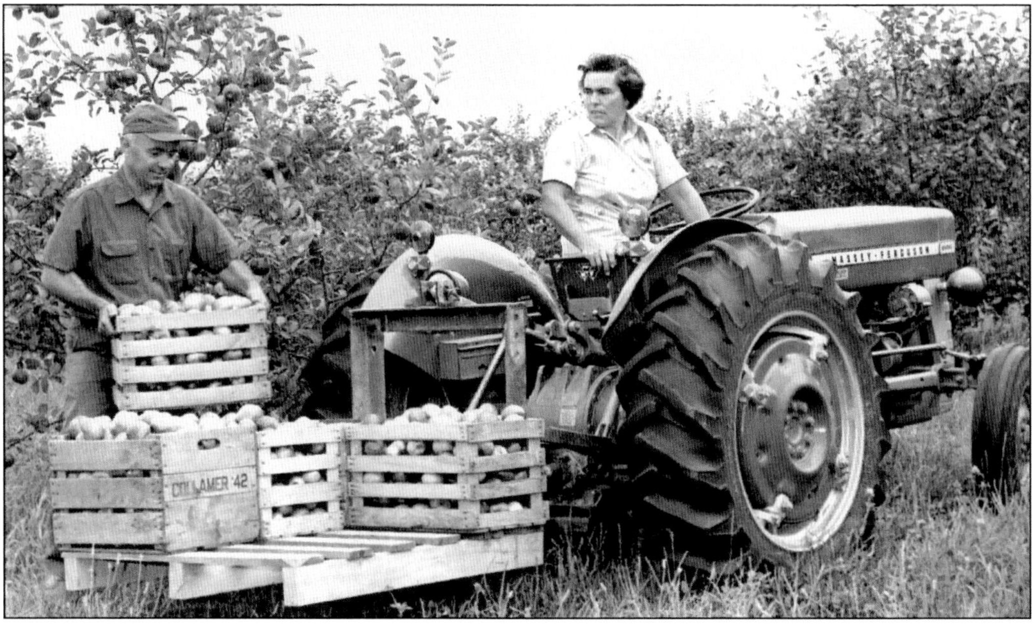

Like the pioneers, many Westfield area families continue to live off the land. Peaches, strawberries, raspberries, blueberries, plums, elderberries, cherries, pears, and apples grow in abundance. Will Larymore Smedley aptly described the fruit belt's beauty: "Great piles of golden and ruby-colored fruit lie among the orchard trees waiting to be shipped or stored for winter and the grapes hang in heavy clusters melting on the vine." (The Post-Journal, Jamestown.)

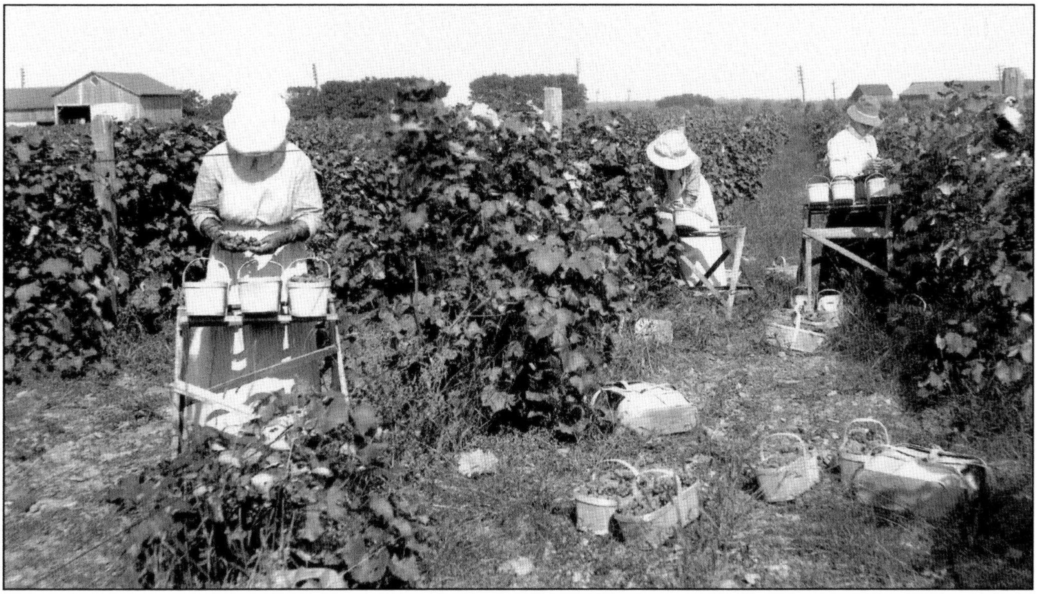

Despite the physical labor, many men and women anticipated making some extra money during the annual harvest, the time when grapes reached their peak of flavor. Backbreaking picking and sorting is now done in days by the mechanical harvester that revolutionized the grape industry. (Peter Flagg.)

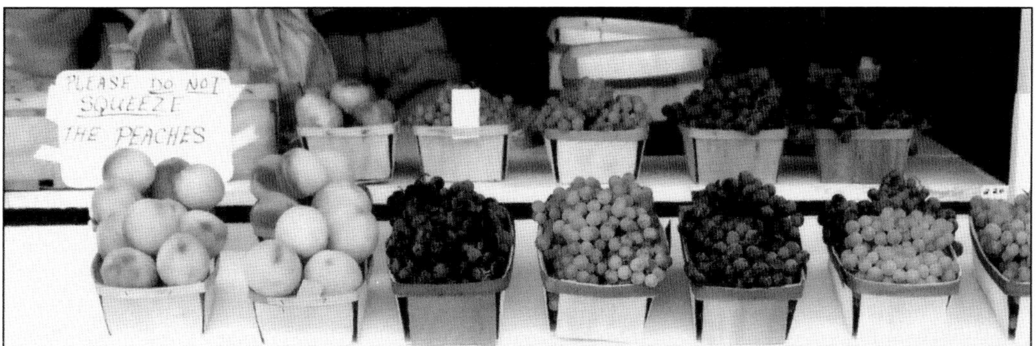

Columnist Anna R. Swanson remembered watching "the neighbor ladies be picked up by a big truck . . . to help with the grapes. In the spring, they pruned and tied the grapes . . . In the fall, they helped harvest. In those days most harvesting was done by hand. Today only those sold at roadside are handpicked." (Jane Currie.)

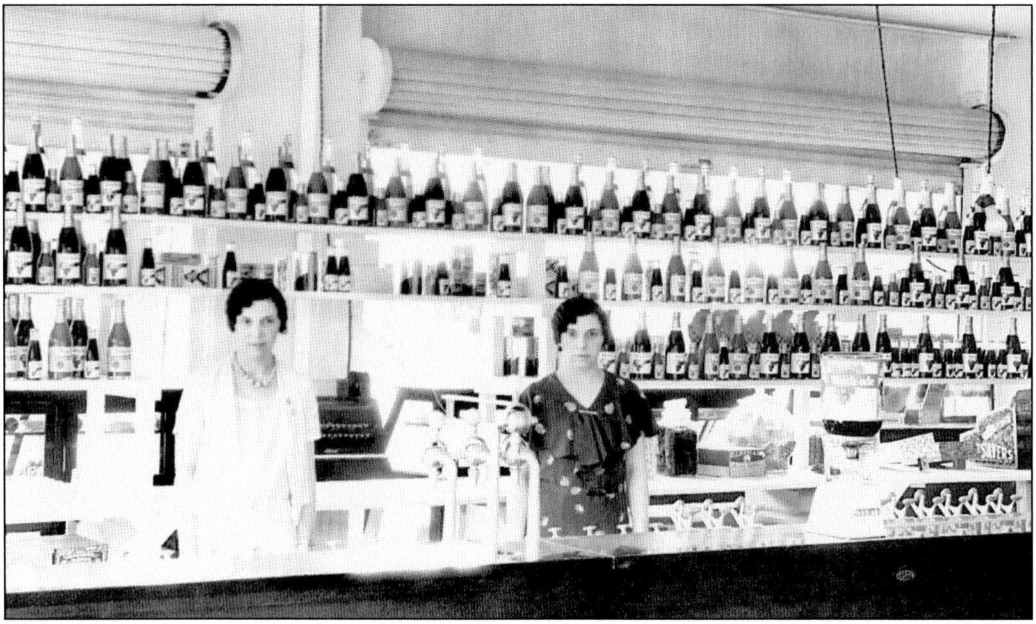

During the summer of 1974, hostesses at the Welch's Refreshment Pavilion on Bestor Plaza at the Chautauqua Institution served Welch beverages in a 1920s-style ice-cream parlor. Dr. Charles E. Welch served as a trustee of the institution from 1909 until his death in 1926. Several of his family members continue to reside on the grounds during the summer season. (The Post-Journal, Jamestown.)

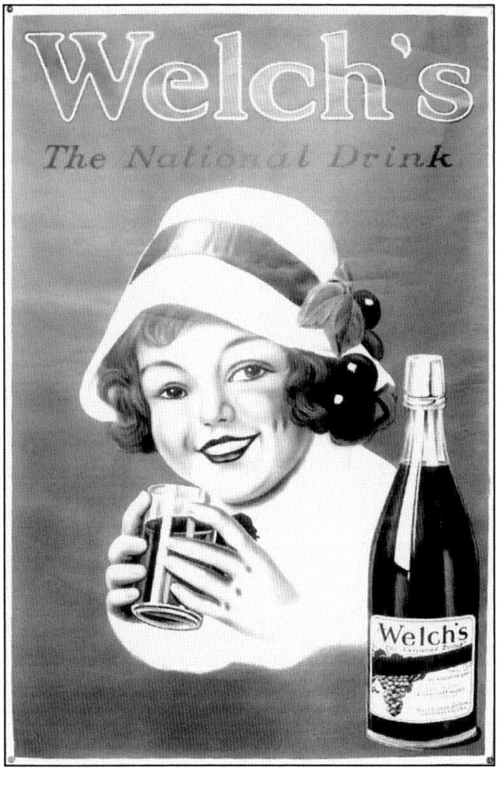

Dr. Charles E. Welch's vigorous advertising campaigns that "set the standard for progressive marketing techniques" aided his company's growth. Begun in church magazines and newspapers, sales and "sampling" were promoted at conventions, county and state fairs, on the Atlantic City Boardwalk, and at the 1901 Pan American Exposition in Buffalo. "Marketed for fountain, medicinal, beverage and sacramental purposes, Welch's grape juice was advertised in over 30 magazines in 1913 alone."

Six

Transportation and Recreation

Located on the main artery of the transcontinental highway midway between Cleveland and Buffalo, Westfield is the gateway to the Chautauqua region and western Pennsylvania. By 1860, railroads connected rural communities and stimulated growth. William H. Seward was praised for his local contributions: "The railroads which to-day cross our county in every direction, whistling upon every hill-top and screaming in every valley, date back to his influence."

Further progress was recorded in this scrapbook entry: "Mr. William Broadhead wanting some business supplies . . . drove an ox team over the Portage Road from Mayville to Westfield . . . wading through mud up the steep hills, taking the greater part of two days to accomplish this journey. [Years later] he made the same trip in a luxurious trolley car in 22 minutes." This occurred after September 1906, when the Chautauqua Traction Company, owned by the Broadhead family, extended its line from Mayville to Westfield. An enthusiastic crowd of 2,000 people flocked to see the four trolley cars arrive from Jamestown. The Westfield Board of Trade presented Almet N. Broadhead with a loving cup for his role in connecting Westfield to the larger county.

The dependable system was used for passengers and freight travel but also provided recreation for Patricia Appleyard Parker. "The track was a natural route for walking. We had contests to see who could balance the longest on the rail without falling off. In bare feet, you either had to do this or stick to the ties; the stones were painful to step on. We walked to our favorite strawberry picking meadow along the tracks and [to the path] by which grandfather took us to Sunday school in Hartfield."

In addition to the Barcelona harbor, residents and tourists also frequented the broad sandy beaches along the Lake Erie bluffs including Bourne's Beach, Walker Beach, Shore Haven, and Forest Park. In fact, many lovely summer homes were built in this locale.

Since the late 1800s, Westfield has had its share of culture and entertainment. In 1883, the Shakespeare Club studied travel, history, art, and literature. In addition, summertime band concerts, the Wells Opera House, the Orpheus Society, the high school's music programs, and the Westfield Music Club attracted participants and large audiences. For 32 years, the extraordinary Das Puppenspiel Theater of Westfield has performed for county students and adults as well as conducted puppetry workshops for teachers and librarians. The talented troupe has toured several states, including Alaska, California, and Texas.

The Chautauqua Rails-to-Trails organization has converted miles of scenic abandoned railroad corridors in the county into safe, off-road recreational trails used for hiking, biking, cross-country skiing, horseback riding, and bird-watching. One of several, the five-mile-long Alison Wells Ney Trail, on the escarpment south of Brocton, also affords a glorious view of Lake Erie from its overlook. The peaceful, serene trail is a fitting memorial to Alison, her family's "official" wildlife spotter, to encourage others to enjoy "the great beauty and gifts of nature" so highly cherished by the Ney family of Jamestown.

In 2003, an agri-tourism initiative was proposed by local developers in conjunction with Cornell University's Community Food and Agricultural Program. The purpose of the 125 business members of the Lake Erie Concord Grape Heritage Association is to encourage visitors to experience the past and present of the region; the many activities associated with grape production are "part of its culture, characteristics, and attractions." Along with the Seaway Trail, a 454-mile scenic route from Lake Erie to the Niagara River onto Lake Ontario and the St. Lawrence River, promoters hope the signage will attract travelers to related centers and "museums without walls." In the local Grape Belt, the objective is to ensure economic stability in its region that sustains 30,000 acres of vineyards.

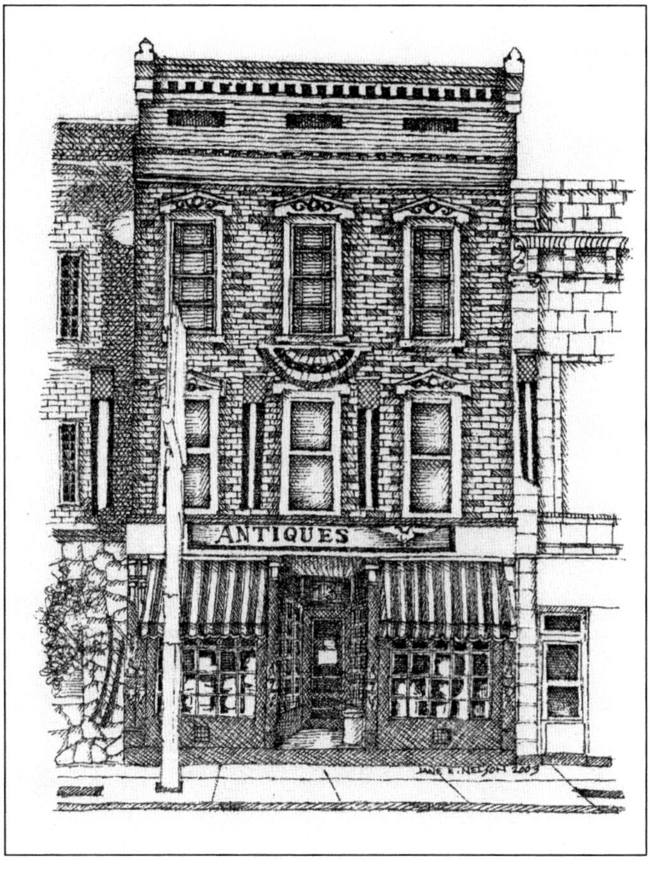

The Annual Westfield Antiques Show and Sale at Eason Hall, the major fund-raiser for the Chautauqua County Historical Society, is always "a glittering emporium which delights vendors and visitors alike." (Jane Nelson.)

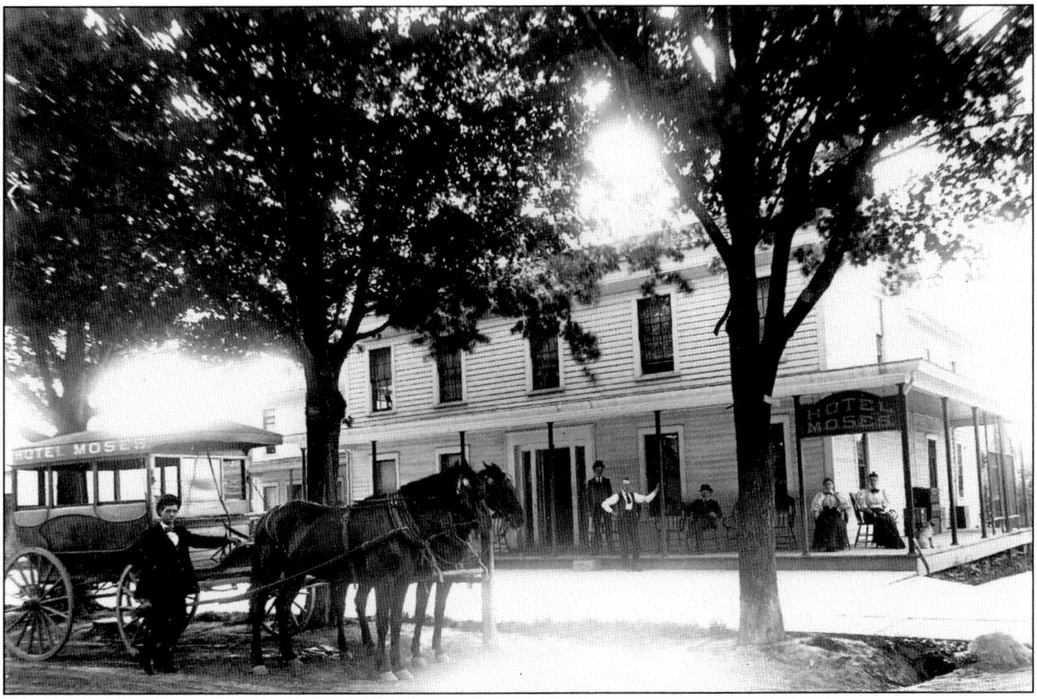

The Westfield House, at the corner of Portage and Main Streets, built by James McMahan in 1829, was a stagecoach stop. Patrons of the Hotel Moses, located at the corner of Clinton and Franklin Streets, were conveyed back and forth to the depot by this horse-drawn taxi. Lodgers at the Westfield Hotel simply carried their luggage across the railroad tracks to their accommodations on English Street. (Sydney S. Baker.)

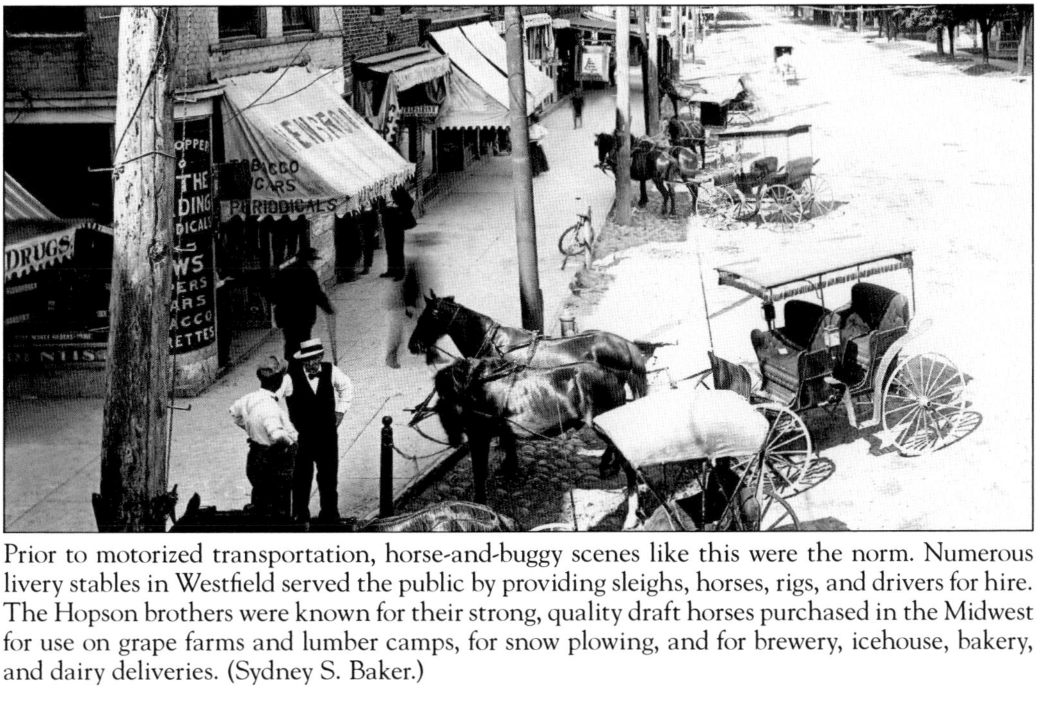

Prior to motorized transportation, horse-and-buggy scenes like this were the norm. Numerous livery stables in Westfield served the public by providing sleighs, horses, rigs, and drivers for hire. The Hopson brothers were known for their strong, quality draft horses purchased in the Midwest for use on grape farms and lumber camps, for snow plowing, and for brewery, icehouse, bakery, and dairy deliveries. (Sydney S. Baker.)

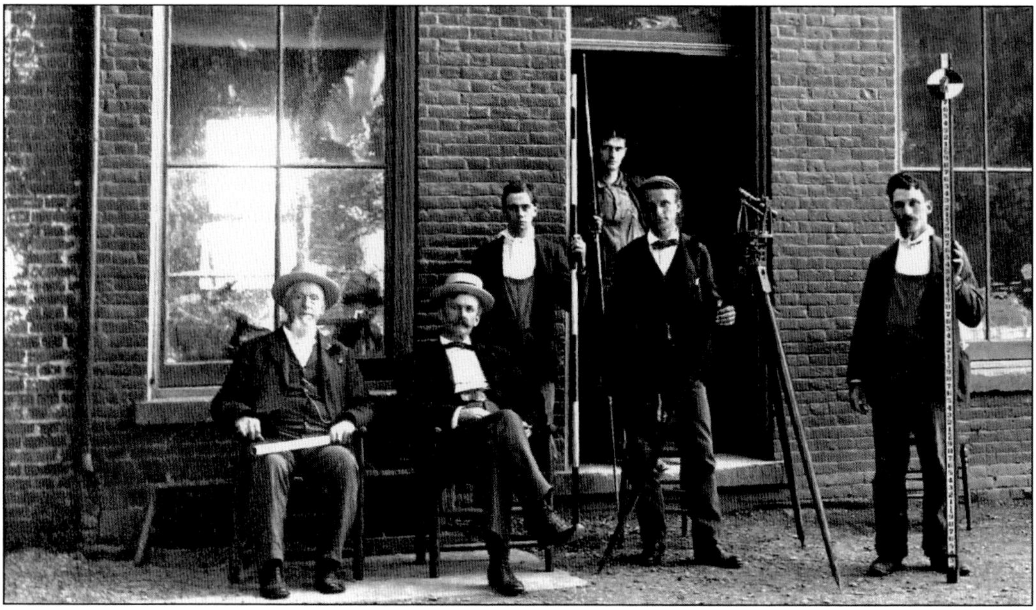

Surveyors for the Chautauqua Traction Company inspect Portage Street where the Welch Building now stands; tracks were subsequently laid along that highway from Mayville to Westfield. When regular service began in 1906, the trolley traveled north through the village to the Nickel Plate railroad station. By 1909, a single-track car traveled on an additional line connecting the station with the Barcelona shore.

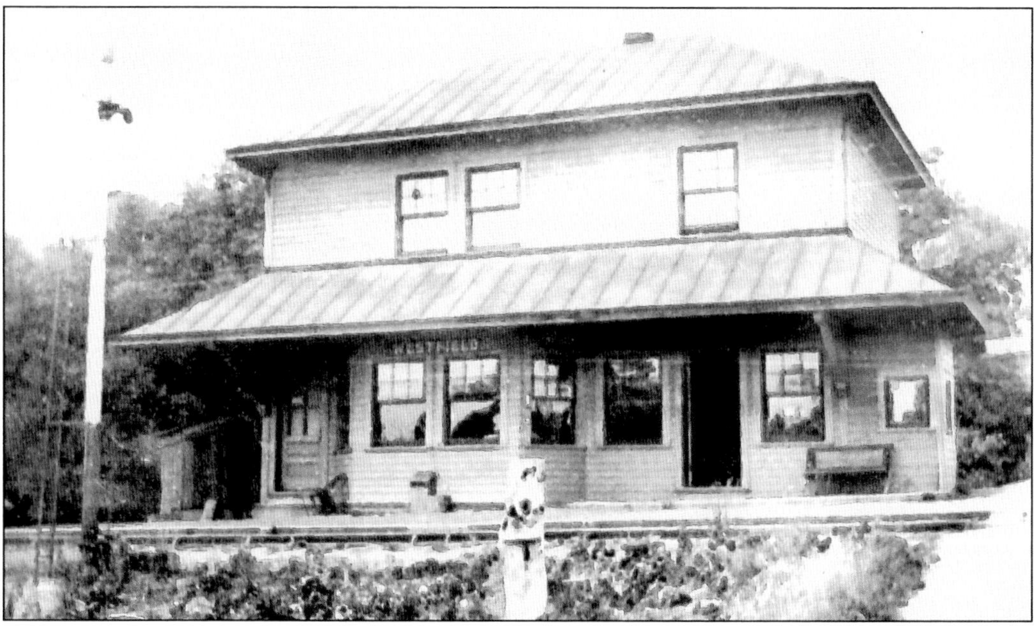

William Broadhead and his sons Almet N. and Shelden B. Broadhead, owners of the Chautauqua Steamboat Company, the Chautauqua Traction Company, and the Jamestown, Westfield, and Northwestern Railroad Company (JW&NW) encouraged county residents to travel beyond their own neighborhoods. A station or depot was located at each transfer point to accommodate passengers. Many resembled this one located on the Westfield viaduct.

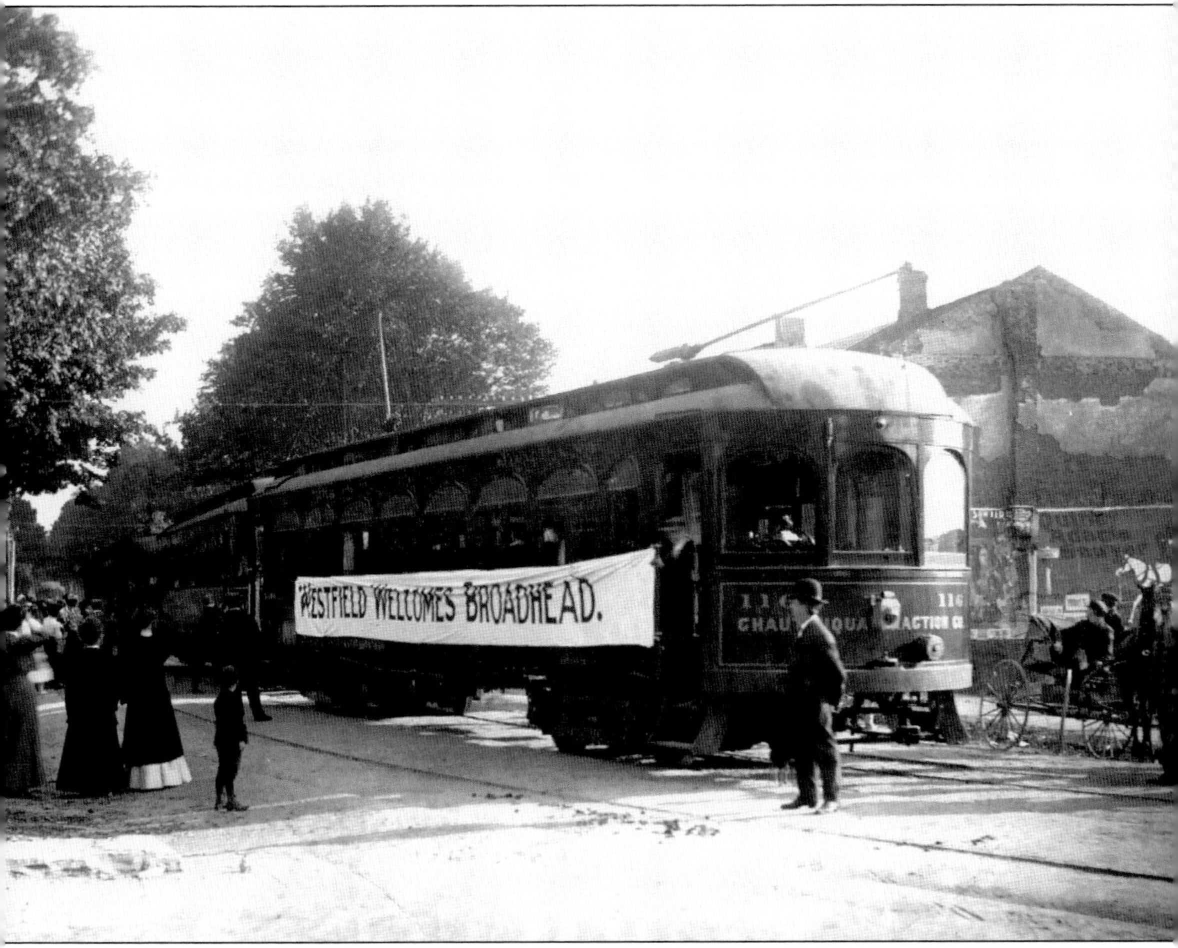

Westfield residents thronged to welcome Almet N. Broadhead, excited that Westfield was finally connected to Chautauqua Lake and to Jamestown about 30 miles away. The downhill section between Mayville and Westfield was extremely slick in the winter due to icing on the tracks. One passenger remembered her rides through the gorge during other seasons of the year: "Descending at the rate of 100 feet to the mile, [the trolley car] passes through deep cuts, over high but substandard trestle works, winding among the hill along dark chasms and wild scenery, until the blue waters of Lake Erie appear . . . terminating in Westfield, close by the precipitous bank of Chautauqua Creek." (Sydney S. Baker.)

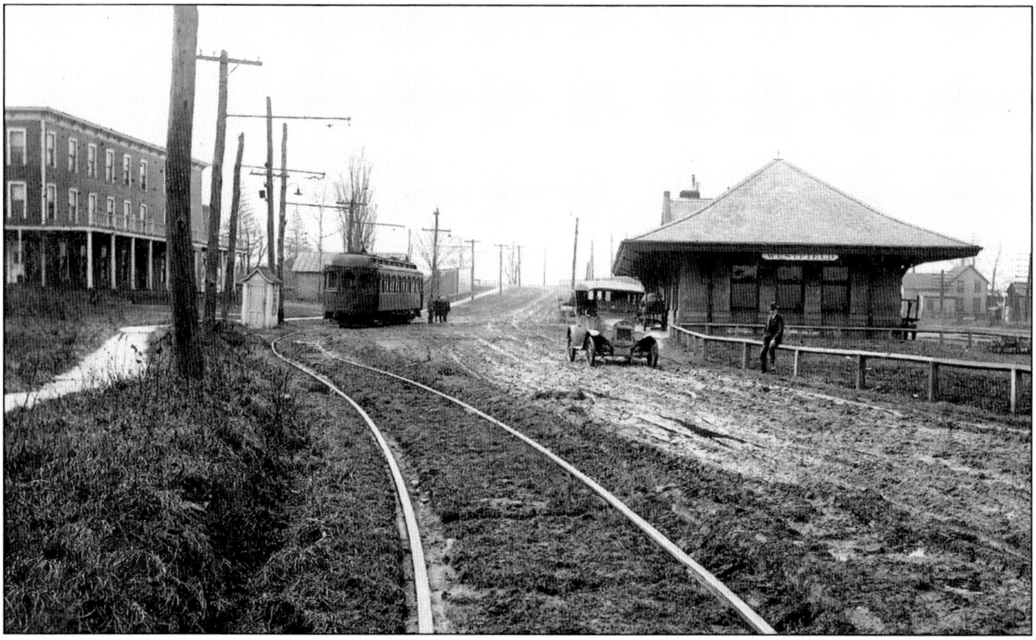

In the mid-1800s, railroads greatly improved Westfield's economy. The Lake Shore and Erie Railroad was the first line to pass through Westfield; with increased traffic, its yards were moved from Erie, Pennsylvania, to Westfield. The Westfield depot accommodated 25 passenger trains that made daily stops on the New York Central and the Nickel Plate Railroads. (Sydney S. Baker.)

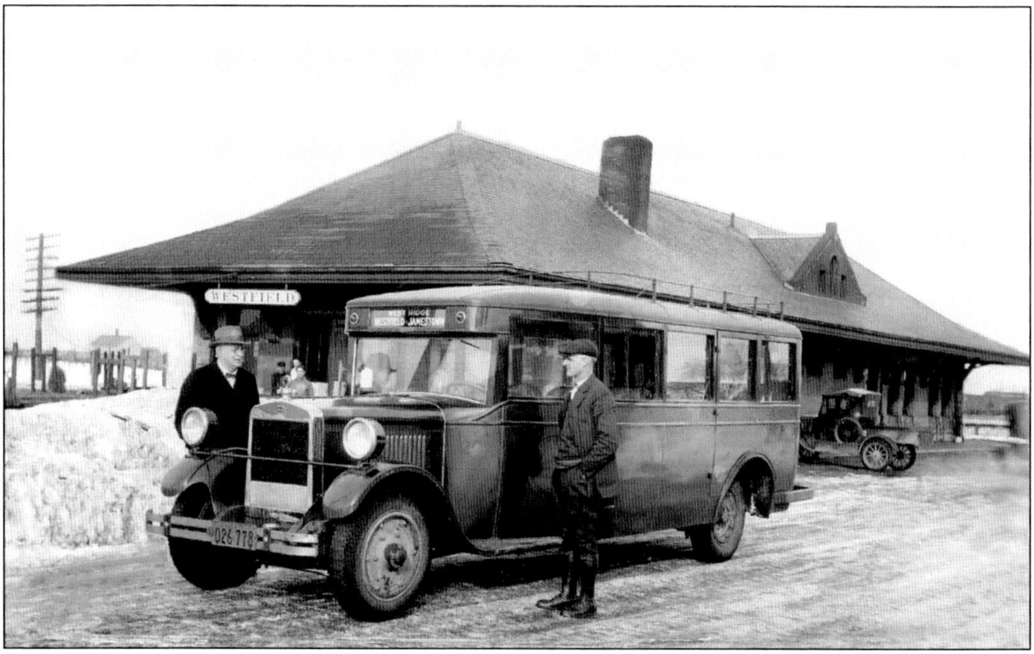

In 1926, Harry Raynor was granted a franchise for the West Ridge Transportation Company to schedule runs between Westfield and Mayville. In the photograph above, the bus is parked beside the railroad depot across the tracks from the Westfield Hotel. When the interurban trolley passenger service ended in 1947, motorbuses were enlisted to convey travelers to railroad depots.

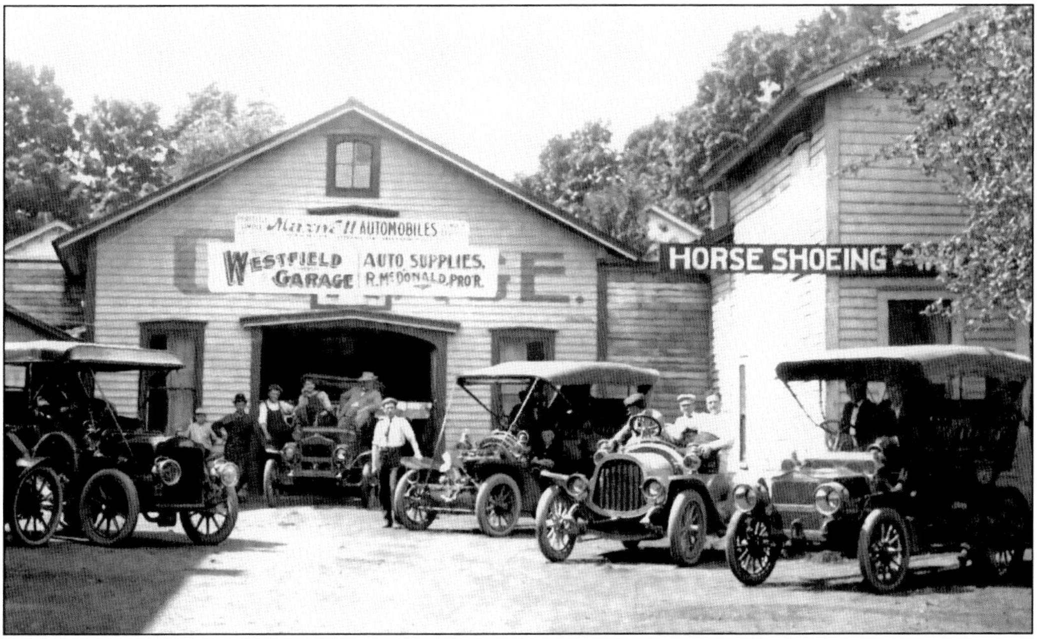

Prior to the devastating 1909 fire, R. M. MacDonald, proprietor of Westfield Garage and Auto Supplies, and blacksmith E. M. Johnson shared an area of the Minton House Hotel barns. Strangely enough, although the trolley ran on Main Street in front of the buildings, the horseless carriage and horses provided alternate modes of transportation at that same time. (Sydney S. Baker.)

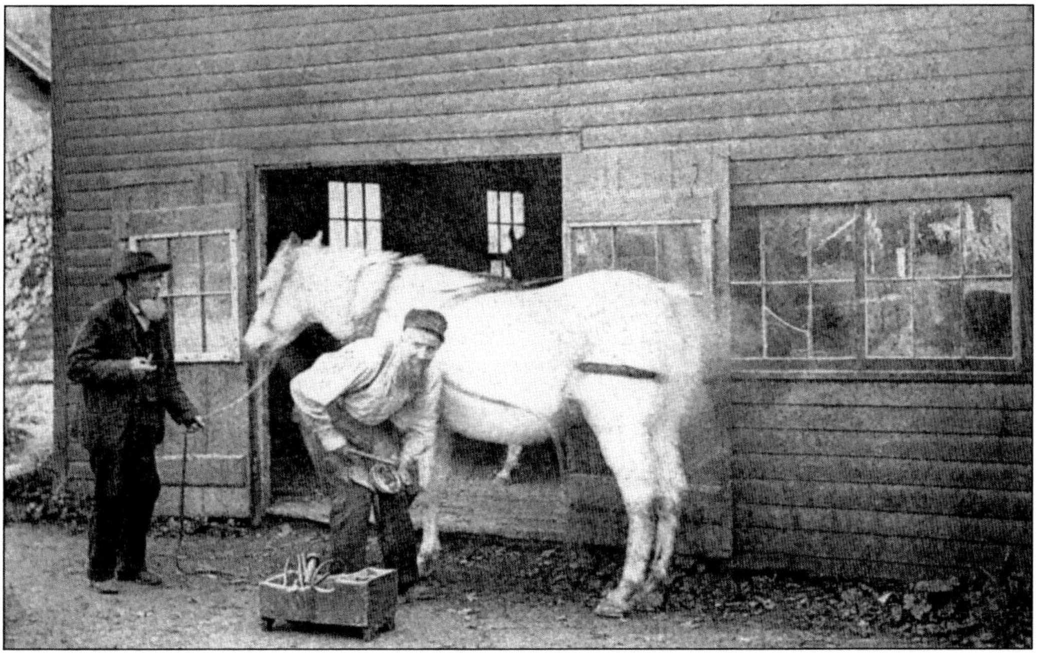

John McCarty's blacksmith shop opened in 1875 on West Main Street. After a fire in 1902, John and his son Bill moved their business to Union Street, where they were in operation for decades. Jinny Griffin remembers riding into town from her family's farm to have her horse shod by the experienced McCartys. (Ray and Kate Lawson.)

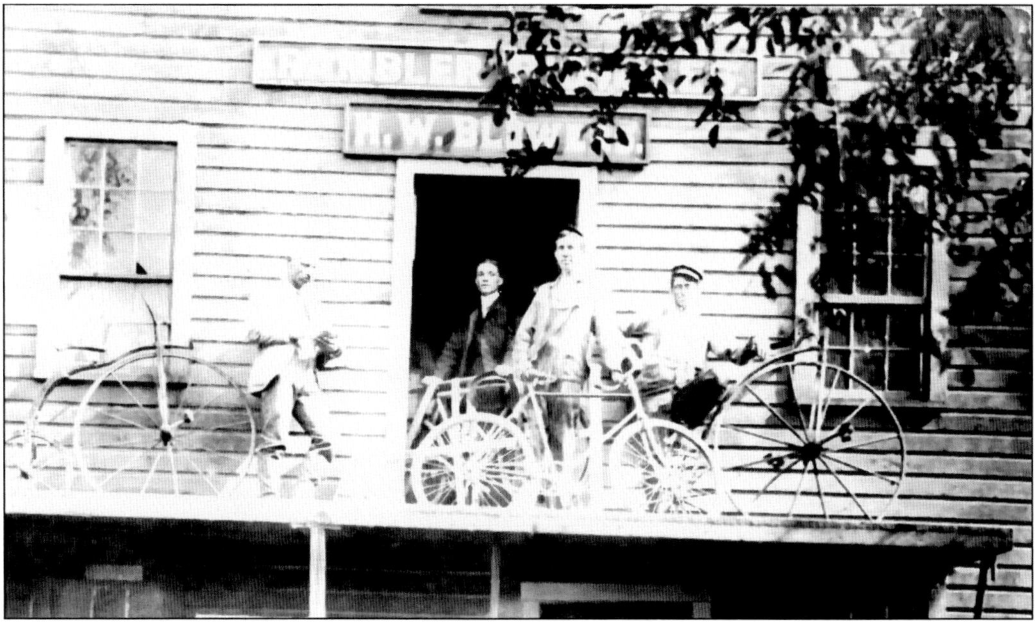

After the Civil War, "large crowds gathered to watch young men on those old-fashioned high wheel bicycles" at the Old Fairgrounds. In 1905, Harry Blowers (left), a fruit farmer, opened a bicycle shop on Elm Street, now the site of Eason Hall. Harry's brother Roy Blowers, who became a bicycle-racing (and later motorcycle) enthusiast, most likely participated in competitions, peddling between Westfield and Erie, Pennsylvania. (Richard Galloway.)

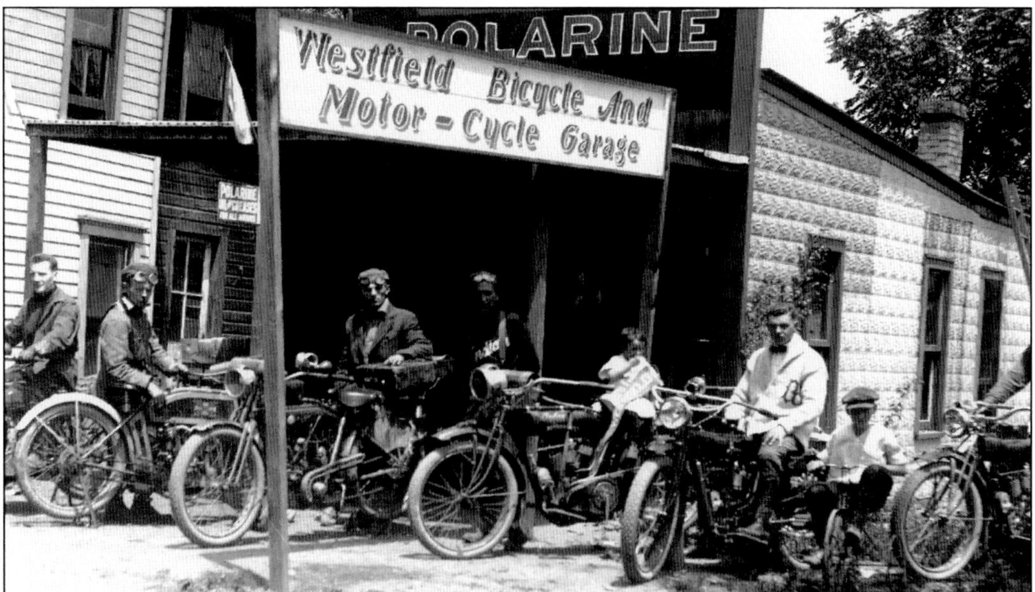

Boys of all ages seem to have an affinity for vehicles. This Westfield Bicycle and Motor-Cycle Garage was probably an adjunct of the garage behind the Minton House. The age of automobiles created the need for filling stations; automobile supply, wrecking, and body shops; and car dealerships. Many such businesses on Main and North Portage Streets continue to cater to community needs. (Dan Chapman.)

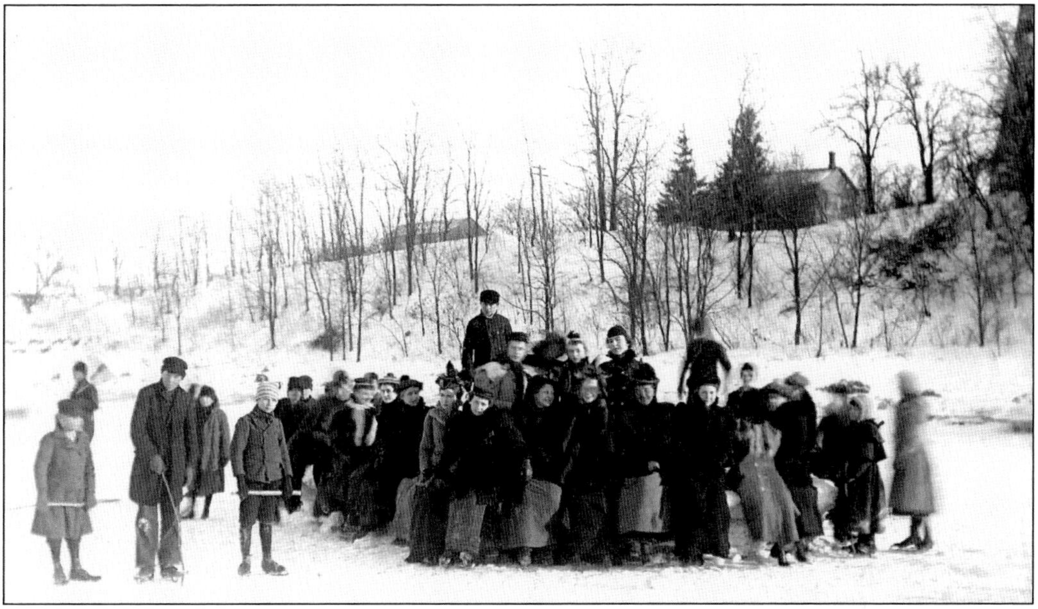

On frosty winter evenings, families would huddle around their coal stove, but during the day, they might venture out onto frozen Lake Erie near Barcelona, as did this bundled-up skating party in January 1894. While "ski trains" from Cleveland came to the county in the 1930s, snowmobiling has become the modern craze. In 2004, six county clubs accommodated more than 3,000 registered snowmobilers. (Chautauqua County Historical Society.)

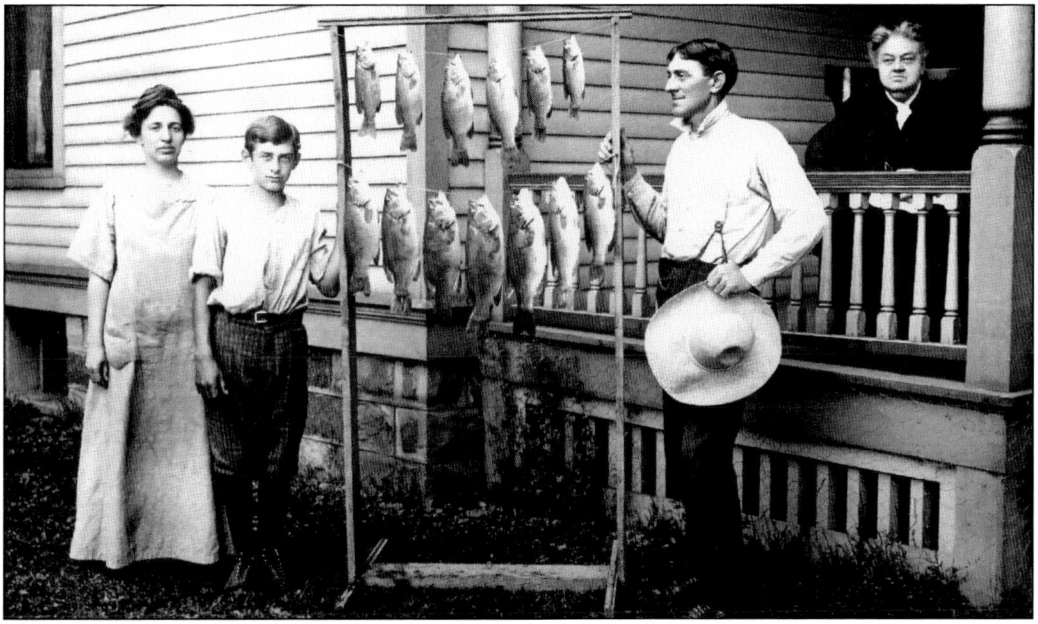

The abundance of wildlife and fish in Westfield, as in all of Chautauqua County, attracts thousands of sportsmen annually. Members of the Westfield Fish and Gun Club host an annual turkey shoot. Oftentimes, muskellunge, small and largemouth bass, walleye, panfish, and trout may find their way to a dinner plate via a rack like this one, despite the disdain evidenced by the woman on the porch.

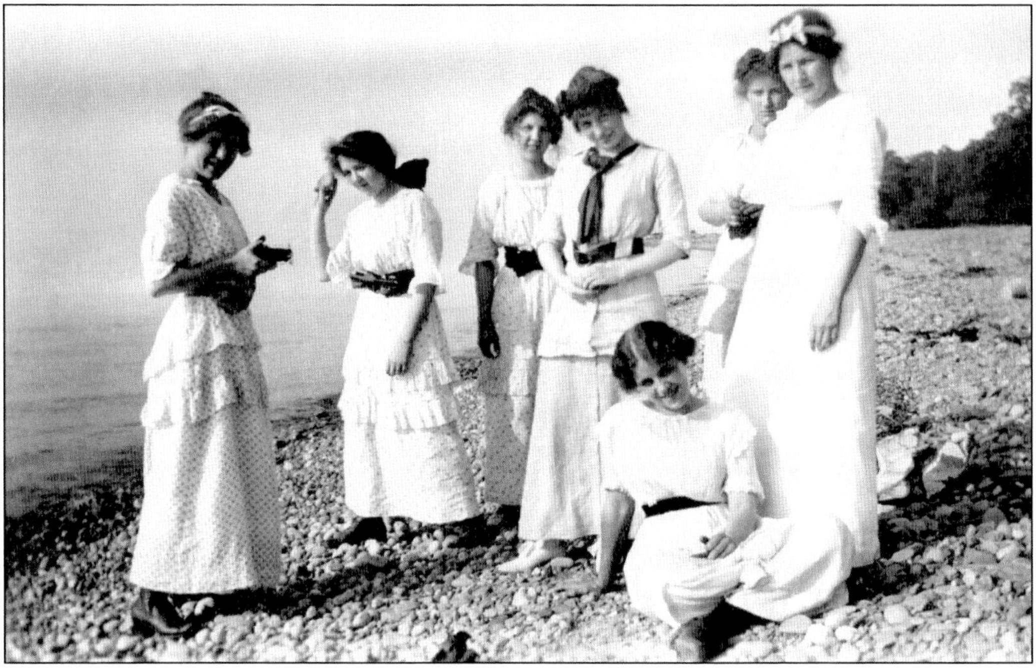

Lake Erie, like nearby Chautauqua Lake, provided a recreational haven in the summertime. In her February 1838 diary entry, Mary Peacock, age 17, who might have been visiting Harriet Goodrich, wrote that she attended a great ball at Westfield, "a splendid affair" and in June "went down to the Lake. There we stayed and walked along the beach for a long time . . . found some very pretty stones and shells." (The Gollnitz family.)

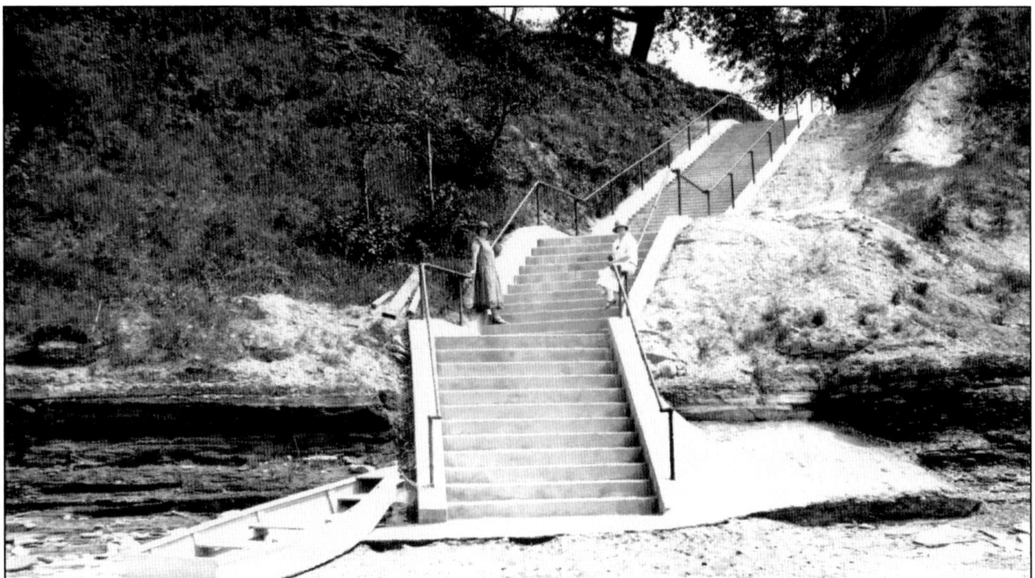

Hawthorne Beach is readily identified by its steps, which, over the years, have fallen and crumbled due to erosion. In 1929, Harry Hopson and Herbert Crandall created and promoted the Lake Erie Beach as an attractive summer resort. Its special features were a stable and two trotting tracks for driving and riding horses.

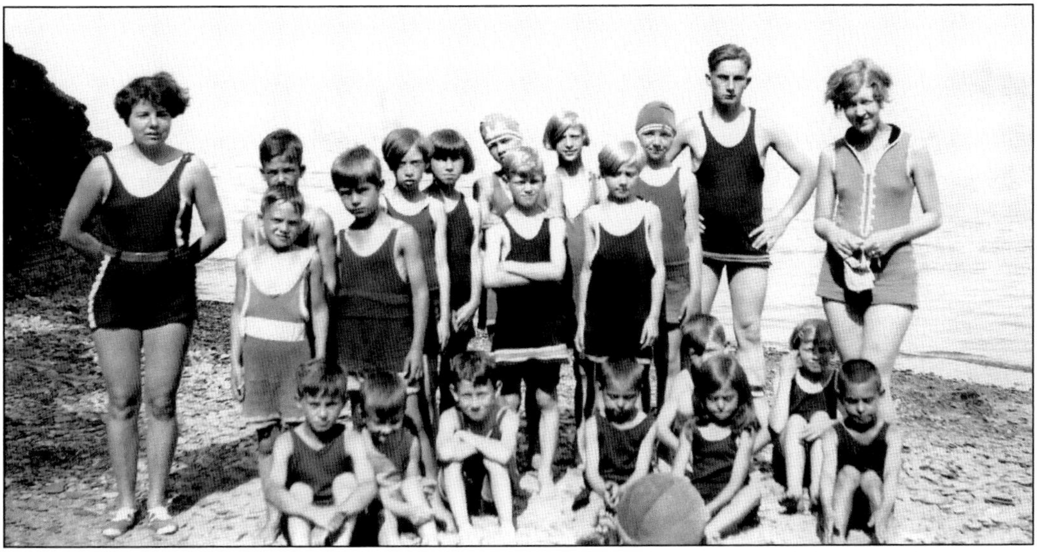

During the Depression, the Westfield Business Girls Club, a group of "live-wired employed women," solicited donations from the community "to provide good food and fun in a healthy environment for the children of Westfield." Beginning in 1930, 21 children were enrolled in their Health Camp at Ottaway Park.

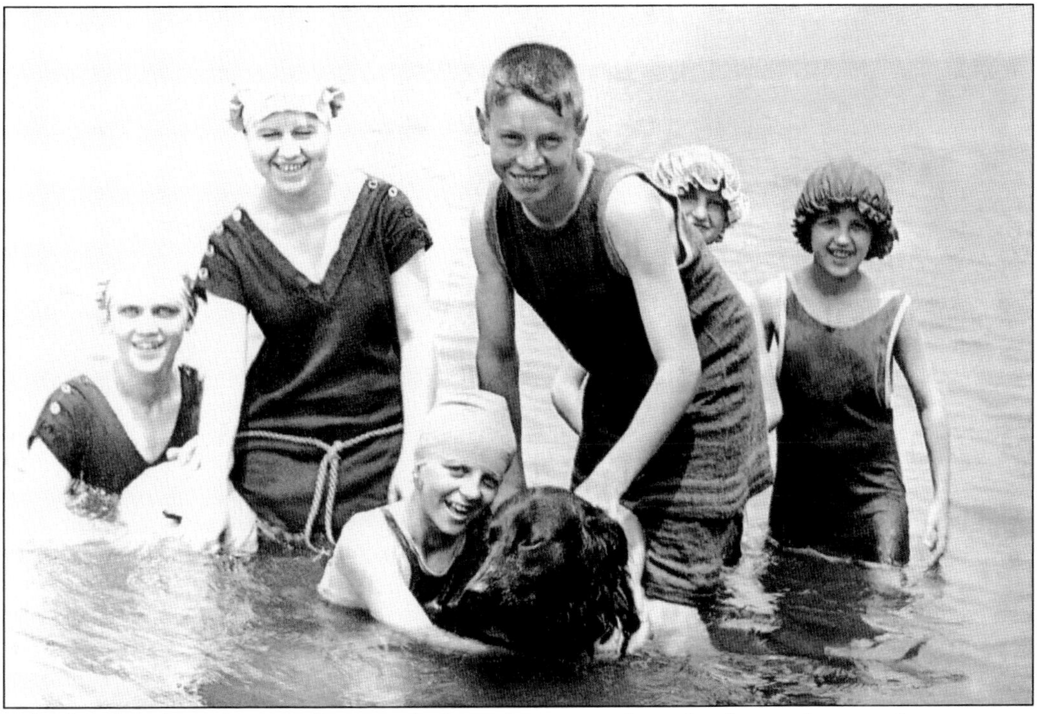

Whether beachcombing, collecting driftwood, or attending the firemen's annual ox roast at Ottaway Park, Lake Erie has been a perfect spot to cool off with friends, canine or otherwise. Prior to Westfield's annual Fourth of July parade, picnicking families might have enjoyed "lunch baskets of potato salad, freshly baked loaves of graham bread, and Boston baked beans, followed by Devil's food cake." (The Gollnitz family.)

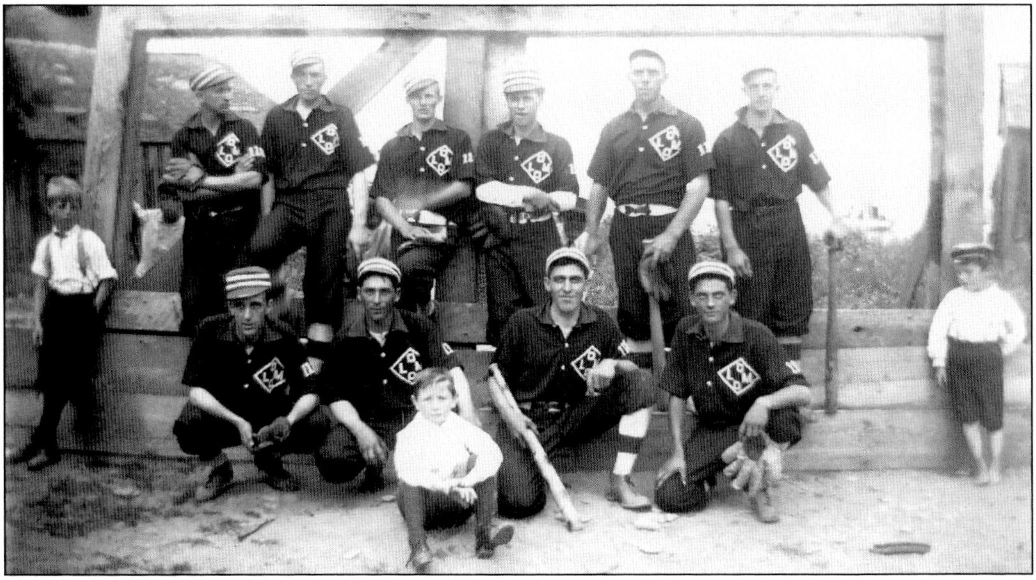

Fishing and boating were not the only activities in Barcelona. Someone took time to label this image of these early baseball players lined up behind Carlisle McLean, the batboy or team mascot. From left to right are (first row) unidentified, Fred Oakes, Ralph Schoenfelt and John Nichols; (second row) unidentified, Roy Cleveland, John Lawson, George Ellis, Fred Anderson, and George Holbrook. (Barcelona Commercial Fishermen's Museum.)

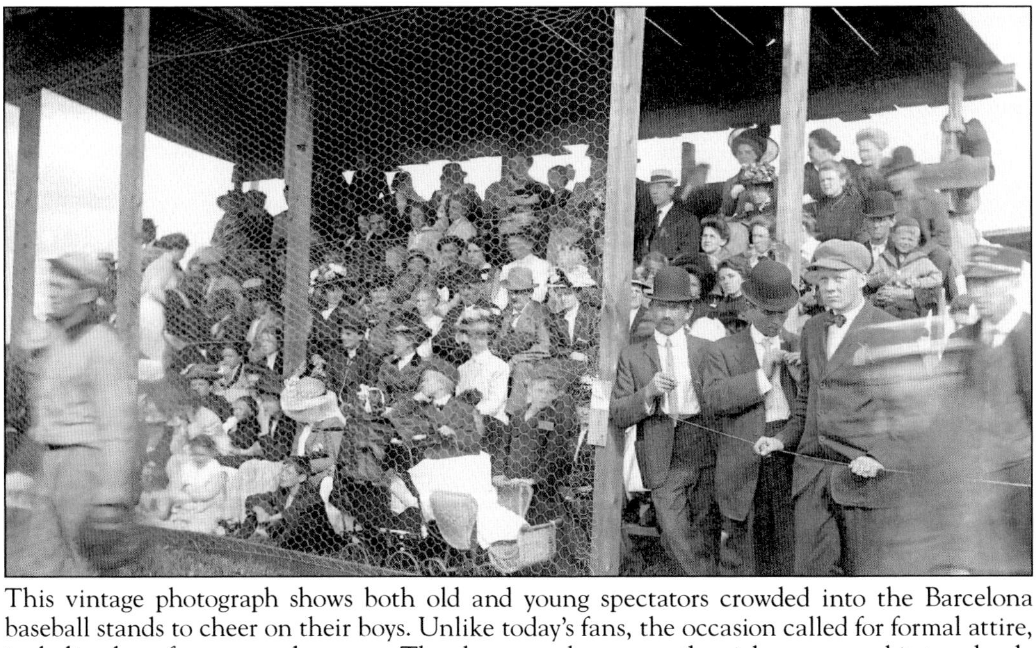

This vintage photograph shows both old and young spectators crowded into the Barcelona baseball stands to cheer on their boys. Unlike today's fans, the occasion called for formal attire, including hats for men and women. The three gentlemen on the right appear a bit too dandy for this occasion; a horse race might have been more to their liking. (Barcelona Commercial Fishermen's Museum.)

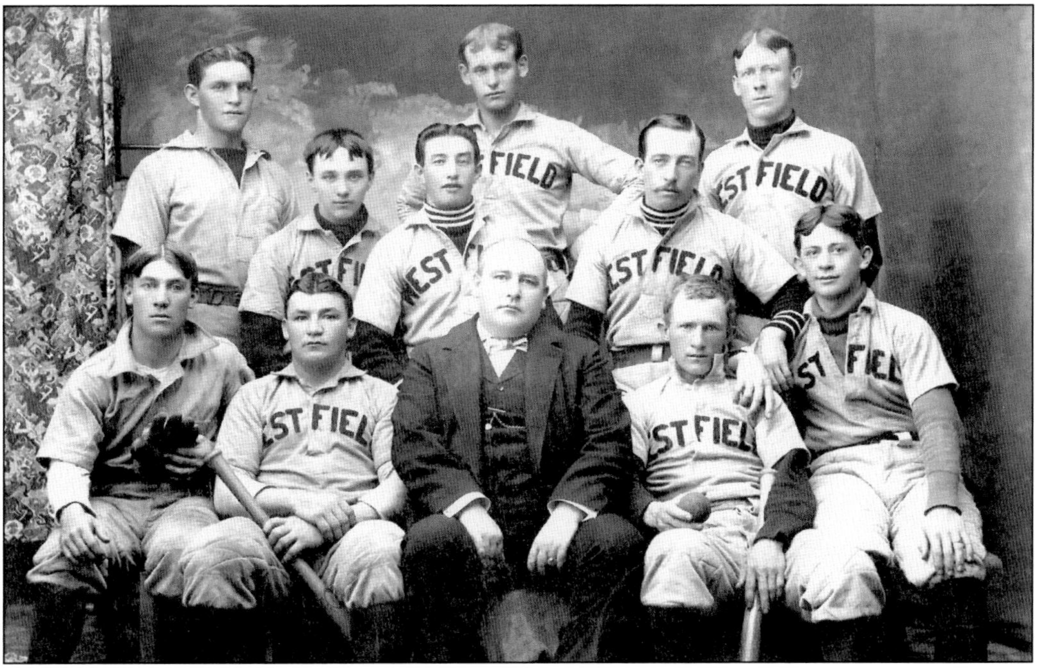

Only surnames were identified on this 1897 photograph of the Westfield baseball team. From left to right are (first row) Hopper, Lehrman, manager C. C. Miller, Kline, and Patrick; (second row) Householder, Pratt, O'Hara, Barker, King, and Slicker. (Chautauqua County Historical Society.)

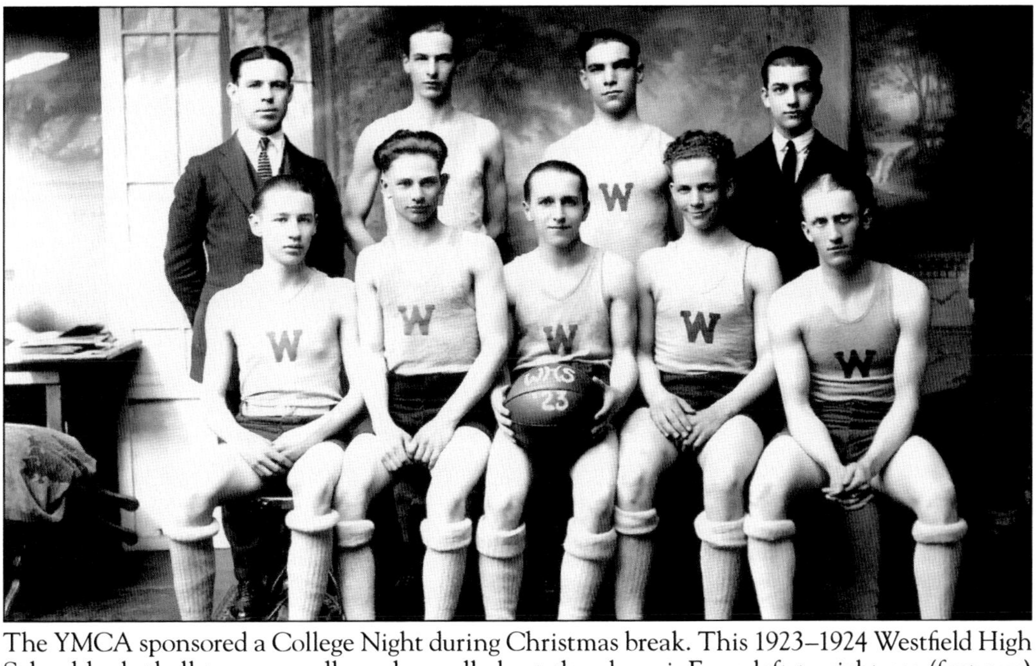

The YMCA sponsored a College Night during Christmas break. This 1923–1924 Westfield High School basketball team soundly and proudly beat the alumni. From left to right are (first row) Ted Skinner, Charlie Ellis, Jimmy Sullivan, Joe Clark, and Nellie Wantshouse; (second row) coach Alton Doud, Ray Hunter, Wilson Forbes, and Paul Cutting. Coauthor Kathleen Crocker's father, Jimmy Sullivan, team captain, treasured those lifelong friends. (Kathleen Crocker.)

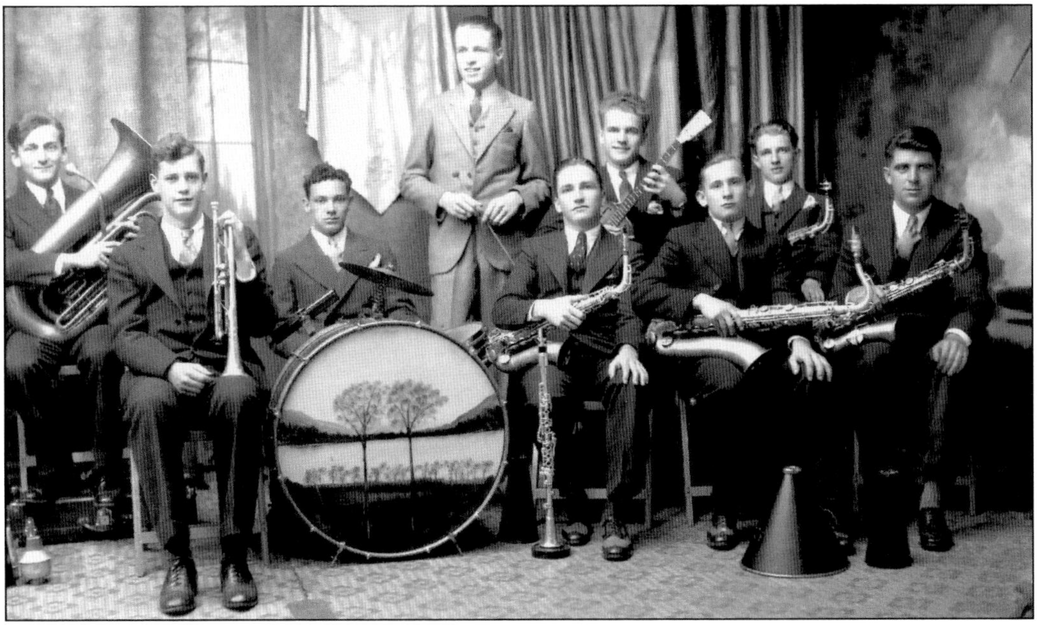

Kent Brown's orchestra was formed in 1928 when "the economy wasn't the greatest and a little cheer seemed a good idea." Among those pictured in this William Sherman photograph are Joe Clement, Brown, Austin Judd, Earl Dascomb, Bill Hall, Don Douglas, Vincent Hopson, and Ernie Morse. Unable to afford a ticket to the big bands at the Casino in Bemus Point, Brown admitted listening from a distance.

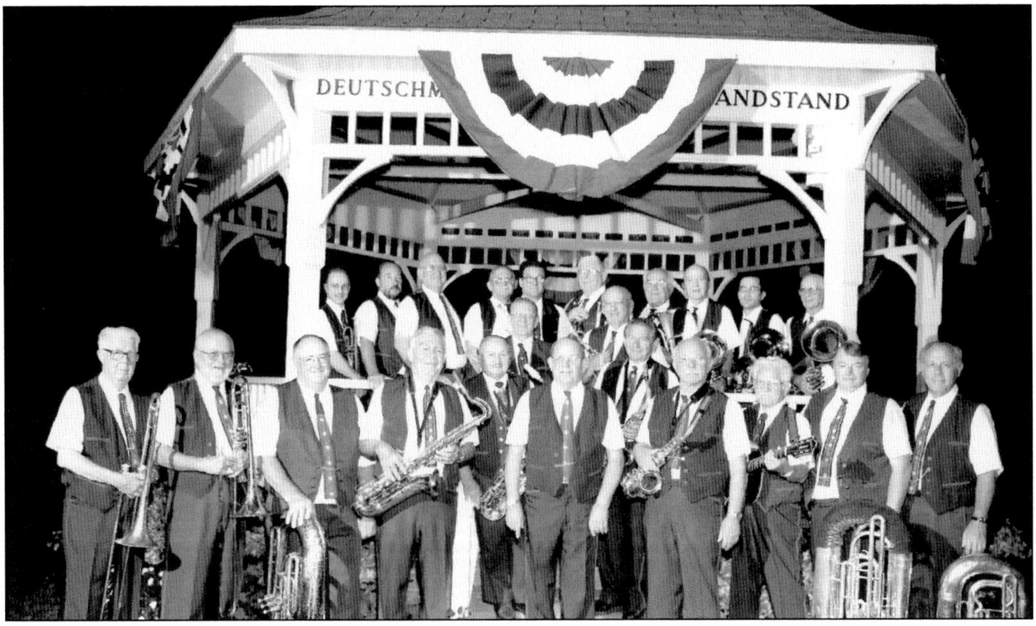

Named for a German march, the Deutschmeister Band originated in the 1960s as part of Westfield's adult education program. The skilled musicians, representing diverse occupations, continue to entertain locally, specializing in marches, waltzes, "golden oldies," Dixieland jazz, and big band numbers. On August 10, 1985, this bandstand in Moore Park was dedicated in memory of group organizer and leader Alva "Matty" Matthews. (Jane Currie.)

Seven

THE VILLAGE

The bicentennial of the first European settlement in Chautauqua County, when James McMahan arrived in the Crossroads in 1802, was celebrated in grand style in Westfield in July 2002. *The 2004 Town of Westfield Community Profile* compiled by Deborah Williams, director of the Patterson Library, affirmed that "the 5,232 residents of the Town of Westfield hold dear all aspects of community life. They take special pride in the unique architecture and historical heritage of the town and village."

The village of Westfield has always been known for its attractiveness. At the dedication of the Patterson Library in 1908, George Vincent, Chautauqua Institution's president remarked, "You have a village among the most beautiful in all the land. I have from my boyhood known your lawns and trees and hospitable houses. You may well take pride in all the loveliness by which your daily lives are surrounded."

The village is widely recognized for its shade trees and beautiful homes with spacious grounds "many of which," wrote Daughters of the American Revolution historian Mattie B. Sullivan in 1917, "testify eloquently to the prosperity which attended the grape harvest in former years." Its Main Street remains "the natural beat of its heart, is kindly and protecting—a neighborly warmth a city never acquires."

In 1928, Amorette E. Fraser summed up the essence of Old Westfield: "its quiet streets, shaded and embowered with massive locust trees which, in their summer blooming, shed a wealth of fragrance over all the town; its bright green Common, the beauty spot of the Village; its deep, full roaring creek, dashing with swift current through the gorge; the stately hills clothed with dense forests and rising in the majesty to meet the sky; the primeval forest, an unbroken barrier between the village and the Lake."

"The mute but eloquent testimony of the old buildings, tied up with that history, speaks louder than any print, of the life, drama, the personalities and eccentricities, of the hardy pioneers . . . The preservation of these land-marks seems imperative, their loss through neglect, or lack of interest, [or] funds, seems a crime against posterity," wrote Emma Piehl.

Leave it to dear Billie Dibble, the current historian, to say it best: "Westfield was a charming village a century and a half ago. She may need a face lifting but I think we can safely say she is growing old gracefully."

Moreover, its residents have also made it a unique place. The Westfield Antique Show and Sale at Eason Hall hosts about 25 reputable dealers annually from all over the country. Several fine shops with knowledgeable owners were established back in the 1800s. Two of the most prominent remain Priscilla B. Nixon Antiques and Vilardo Antiques. Militello Antiques on Jefferson Street, now operated by Julia Militello, has been in her family for over a century. Serious dealers and collectors visit Westfield's many dealers to purchase fine china, pressed and cut glass, miniatures, dolls, musical instruments, lamps, textiles, furniture, quilts, artwork, and Welch Grape Juice Company memorabilia.

Founded around 1880 by eight women including Hannah Patterson and Jane Wright, the Union Relief Association was the first organization in Westfield to provide food and clothing for the needy in the community. During the Depression, the group even served lunches to children in the primary grades. The year 2005 marked the 84th Union Relief Charity Ball fund-raiser.

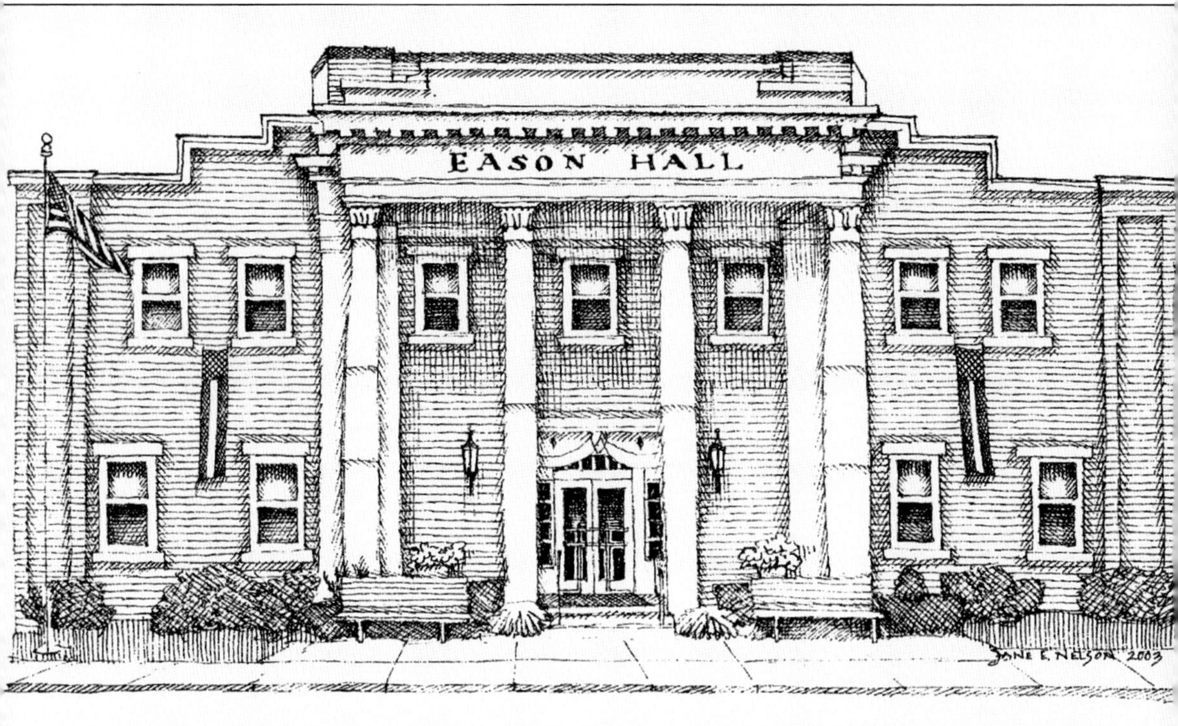

Backman's Skating Rink and Stage were once located in what is now Eason Hall, the Greek-pillared community gathering place donated by Clara Eason, who bequeathed $26,000 for a municipal building to honor her parents David and Margaret Woodside Eason. She stipulated that jail- and fire-related purposes were to be excluded in favor of town and village offices. Dedicated in 1925, the building's four pillars represent love, design, work, and wisdom. (Jane Nelson.)

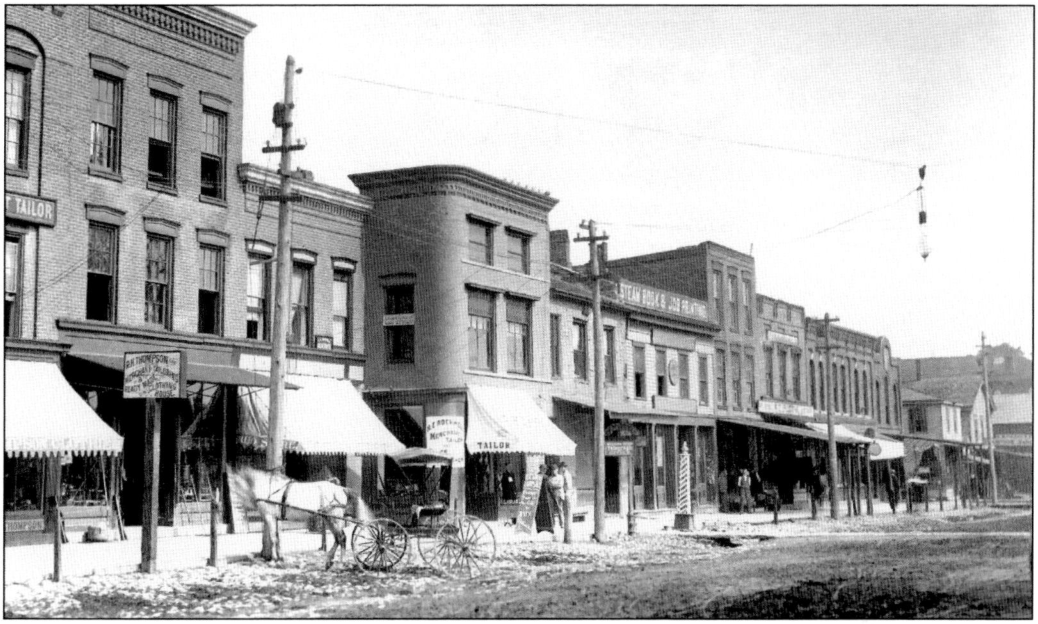

The Irvine E. Jones's Corner Drug Store, W. G. Norton's Furniture, and M. A. Lyon's Central Drug Store are seen above. This row of frame business buildings fronted by brick sidewalks and hitching posts extended from North Portage to Market Streets. In 1909, flames consumed the block from Market Street east to the Minton House Hotel. (Sydney S. Baker.)

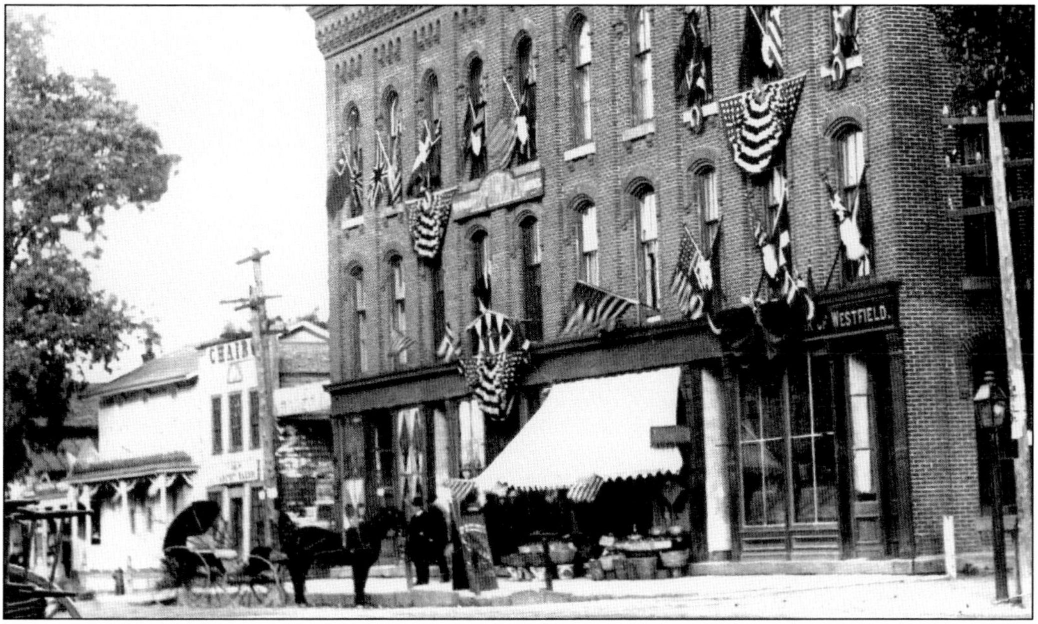

In 1864, the Brewer Block, at the corner of Main and Elm Streets, faced the Spencer Block, the business row above. The First National Bank (at the far right), the post office, and retail stores were its occupants. The power lines and poles, seen at each side of the photograph, were in place long before the Chautauqua and Erie Telephone Company building replaced the bank's office there.

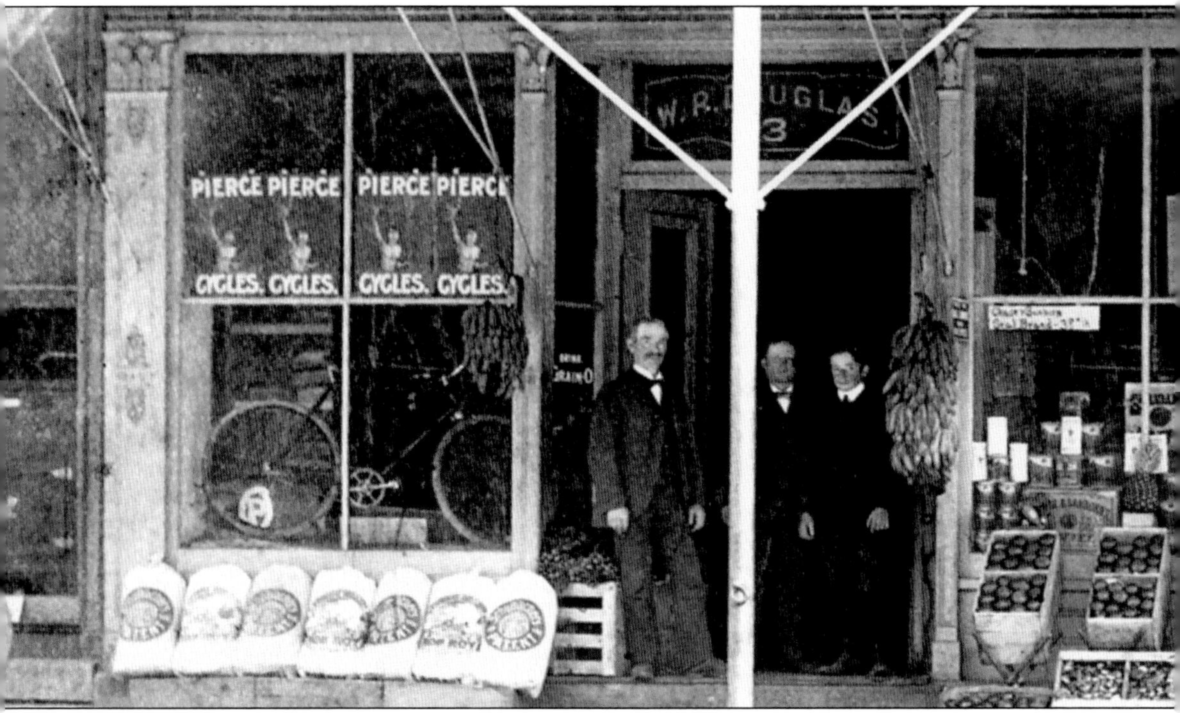

William R. Douglas came to Westfield in 1863 from Ireland and, in 1870, became an associate of Robert Shaw. Begun as the Cosgrove and Shaw store in the Shaw Block, William R. Douglas's lucrative business endured from 1882 until his death in 1912. "The two stores Nos. 3 and 4 were united by arched passageways. Store No. 3 was used as a grocery department, while No. 4 sold

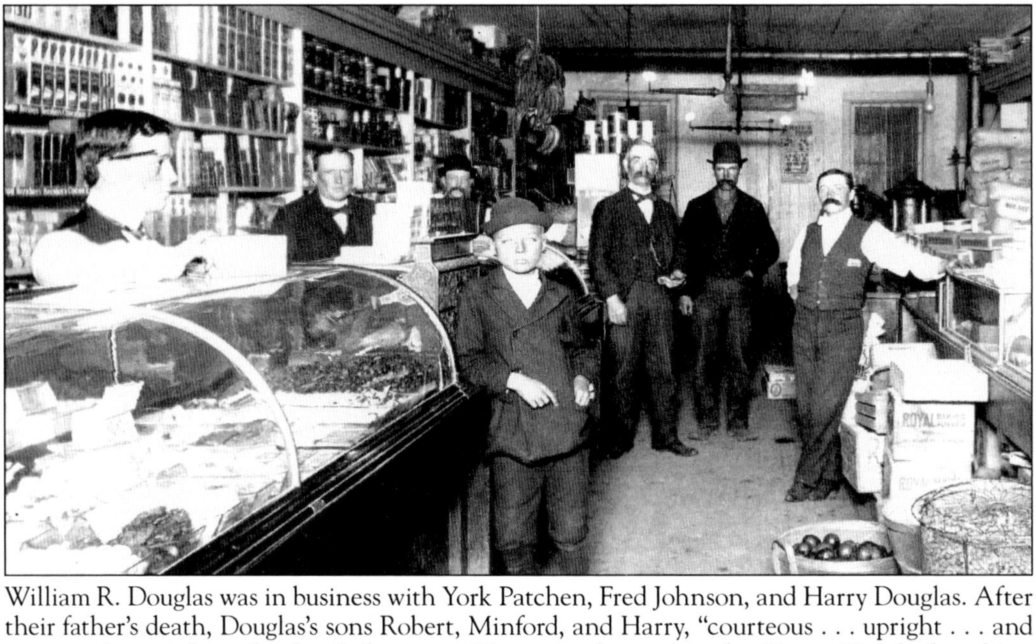

William R. Douglas was in business with York Patchen, Fred Johnson, and Harry Douglas. After their father's death, Douglas's sons Robert, Minford, and Harry, "courteous . . . upright . . . and generous," carried on the family business. The sons also procured a Pierce Bicycle franchise. (Chautauqua County Historical Society.)

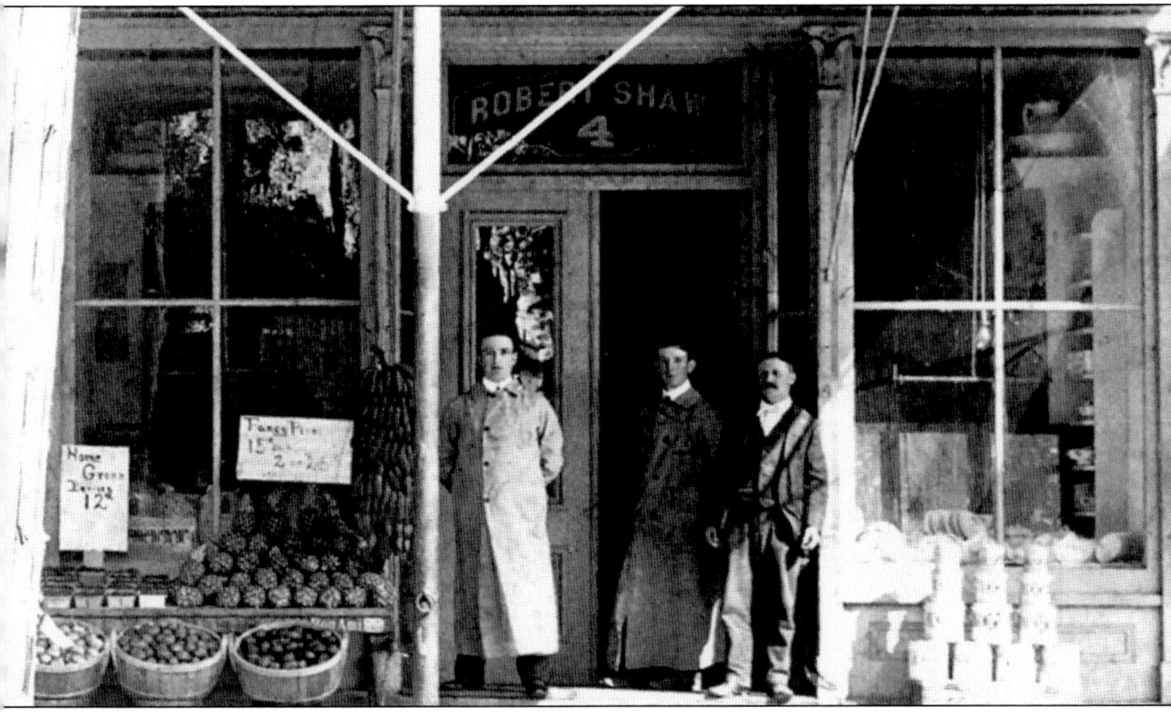

crockery, glassware, elegant china, and lamps." The second floor was used as a "cheese room" and held reserved stock. The entire building was protected in the front by an awning, which extended the length of the walkway. After 70 years, the building converted to the well-known Pinter's Restaurant.

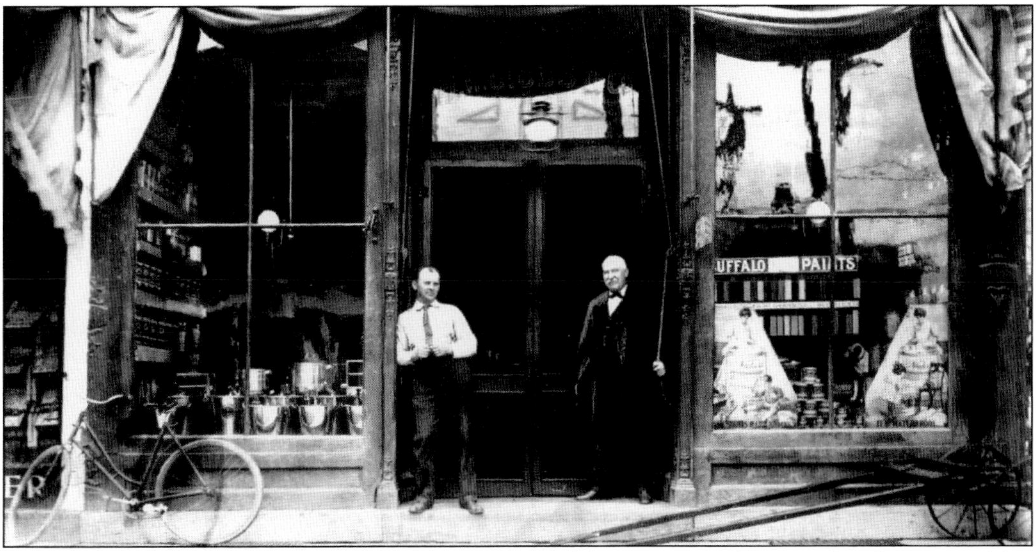

In 1901, Gus Gollnitz worked with Harlow W. Gibbs, seen standing in the doorway of his three-story hardware establishment at 31 East Main Street. Gibbs "was the ranking merchant on Main Street for his length of service." For more than 150 years, the building has housed other hardware stores operated by numerous men, including W. R. Reid, Clarence and Will Bell, F. Ryan, and L. B. Waite. (Vinnie Calarco.)

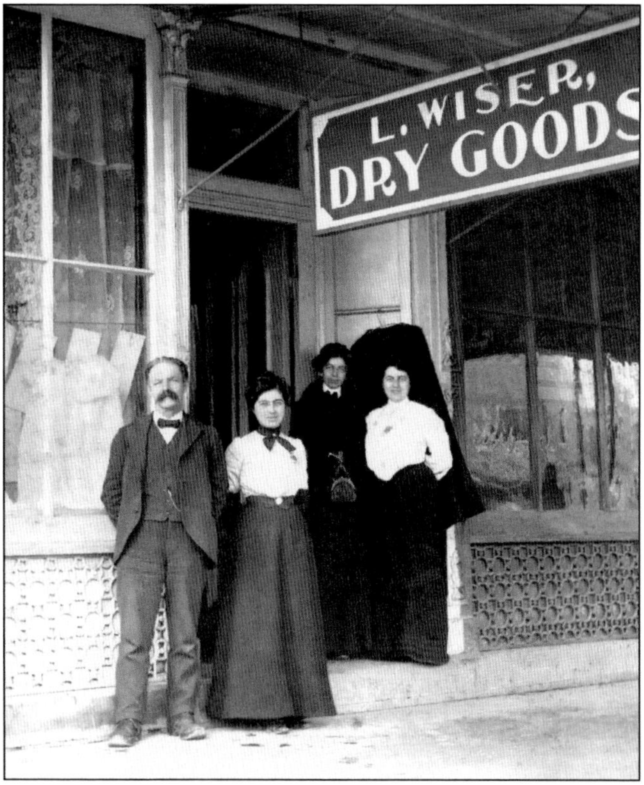

German-born Lawrence Wiser, a shoemaker and peddler, once lived with Dr. Francis Beattie Brewer, whose loan helped him become a successful Westfield merchant. Interesting bargains included "muslin underwear and corset covers, 19 cents to $1, night gowns, 50 cents to $2, and white petticoats, 50 cents to $4.50." After his death, his daughters Mary and Fanny maintained a dry goods, millinery, and jewelry business on the premises.

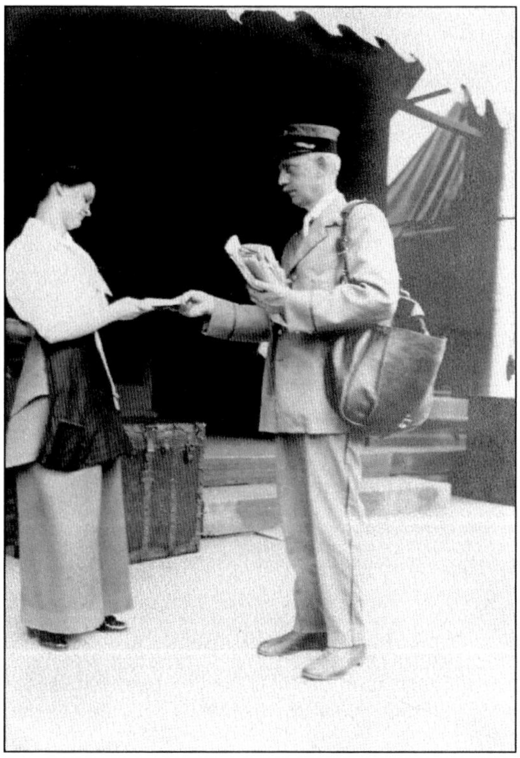

James McMahan was the first postmaster of the Chautauqua Post Office at the Crossroads from 1806 until 1818 when it was moved and renamed the Westfield Post Office. It has been located in the Brewer Block, the Welch Block, and the Kent Block on North Portage Street. It was typical for store clerks to greet their carrier as he made his rounds in the business section. (The Gollnitz family.)

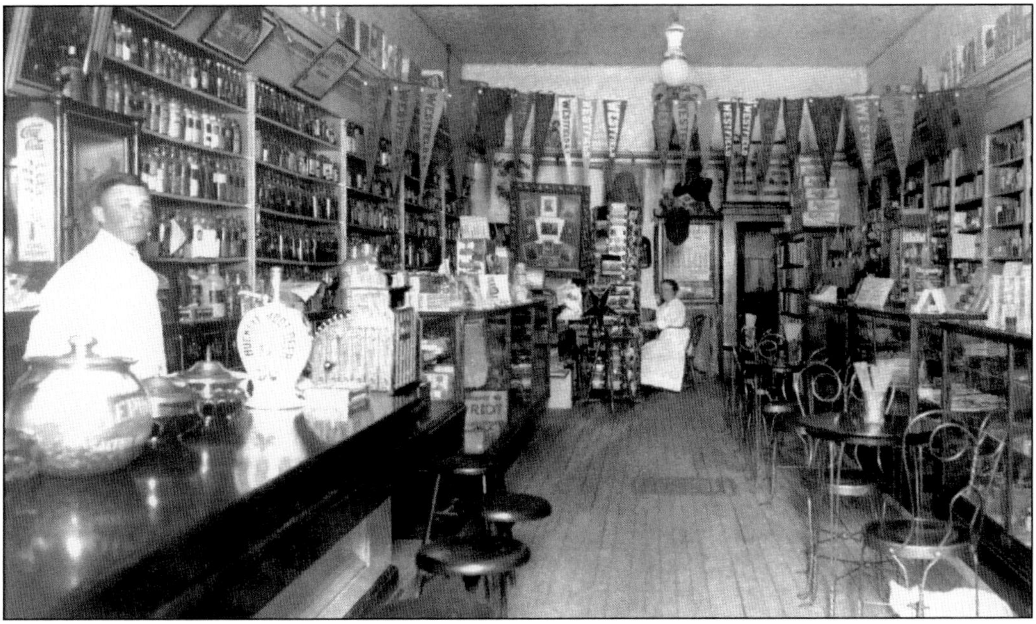

The Corner Drugstore at 1 East Main Street, in the Spencer Block, was first owned by Byron Fenner and then James V. Minton. When Julia Poole of Clymer, New York, purchased it in 1910, it became a popular hangout. In addition to pharmaceuticals and a soda fountain, she featured a rental library for children and one of the first racks of postal cards.

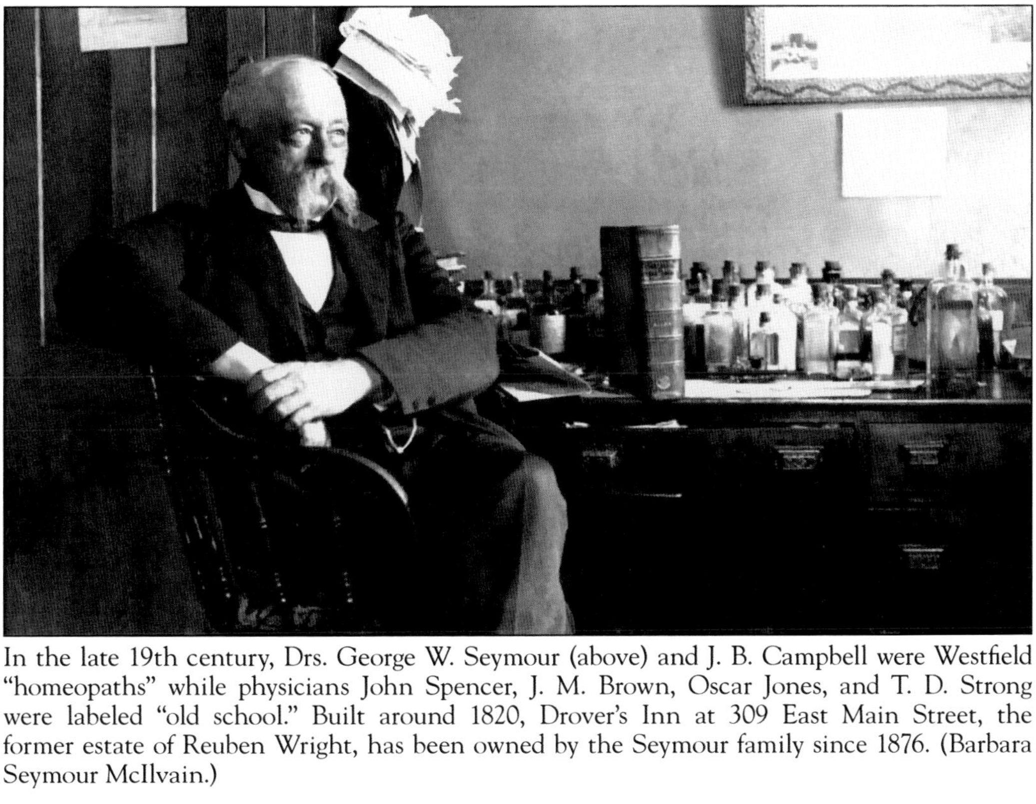

In the late 19th century, Drs. George W. Seymour (above) and J. B. Campbell were Westfield "homeopaths" while physicians John Spencer, J. M. Brown, Oscar Jones, and T. D. Strong were labeled "old school." Built around 1820, Drover's Inn at 309 East Main Street, the former estate of Reuben Wright, has been owned by the Seymour family since 1876. (Barbara Seymour McIlvain.)

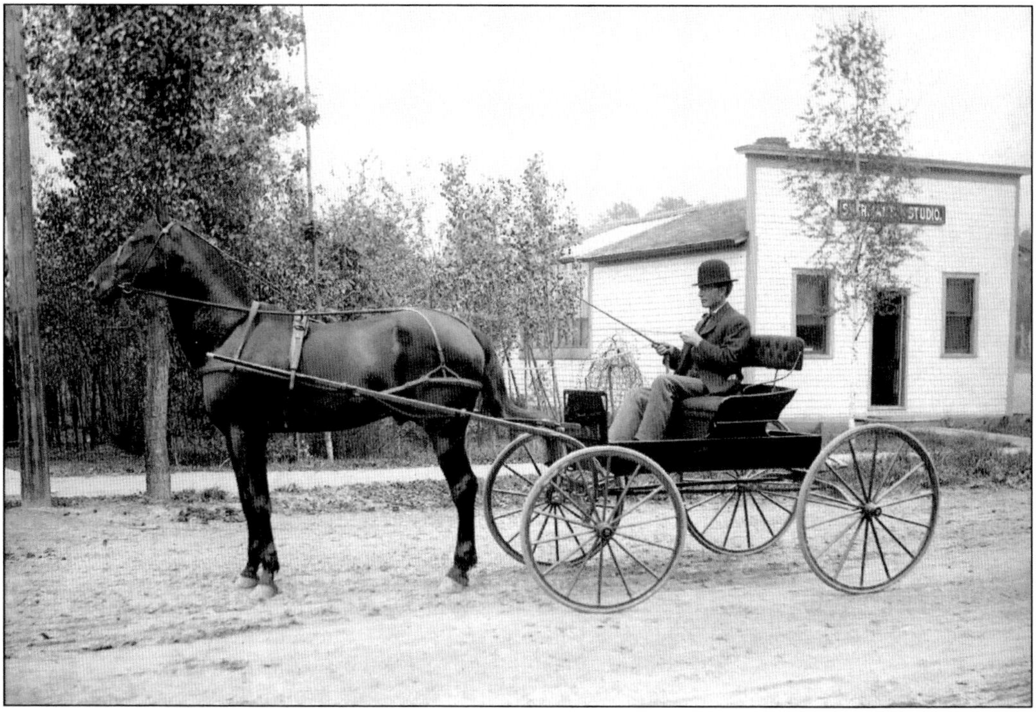

Some of the premier photographs of early Westfield were collected over the years by Ed Mateer, who generously donated them to the Patterson Library. His extensive collection includes images taken by William Sherman, whose Elm Street studio is in the background. Photographs from Weatherup's studio on South Portage Street are also scattered throughout this publication.

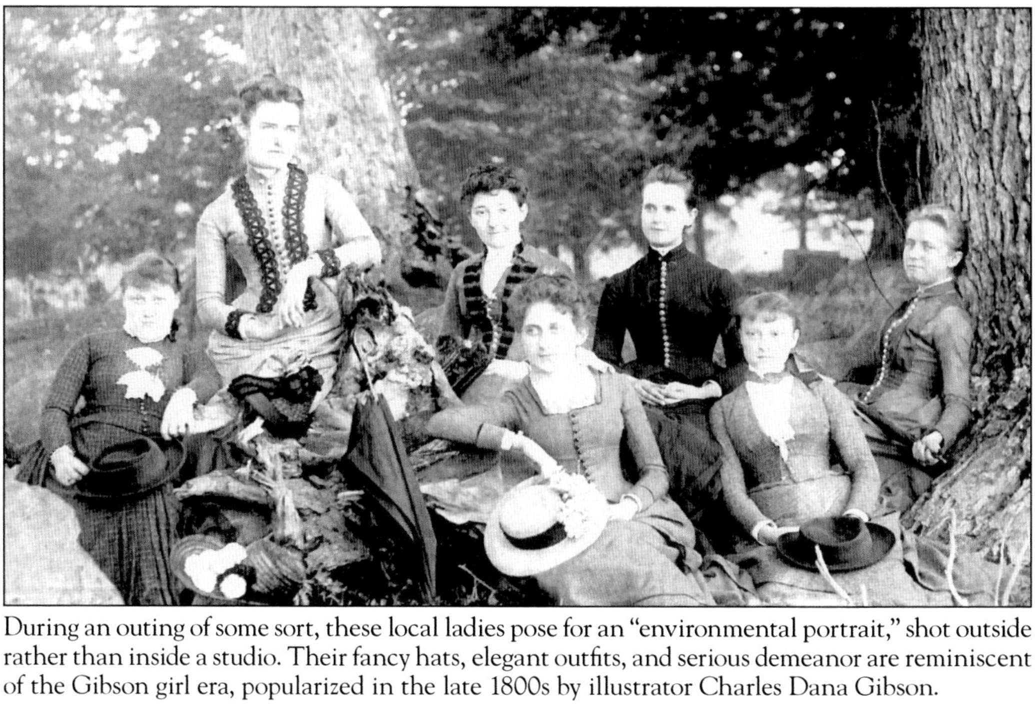

During an outing of some sort, these local ladies pose for an "environmental portrait," shot outside rather than inside a studio. Their fancy hats, elegant outfits, and serious demeanor are reminiscent of the Gibson girl era, popularized in the late 1800s by illustrator Charles Dana Gibson.

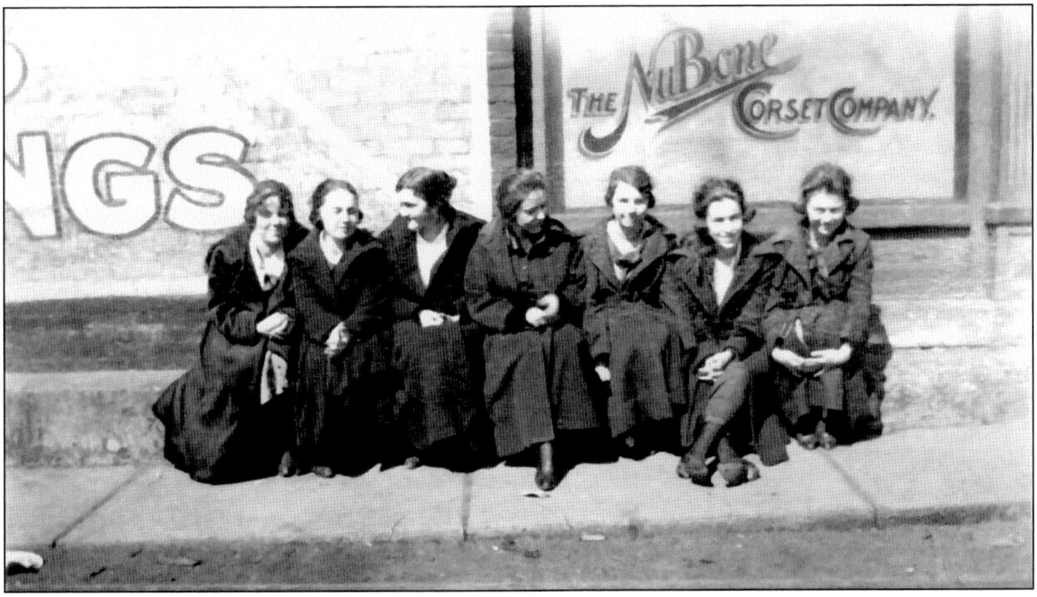

Shopping in the small village was very convenient. Hats trimmed with fur, decorative plumes, or wide-brimmed with lilacs could be purchased at Jenny Macomber's Millinery Shop at Main and Elm Streets. Ladies could buy coordinating materials and buttons at nearby Boult's Dry Goods Store. For intimate apparel, they could amble over to the NuBone Corset Company and seek advice from these shopgirls after their break. (The Gollnitz family.)

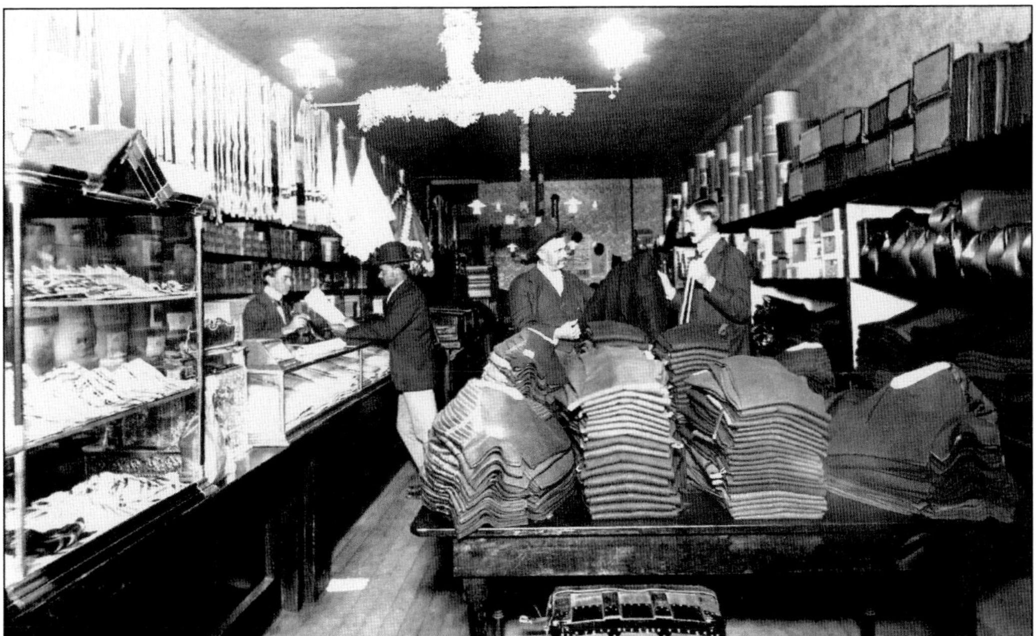

Carl Goetz, the tall man on the right holding the measuring tape, owned this men's haberdashery and clothing store. His merchandise was neatly displayed, including the suspenders hanging upside down on the left wall. Men could also shop for shirts, drawers, hose, gloves, handkerchiefs, neckties, and collars at Gent's Furnishing Goods at 12 Main Street.

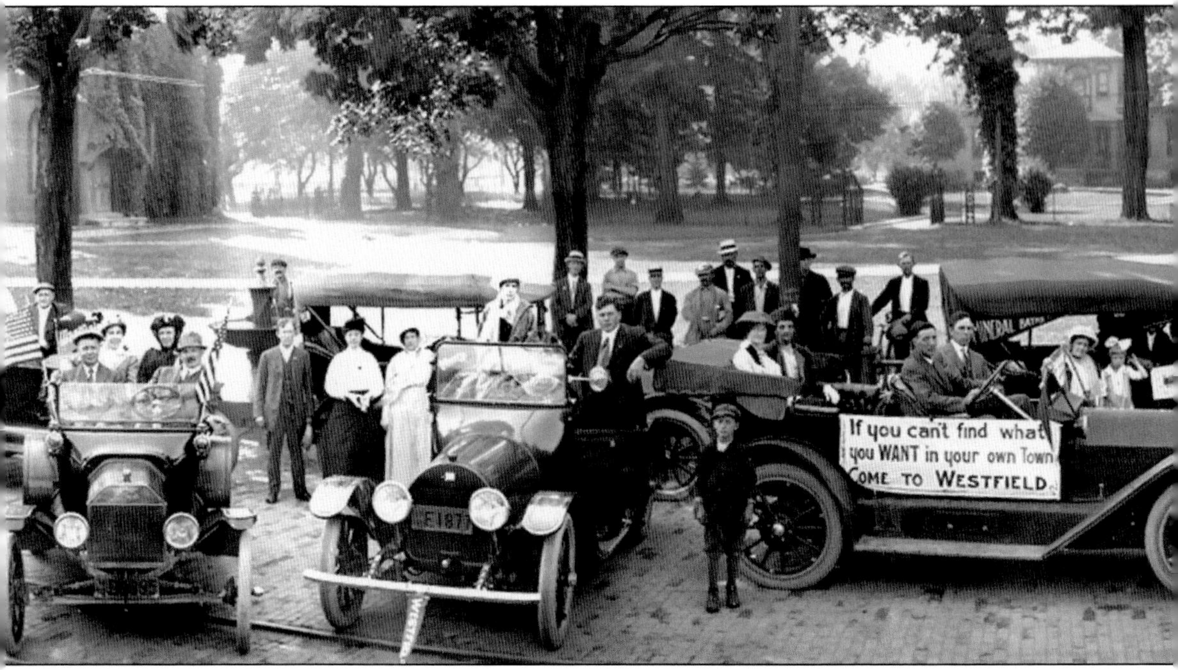

Cars came into vogue in the early 1900s, and for a couple of decades prior to the Great Depression, families prospered. After Main Street was paved in 1921, more automobiles were driven in the village. Travel became a leisure activity, enabling people to venture from their hometowns to other destinations. The Motor Inn restaurant in the Welch Building catered to such folk, as did area inns. Like a contemporary chamber of commerce, this group in front of Moore Park solicited

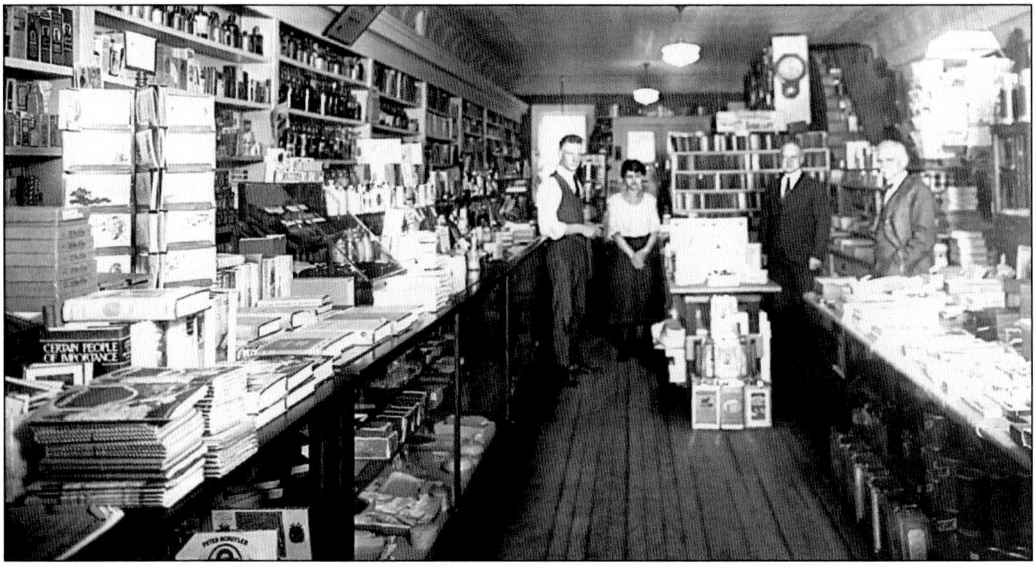

Operated by brothers-in-law, the interior of the Frank B. Lamb and George M. Cowan store in the heart of the village is seen in 1922. On the same site, Gunnard's Drug Store continues to be patronized for its stationery, cards, and collectibles. Virginia Hall, a grand ballroom located upstairs in the Spencer Block, was once a social center "for gentlemen in silk top hats and ladies in sweeping evening gowns."

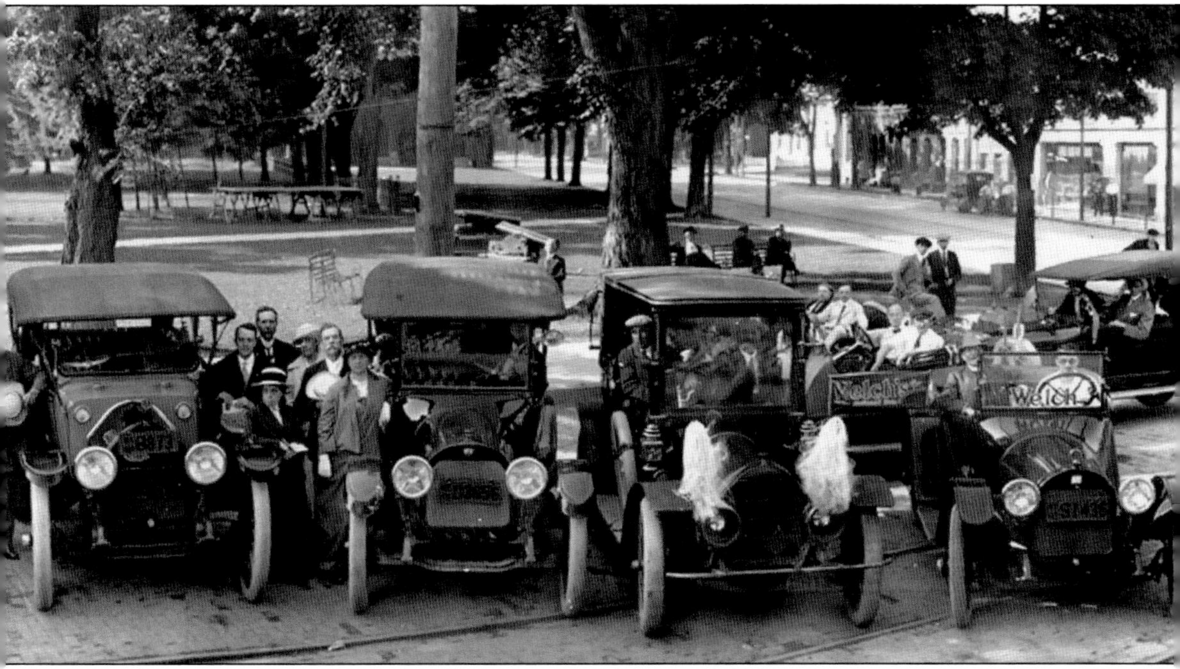

business for their community. Today the mission of the Westfield Development Corporation is to "act as a leader and catalyst for economic development, to work both inside and outside of Westfield, and to create environments conducive to economic growth, economic stability, and an enriched quality of life."

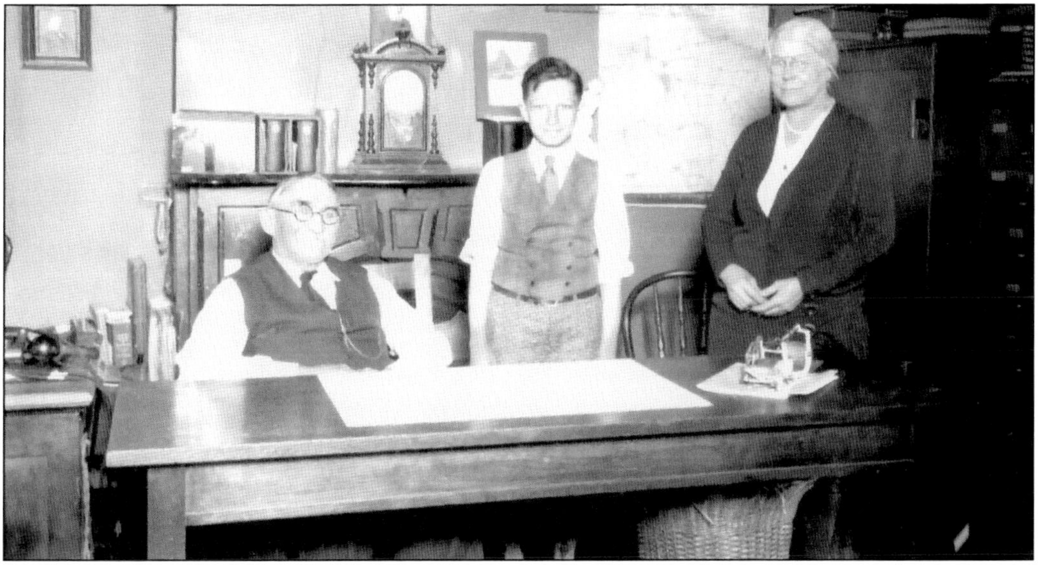

First printed on April 25, 1855, in Fredonia, the *Westfield Republican*, "the first Republican newspaper printed in the United States," was moved to Westfield shortly afterward. Martin C. Rice, its first editor, preceded Hugh "Willie" Thompson (seated) who was editor for 54 years. In 1943, Herbert F. Thompson, above with his father and office manager May Phillips, maintained the weekly newspaper as "an organ of the Republican Party," its founders' mission.

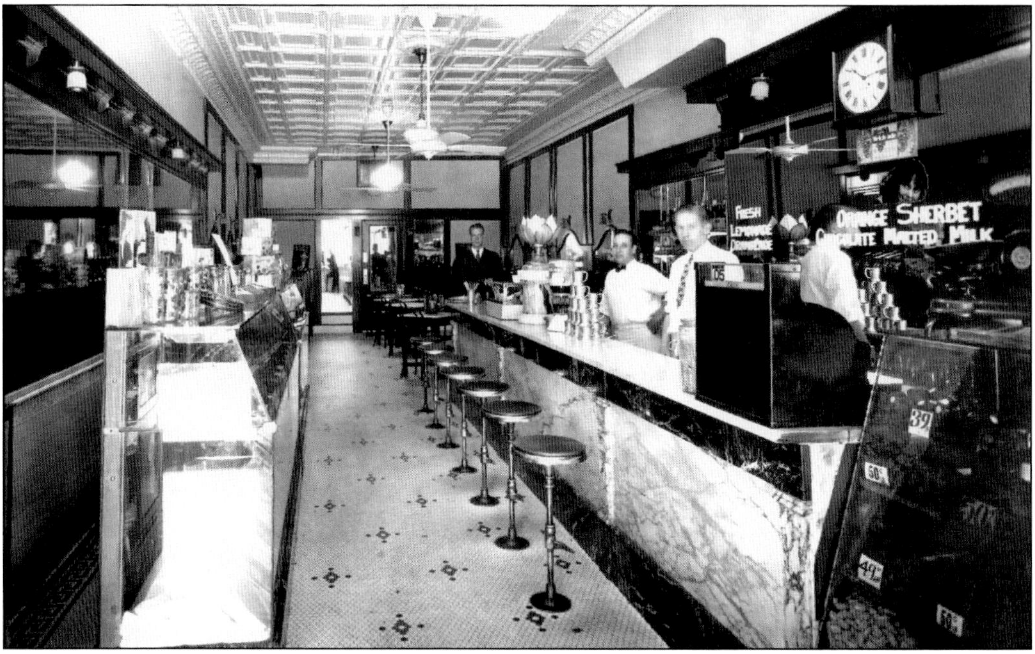

Anthony Caras opened the Olympian on Main Street around 1912. "Tony's," a combination ice-cream parlor, luncheonette, and soda fountain, was a favorite hangout. Although Caras made ribbon candy, peanut brittle, and candy canes, every child in Westfield longed for one of his famous chocolate bunnies.

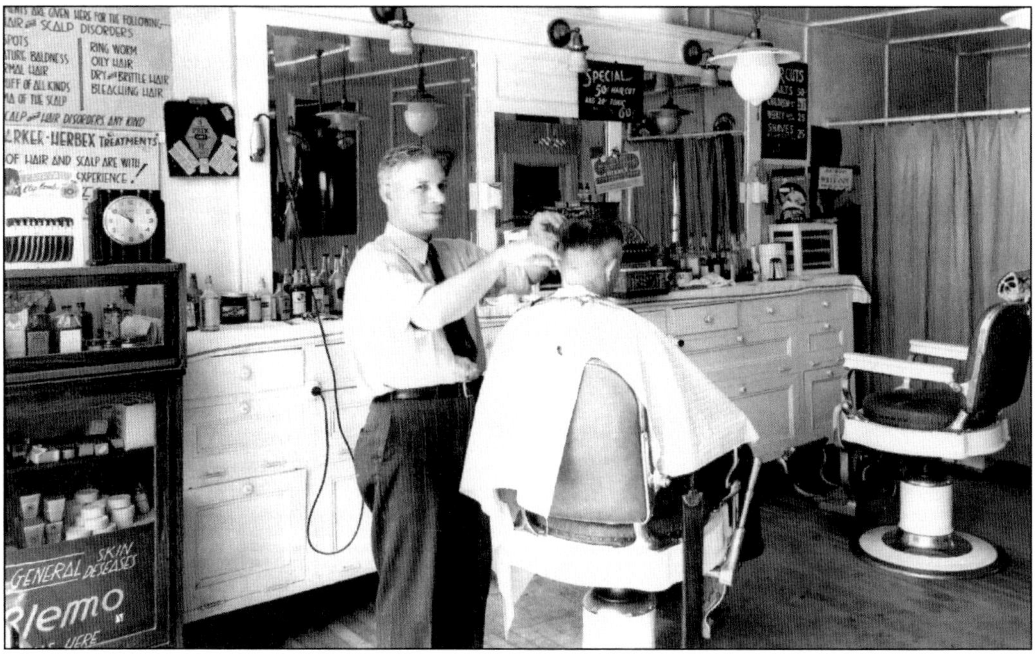

During the 1890s, two barbers matched razors in a beard-shaving contest during a street fair. Two barber chairs were placed atop a grape truck at Main and Elm Streets. "At the sound of the gun, an excited crowd . . . watched, probably expecting some surgery, but there wasn't a scratch." Did John Benanti and Tom Guido pull a similar caper in the 1930s? (Antiques by the Lake.)

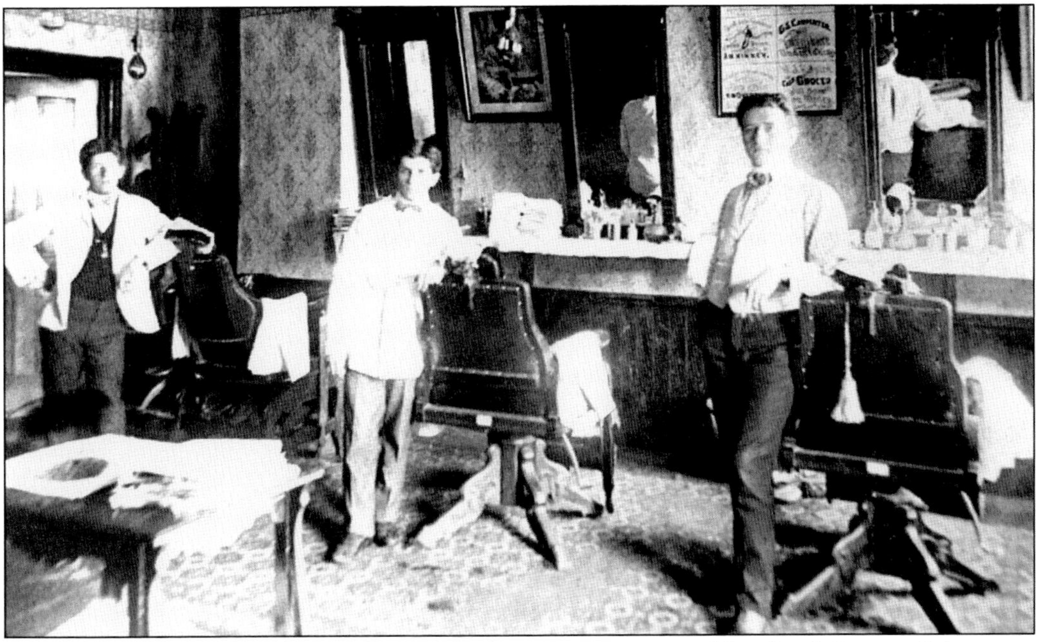

Jack Allen's tonsorial parlor on East Main Street, now occupied by Cora's Beauty Salon, was in operation for six decades. Animated political debates, gossip, and horseplay were the norm. Allen, center, poses with Will Golden to his left. Allen, a village historian, is fondly remembered as "a little man . . . who carried his share of the load in serving the village in many ways and for many years." (Ed Schaeffer.)

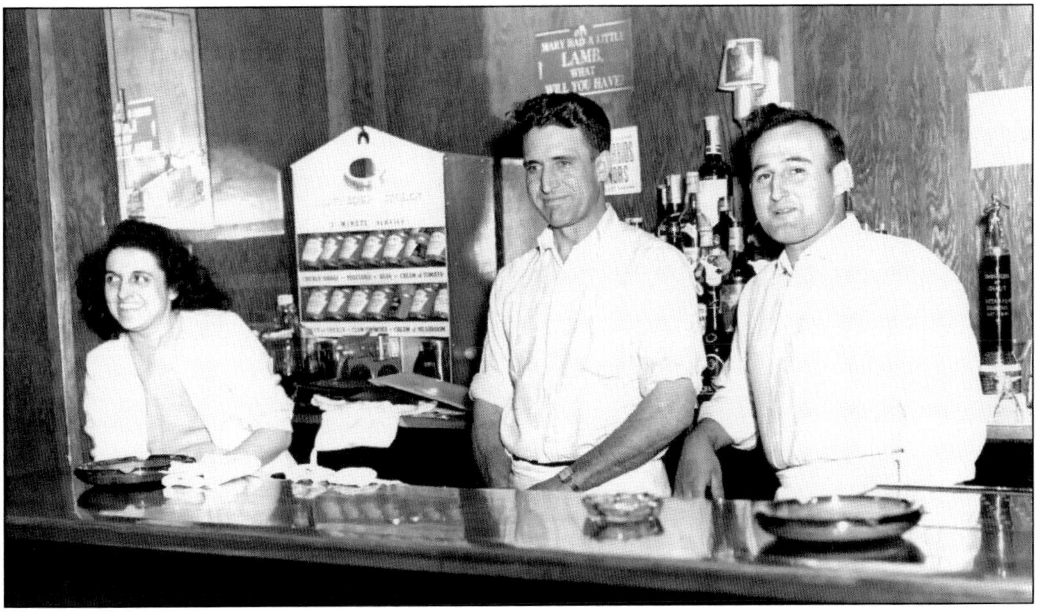

Originating in 1933 as Calarco's Grocery, Calarco's Bar and Restaurant at 15 Market Street is the oldest eating establishment in Westfield. In the 1930s, weekend specials featured "1/2 Springer, potatoes and gravy and glass of beer for 35 cents." Pictured behind the bar in 1949 are Grace Trippi, Bernie Duchaine, and Vinnie Calarco (right). The latter and his wife and daughter continue to maintain the family's business. (Vinnie Calarco.)

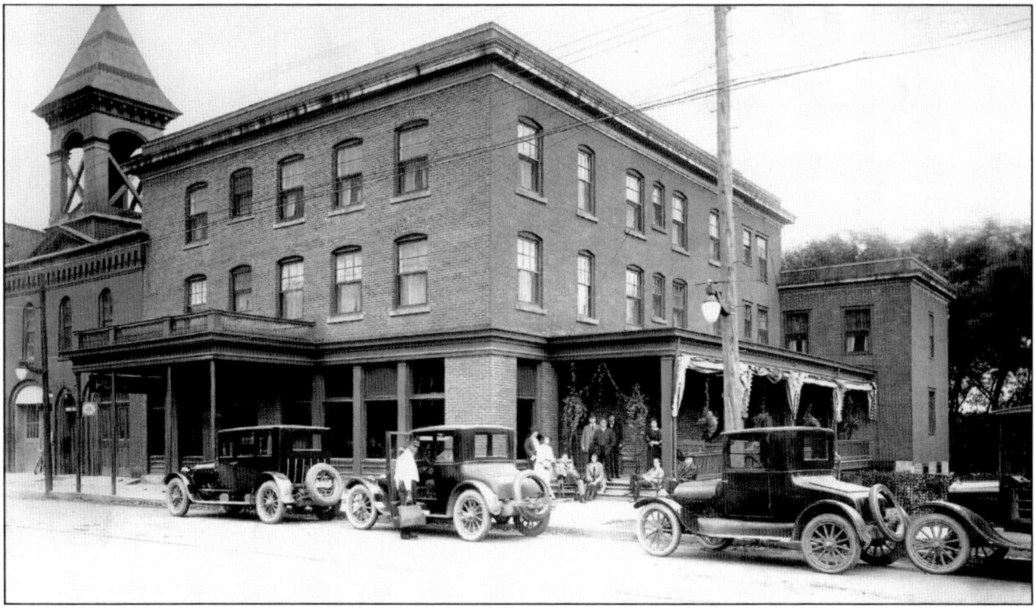

The 35-bedroom Portage Inn hostelry on North Portage Street, near the Westfield depot, catered to commercial travelers. It boasted two dining rooms, a 20-foot bar, reasonable rates, cleanliness, and bounteous meals. Grandma Mattie Sullivan kept copious diaries in which she penned mundane happenings and this intriguing entry on October 10, 1932: "hosted Jamestown Chamber of Commerce luncheon who discussed a bridge over Chautauqua Lake." (Kathleen Crocker.)

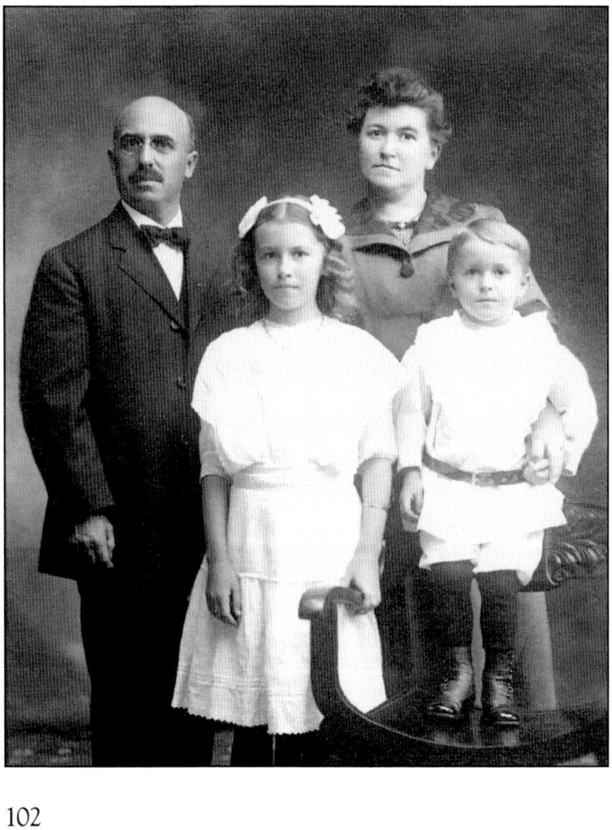

Coauthor Kathleen Crocker's paternal grandparents, Mattie Barrett and Hiram B. Sullivan, shown in this family portrait, bought the Portage Inn from John C. Jones for $25,000 on October 19, 1919, and operated it for 12 years. Previously, Sullivan had worked in the family grocery establishment in Bemus Point. Their son, James Barrett, continued in hotel management while his older sister, Onalee Beatrice, moved to Cleveland. (Kathleen Crocker.)

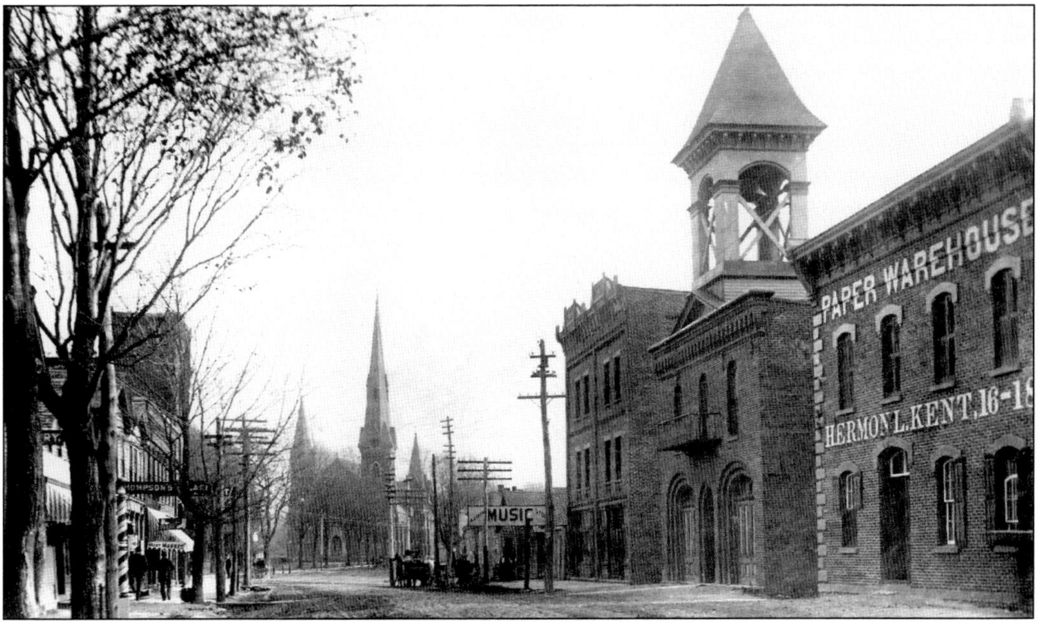

This is an unusual view of North Portage Street, looking south toward the Presbyterian church's spire in the distance. The Portage Inn hotel was built on the site of the former Herman L. Kent Paper Company warehouse in 1908. The cornerstone for the steepled Old Firemen's Hall, to its left, was laid in 1873.

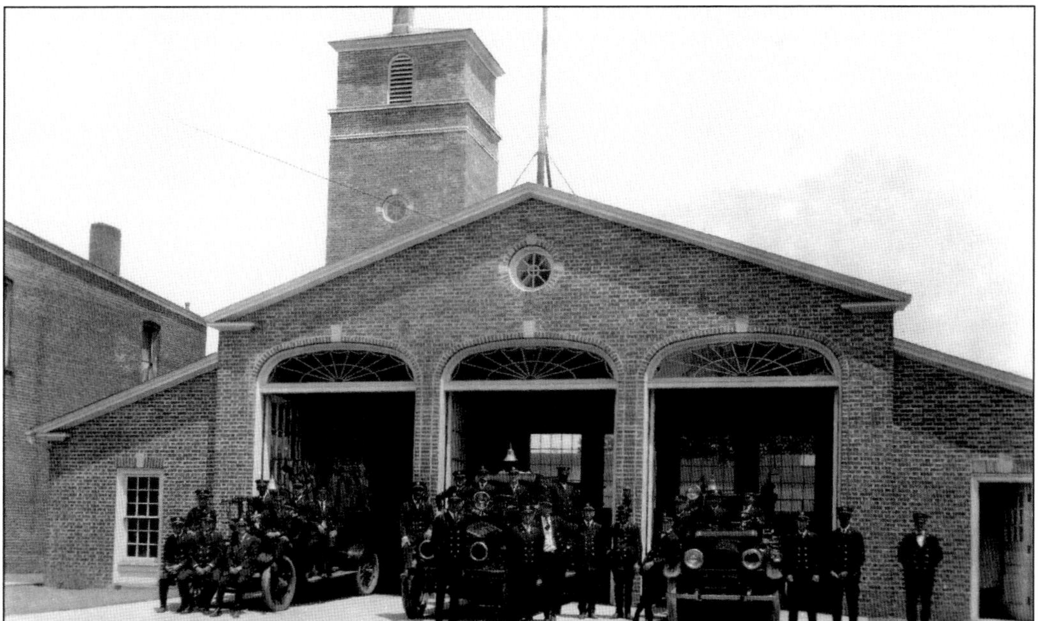

Barcelona established its own fire department in 1920, nearly 50 years after the Westfield Hook and Ladder Company was organized. Following a fire at the old hall, Westfield's station was relocated to Elm Street next to Eason Hall and is now at the corner of Clinton and Market Streets. Throughout the years, its dedicated volunteers battled blazes at homes, churches, and an entire village blocks. (Sydney S. Baker.)

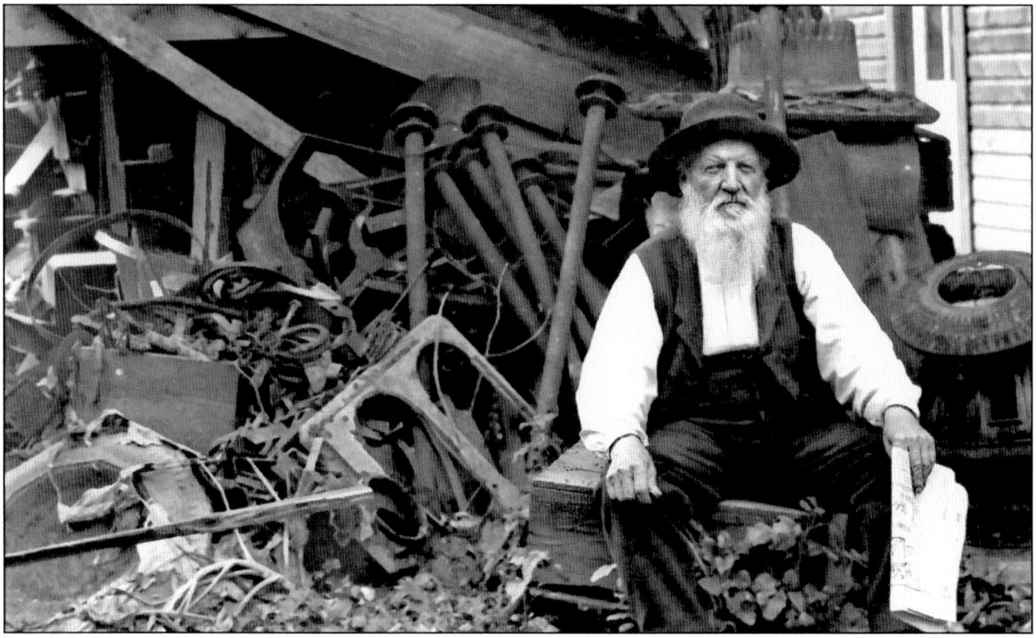

Westfield had its share of characters. Fortis Tew's "Old Curiosity Shop" was located in the center of town. His "recycled wares," much of which sat on the Main Street curbside, consisted of everything from scrap metal to dried codfish, attracting the attention of passersby. Children mercilessly taunted him with calls of "Forty-Tew! Forty-Tew."

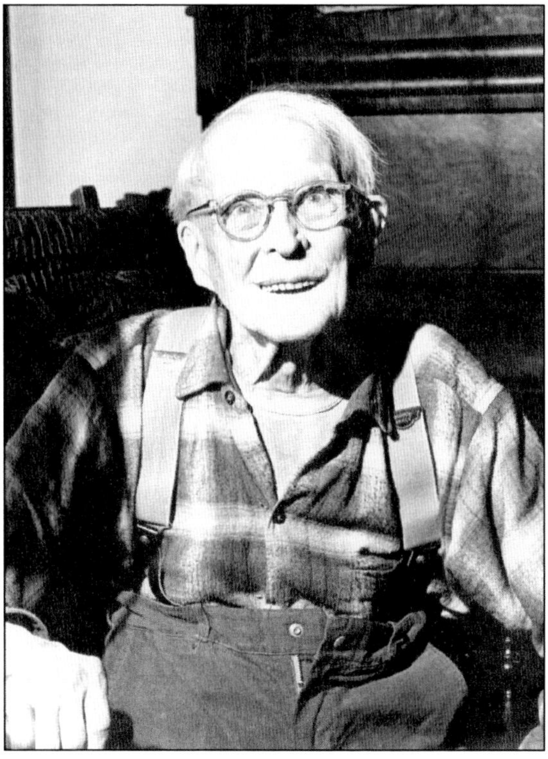

Frank Oldenburg (1869–1967) was a naturalist and rugged individual known primarily as a talented cabinetmaker. He crafted lovely furniture using cherry, walnut, curly maple, and other fine woods. Frugal and eccentric, he took wood from old pianos, broken furniture, and melodeons to convert into miniature chests and other signature pieces. Oldenburg furniture has been exhibited and cherished by many area residents. (John Paul Wolfe.)

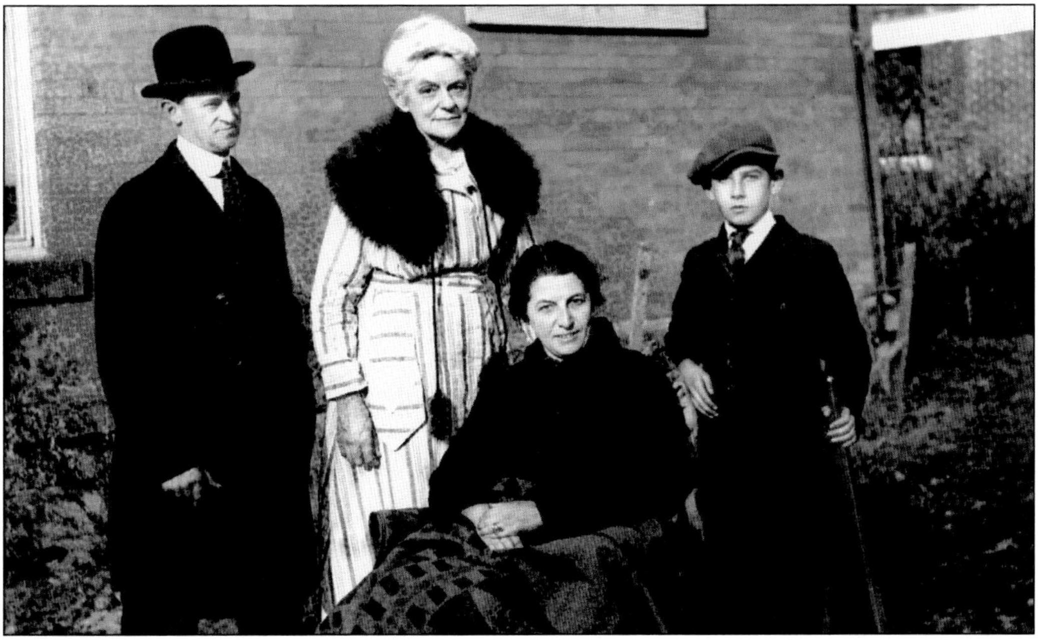

Westfield native Lawrence A. Powers (1908–1948), right, is pictured with his parents, Clement Powers and Margaret Wiser Powers. The prominent portrait artist studied at Pratt Institute in New York City. By 1941, his works were displayed in western New York, western Pennsylvania, and Washington, D. C., galleries. He concentrated on Latin American portraits prior to his untimely death at his Lake Erie home that later operated as the Sugar Shack.

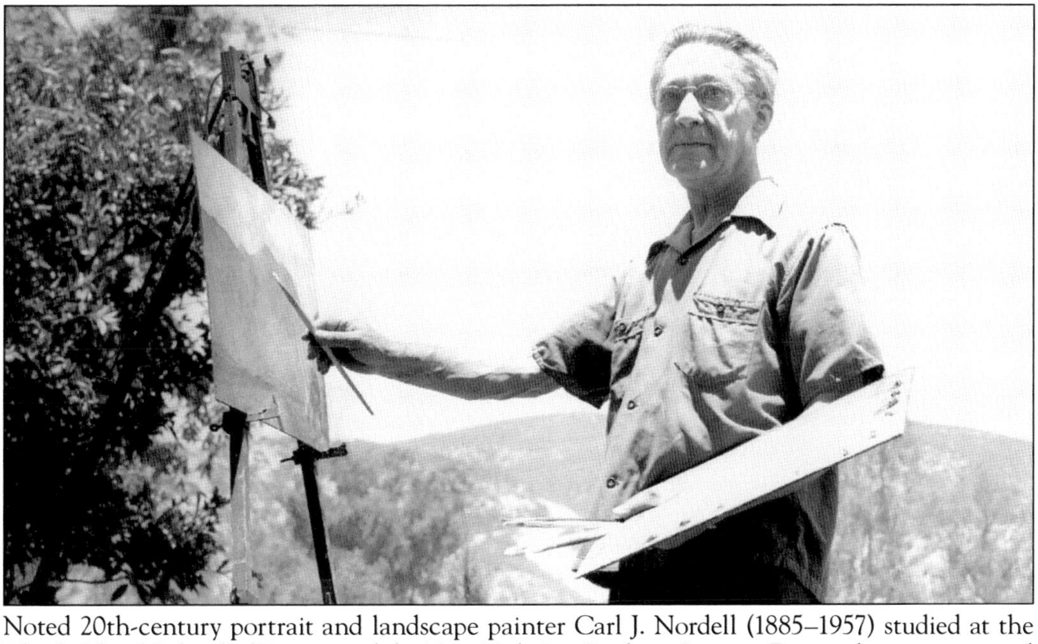

Noted 20th-century portrait and landscape painter Carl J. Nordell (1885–1957) studied at the Rhode Island School of Design and the New York Art Students League. Despite his international fame, in 1937, he relocated to 81 South Portage Street in Westfield to be near the Chautauqua Institution. Nordell and his second wife, local artist Helen Eddy, held painting classes, musical teas, and philosophical discussions in their lovely home. (Jack E. Ericson.)

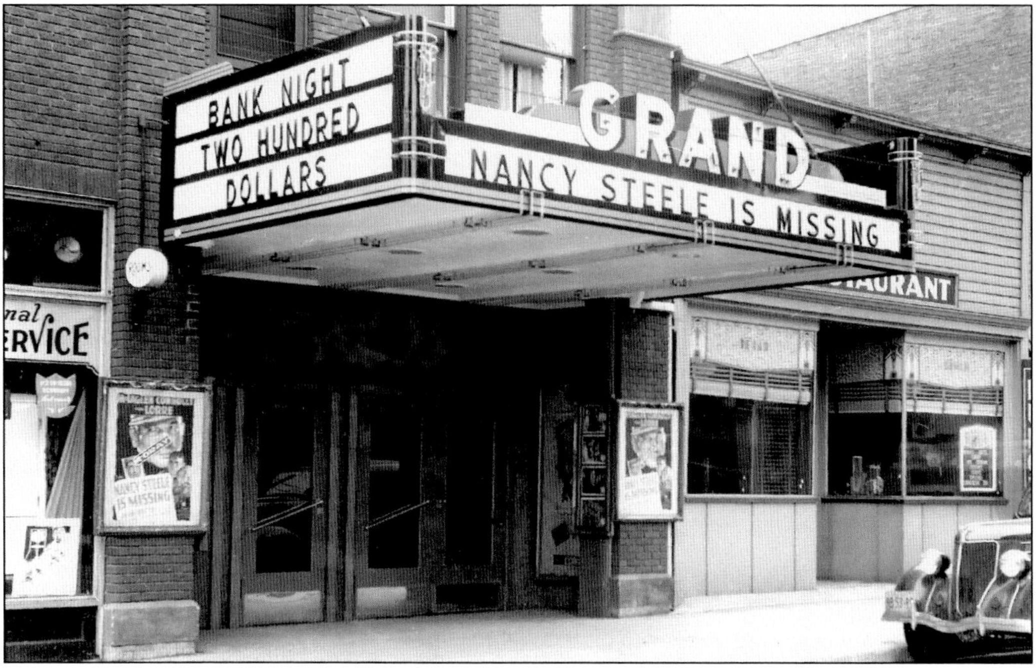

In 1917, the first Grand Theater opened at Main and Portage Streets, the former site of McClurg's Westfield house. According to Donna Chatley, "Times were difficult [in the 1930s] and money scarce but movies were on the corner with lights aglitter." The theater hosted high school class plays and vaudeville acts and often served as a community meeting hall. Many extant diaries chronicled its nightly entertainment. (Chautauqua County Historical Society.)

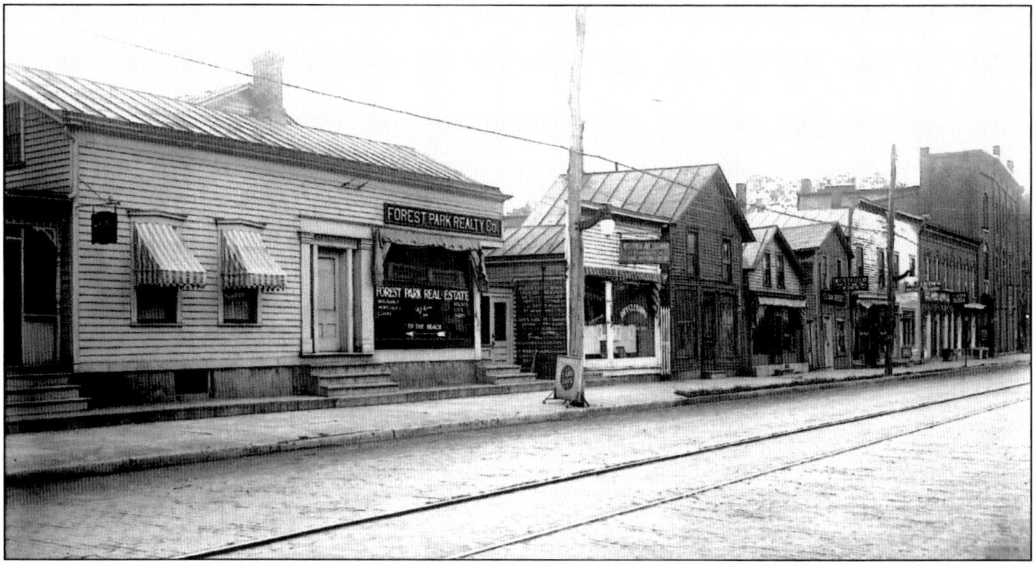

In 1922, to fulfill a lifetime dream, Otto Schultz purchased 70 acres of the Peacock Grove to create Forest Park, a lakeside community. From this office on North Portage Street, he developed a popular summer resort. Catering to out-of-towners, the safe beach area, with no drop-off, has remained open to the public for swimming and picnicking, and 22 residents live there year-round. (Jamie Jaynes.)

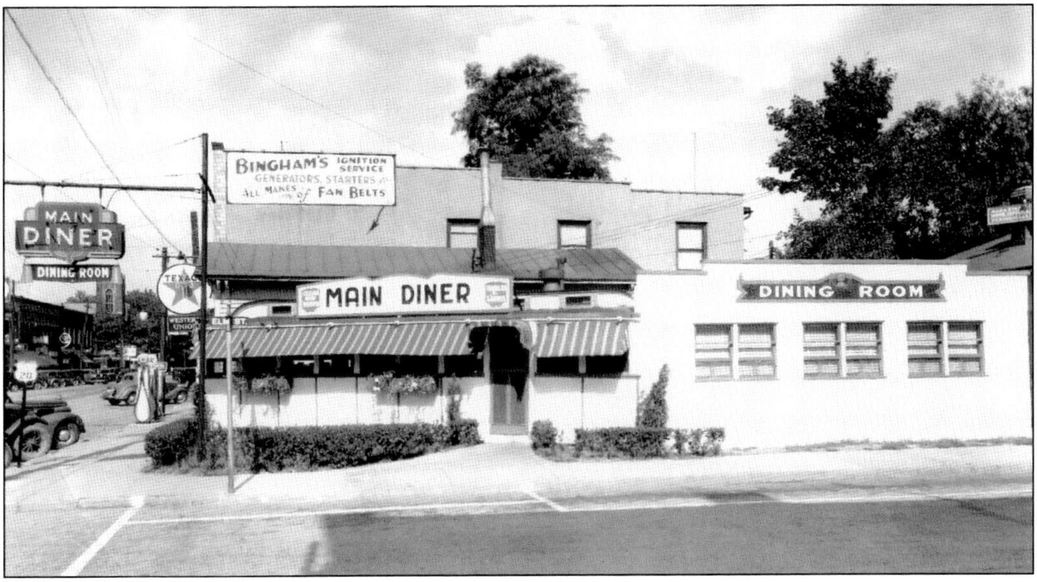

Located on the corner of Elm and Main Streets, the former site of Macomber's Millinery Store, the Westfield Main Diner has been a landmark and favorite family restaurant for decades. In the early 1920s, Harold Washburn and Walter Moore purchased and operated "mammoth diner, the last word in dining cars" there. (Vinnie Calarco.)

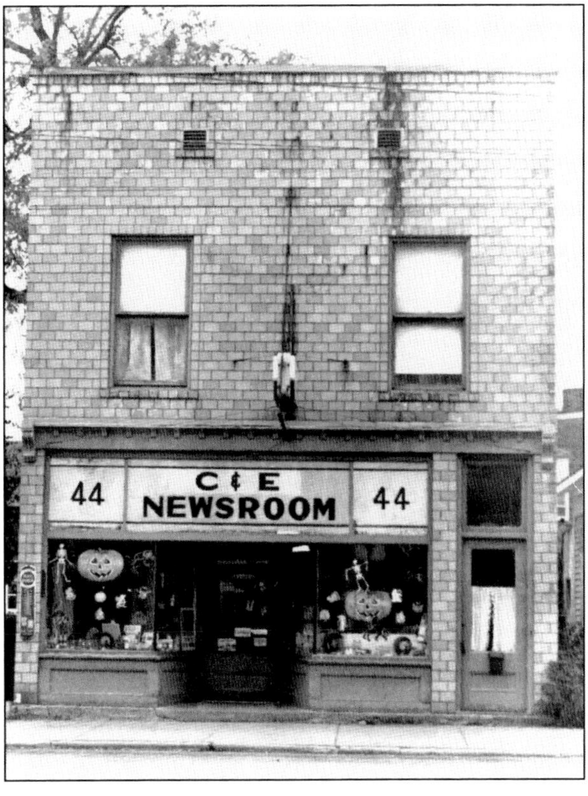

Robert Franklin, former owner and manager of the Jamestown Baseball Club, was an avid sports fan. Despite competition from stores that carried similar merchandise, his newsroom at 44 East Main Street, like the diner, has been a social center for decades. On the former site of the Old Stone Tavern, the newsroom has also doubled as Westfield's bus station.

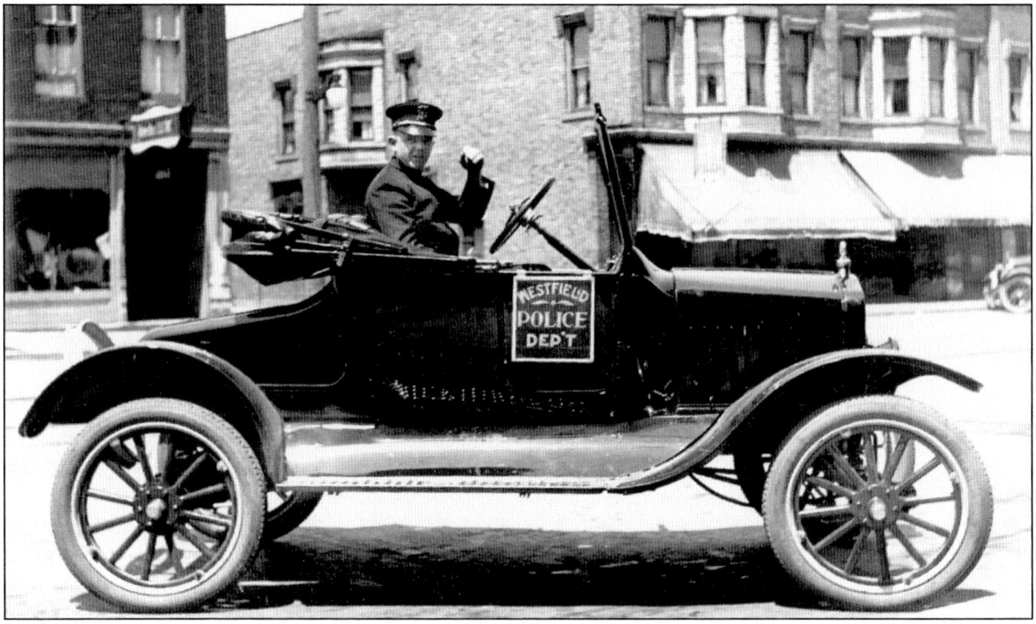

In 1924, the newly organized Westfield Police Department shared facilities on Elm Street with the volunteer fire department. Following a devastating fire, the jail at the rear of the old Firemen's Hall on North Portage Street was relocated to the new facilities. Civil War veteran Philander Bemis served for 18 years as Westfield's deputy sheriff before his appointment as chief of police at the Chautauqua Institution.

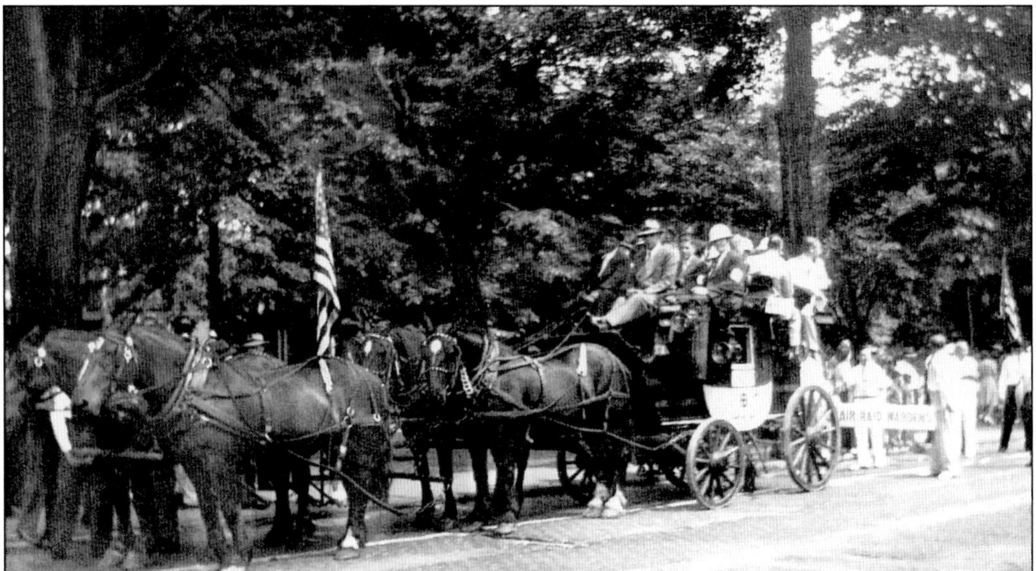

"Buy bonds for bloc busters to bomb Berlin" was the goal of the July 24, 1943, rally and parade. Dignitaries were chauffeured to Eason Hall in Harry Logan's elegant Tally-ho, purchased in England. Accompanied by Ted Skinner, Arthur Scolton drove Wilson Hopson's four-horse team with the owner's assistance. Villagers more than doubled their goal, selling $28,000 worth of savings bonds, which reportedly "surpassed all expectations." (Virginia Hopson Griffin.)

Pictured here with her daughters, Frances Swain, in her later years, lived in the YWCA as the housemother. The group's 1924 New Year's resolutions were "1. Use no slang, 2. Sleep with open windows, 3. Eat green vegetables, 4. Learn to play the piano or other musical instrument, 5. Cook at least one meal a week so mother can rest, 6. Speak in a low tone, 7. Learn to play well a team game, 8. Create. . . by writing, painting, or sewing a thing of beauty.

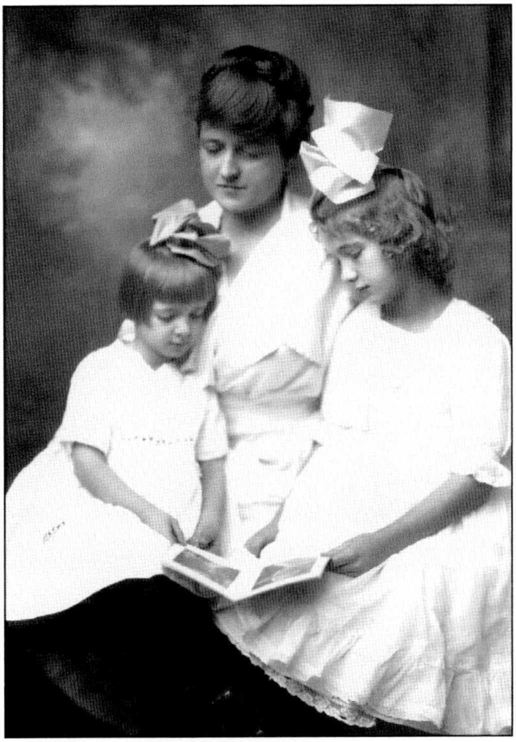

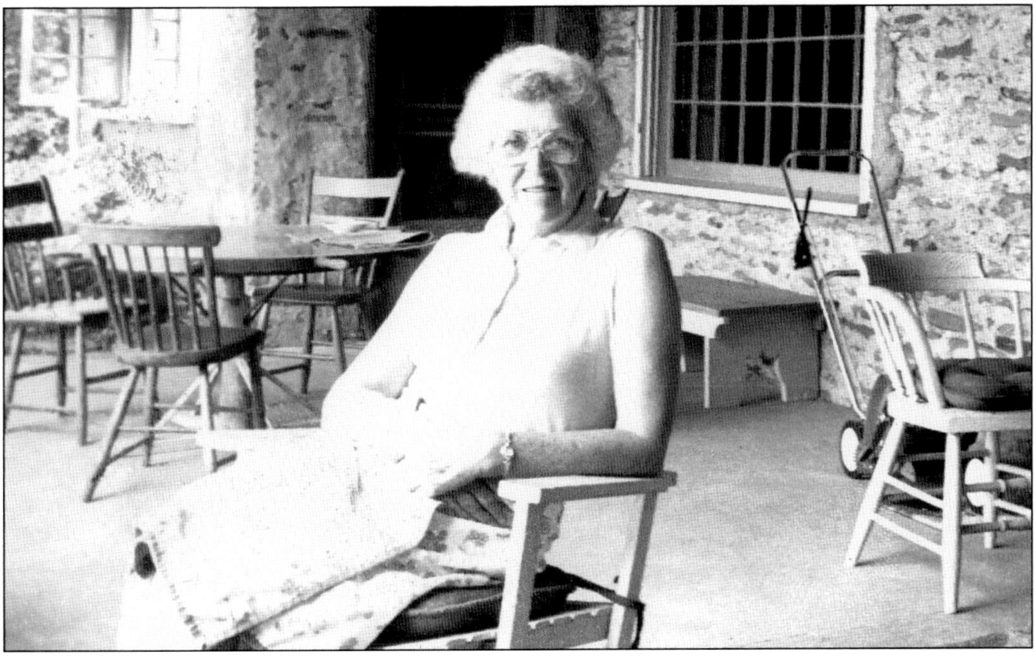

Faith Crandall Scott, granddaughter of George W. Patterson II, earned a degree in library science, was hired locally, and then left to work at Vassar. She retired to Westfield to live year-round in the family-owned Barcelona Lighthouse keeper's cottage. A trustee and member of the Patterson Library Board of Directors and active member of the Board of Education, Scott was an asset to her beloved Westfield.

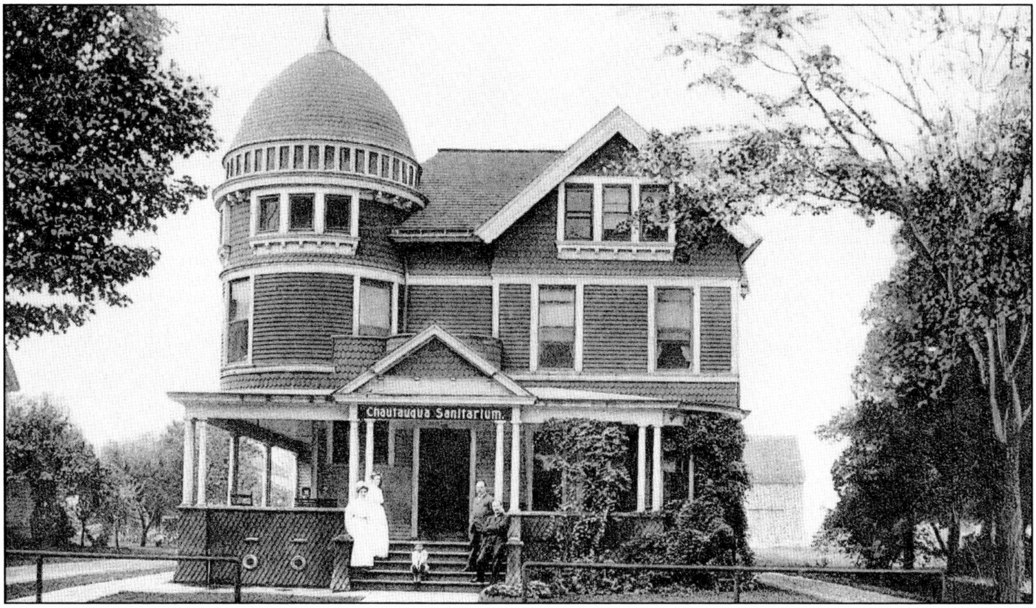

The Soules Hospital and Training School for Nurses, owned and operated by county coroner Dr. Thomas E. Soules and Dr. H. Ralph Willse of Buffalo, was chartered in 1901. Other than room and board at the South Portage site, women ages 23 to 25, during their two-year program, "will receive no allowance, as the teaching given and profession acquired are considered amply equivalent for services rendered." (Sydney S. Baker.)

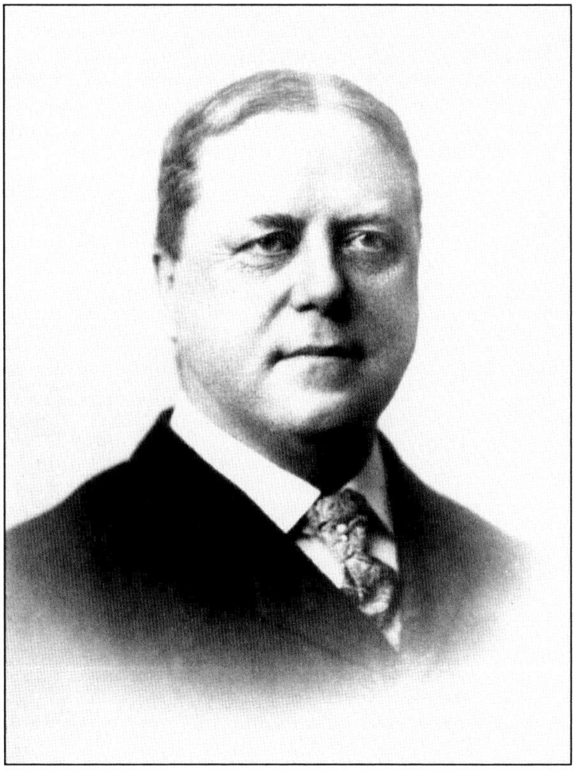

On weekends, Dr. Roswell Park often traveled by train from Buffalo to Westfield to serve as a visiting surgeon at Soules Hospital. Praised by Dr. Kent Brown for his "impeccable reputation," Park founded the world's first cancer institute in Buffalo. He also had the distinction of being the medical director for the 1901 Pan American Exposition and was involved in the aftermath of Pres. William McKinley's assassination there. (Courtesy Roswell Park Cancer Institute.)

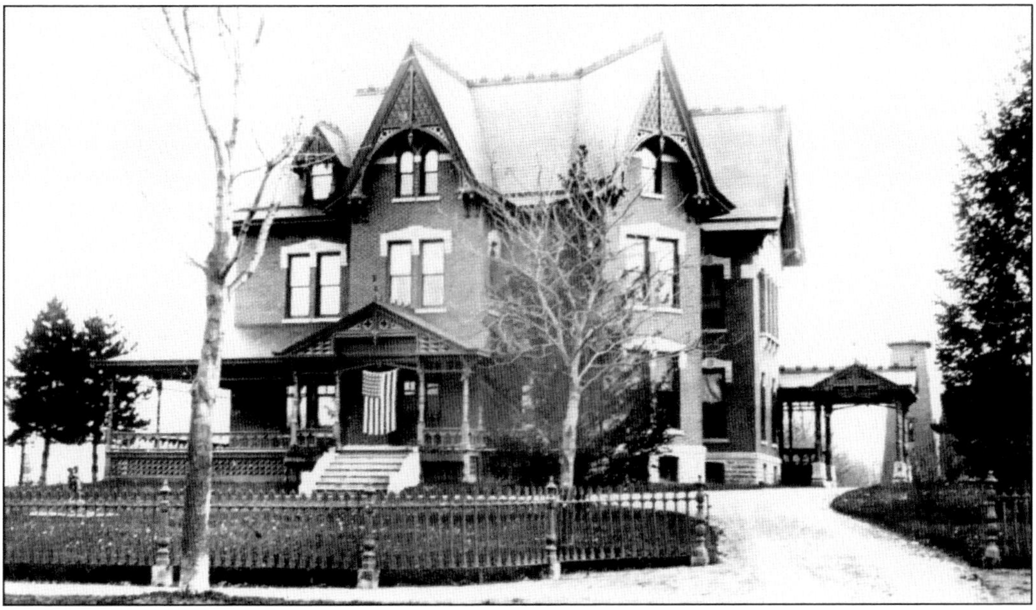

The Dickerman mansion at 158 Main Street was built in the 1860s. In 1905, it was bought by A. W. Rumsey and became the Rumsey Hotel, famous for its black water mineral baths, which were purported to relieve nervous exhaustion, rheumatism, neuritis, high blood pressure, intestinal disorders, insomnia, and partial paralysis, among other maladies. In 1927, it became the Murray Hill Hotel, and in 1957, it was destroyed by fire.

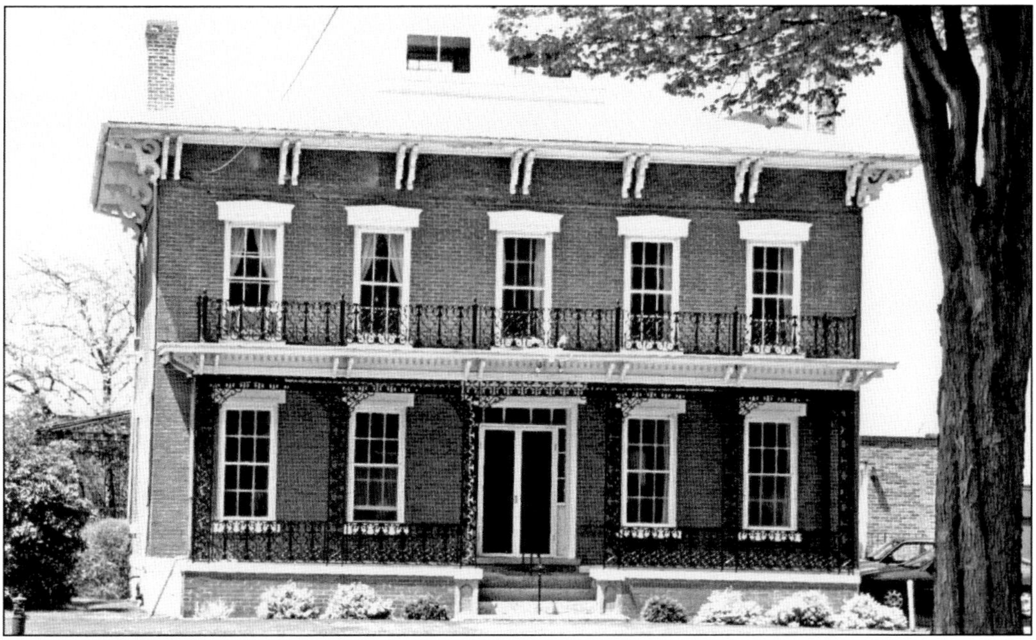

In the 1800s, Dr. John Spencer practiced medicine; his East Main Street home is the current site of Westfield Memorial Hospital. General hospitals were once sparse; prior to its opening on August 31, 1942, residents had to drive 30 miles to Jamestown for medical assistance. An affiliate of St. Vincent's in Erie, Pennsylvania, the hospital now provides specialized and quality health care to patients in the Chautauqua region. (Jane Currie.)

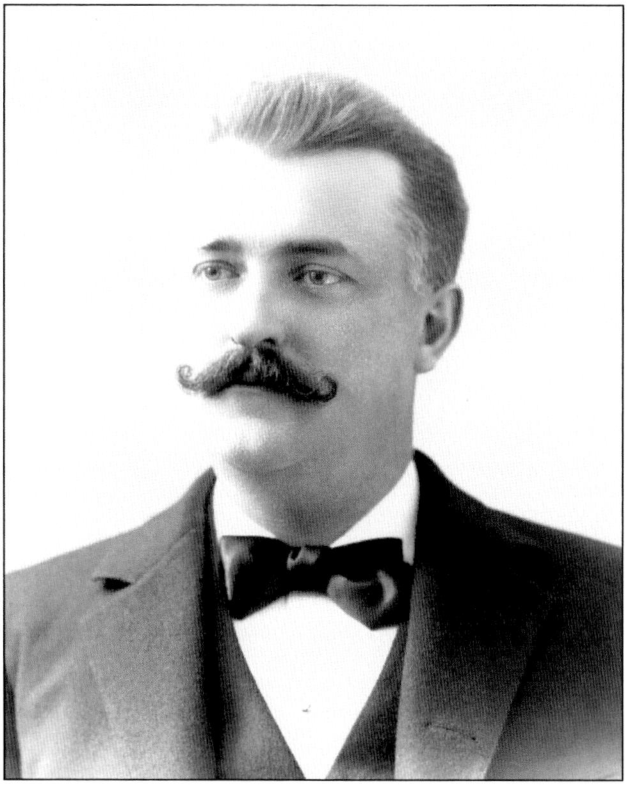

Hon. Samuel Frederick Nixon (1860–1905) was "the acknowledged leader of his town and county for 20 years." Village trustee and then town supervisor, he was one of the Republican Party's "most able, fair, wise, and successful leaders." While serving an unprecedented seven years as the speaker of the New York State Assembly, he initiated a free school tuition law and, as a grape grower himself, fostered agricultural colleges.

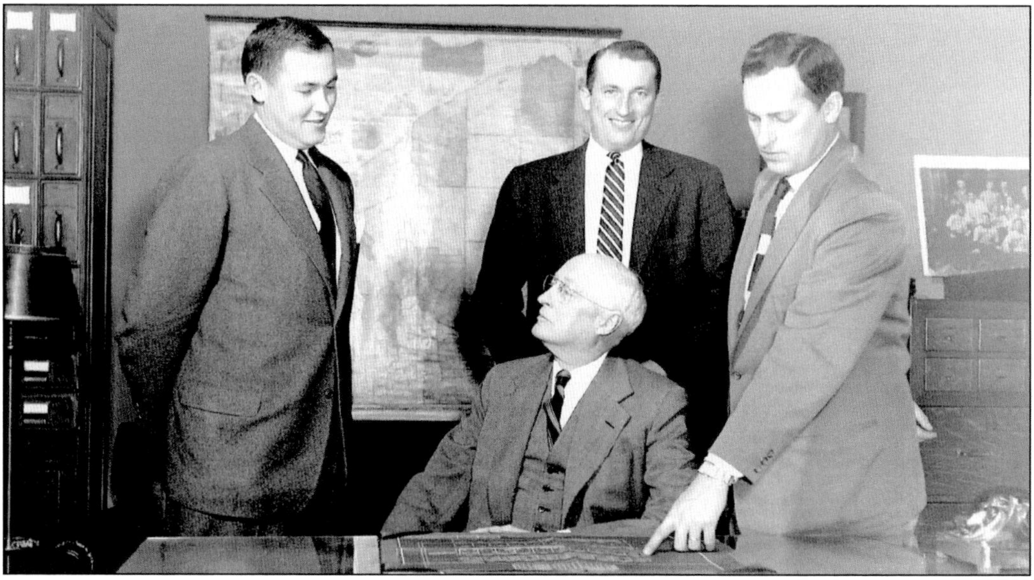

In 1894, Alexander Graham Bell's telephone patent expired, ending his manufacture and installation monopoly. In 1897, S. Fred Nixon founded the Chautauqua and Erie Telephone Corporation to service Westfield and several other communities. Samuel Nixon (seated) and sons, from left to right, Alastair, Roderick, and S. Fred III, maintained the business. In 1997, it was absorbed by Fair Point Communication, making it the oldest independent family-owned local telephone company in America. (Chautauqua and Erie Telephone Corporation.)

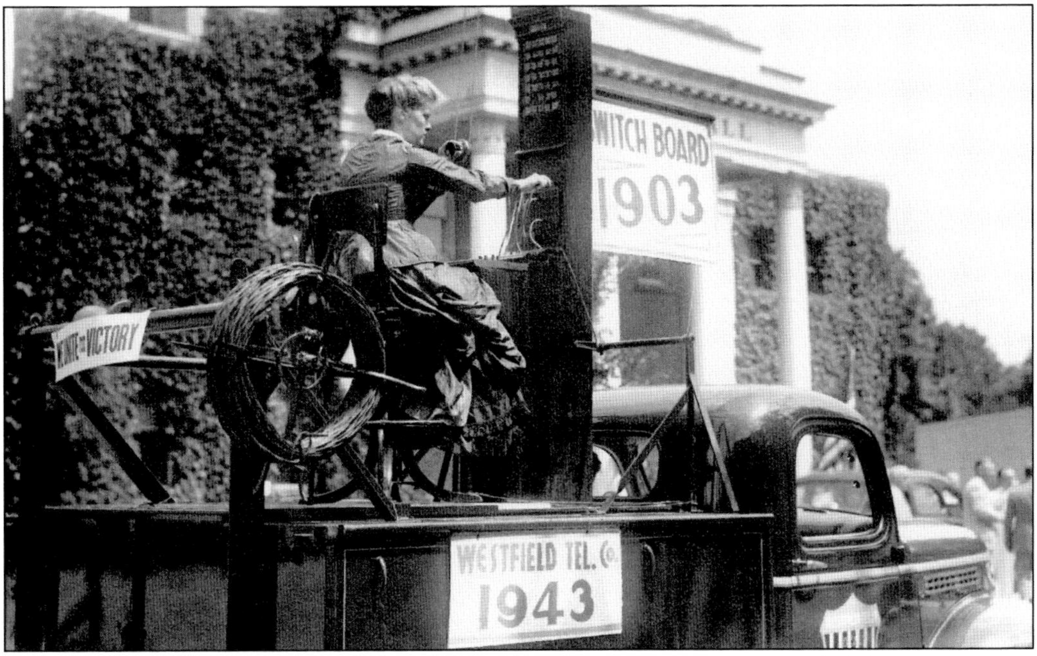

Priscilla Hopson (Robbins) was a Westfield high school student when Samuel F. Nixon, president of the Chautauqua & Erie Telephone Company, selected her to play the role of telephone operator in the July 24, 1943, war rally parade. Many residents were thrilled with the "Secret Service" feature of the new 1938 switchboard, which prevented operators from listening to conversations once the parties were connected. (Virginia Hopson Griffin.)

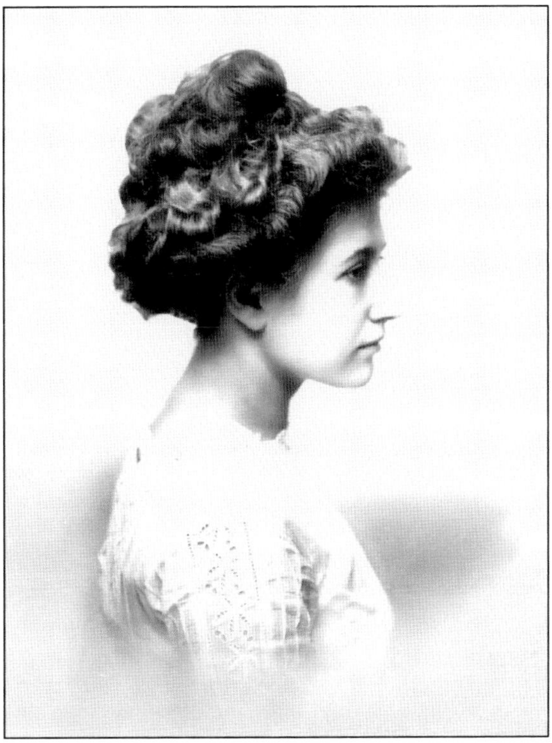

In 1959, when operator-assisted toll calls began, E. Margaret Cooper's 50-year career with the telephone company ended. The legendary operator reminisced: "I think I was the first babysitter in Westfield. Sometimes children would call . . . when they got locked out and say, 'Miss Cooper, where's my maw?' I usually knew. The old-fashioned way was more interesting. More fun. We [operators] looked out for Westfield."

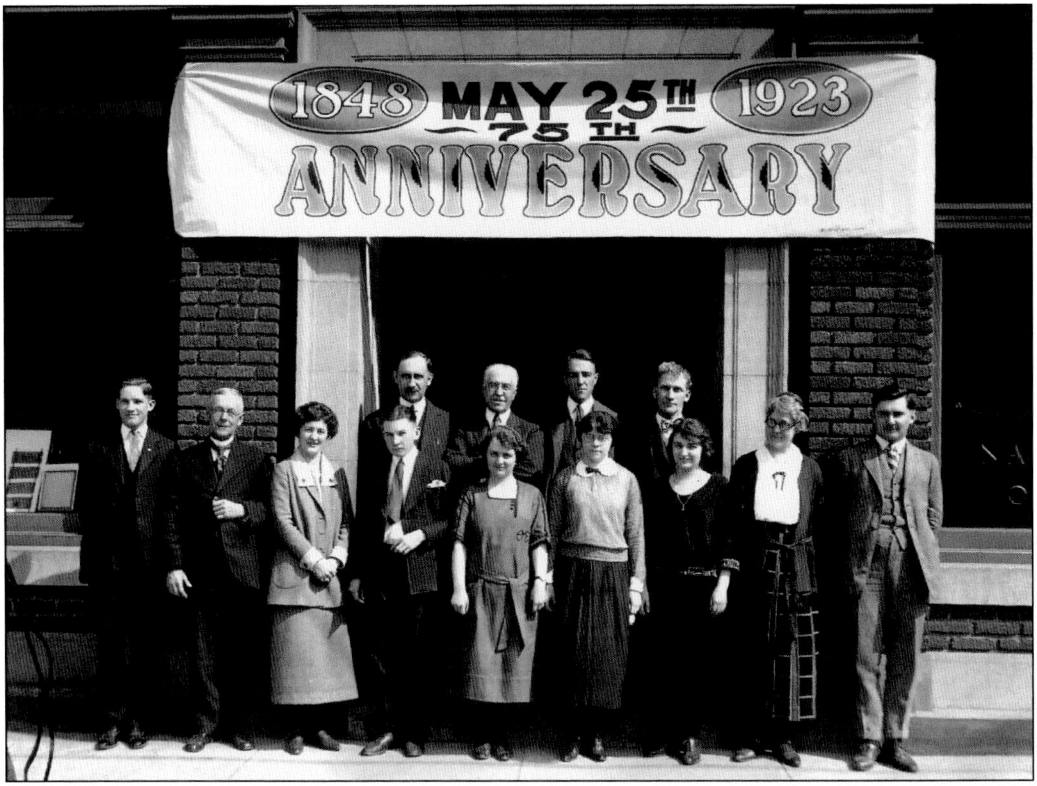

These employees are celebrating the bank's 75th anniversary. Founded by Sextus H. Hungerford in 1848, the First National Bank was eventually located in the Brewer Block, named for Francis B. Brewer, its first president. In 1884, it was renamed the Bank of Westfield. Frank W. Crandall, who rose through its ranks from office boy to cashier to the presidency, held that office from 1912 until 1938. (John Paul Wolfe.)

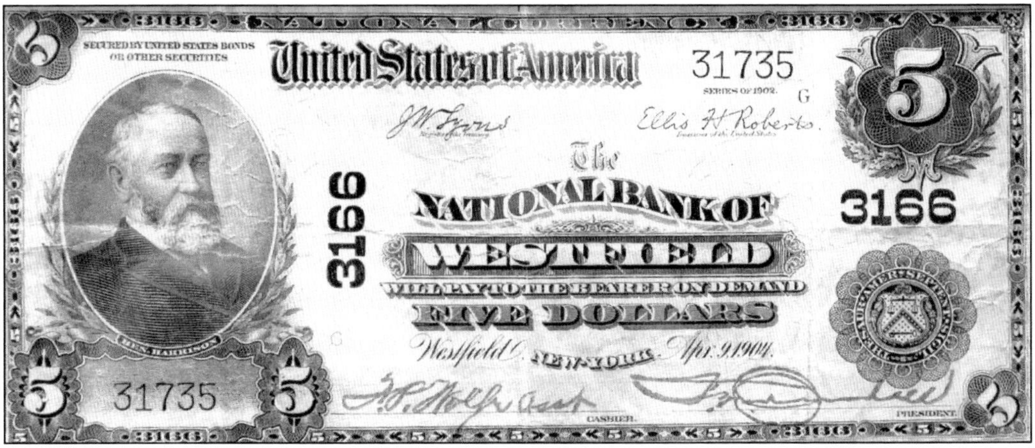

This $5 bill featuring the image of Benjamin Harrison was issued by the National Bank of Westfield on April 9, 1904. Note the signatures of the donor's grandfather Franklin Peter Wolfe, cashier, and Frank W. Crandall, president. The latter's life has been lauded as "a shining example to all young men . . . nothing is needed to succeed but character, determination, and perseverance." (John Paul Wolfe.)

Eight

Historic Treasures

Two unassuming institutions, Patterson Library and the Chautauqua County Historical Society, located in the small village of Westfield, operate with a minimum number of staff. Just steps apart, these acclaimed repositories preserve the complete histories of Westfield and all of Chautauqua County.

Previous to the founding of the Patterson Library in Westfield in 1896, circulating libraries for community members were, for the most part, nonexistent. Hannah Whiting Patterson believed a free public library would be the perfect memorial to her parents Lt. Gov. George Washington Patterson and Hannah Dickey Patterson. Her will instructed her brother George W. Patterson Jr., "a man of wide learning and culture," to institute her plan. Until their deaths, Patterson and his wife Frances D., "were the indefatigable working heads of the corporation." Their children and grandchildren, including George Patterson Crandall, served in various capacities and are credited with leading the "library in its growth into one of America's leading small town libraries."

The Crandall family was interested in the establishment of a modern art gallery and recital studio, "a pilot project to show what can be accomplished with limited funds in a small village." In 1971, librarian James Wheeler was responsible for the development and growth of the Patterson Library Octagon Gallery. The library gallery was the setting in 1972 for an evening of Cole Porter's music since he and George Patterson Crandall had been classmates at Yale University.

Prior to the present building, the library was housed rent-free in the YWCA building on South Portage Street. In 1908, Dr. George Edgar Vincent, dean of the University of Chicago and president of the Chautauqua Institution, gave the dedication address. Patterson Library is considered "one of the show buildings of Western New York, a gem in point of architecture and in artistic finish and coloring" and for decades has been "an object of pride to all inhabitants of Westfield."

During wartime, Patterson Library assisted in the war effort by collecting and forwarding hundreds of books and periodicals to servicemen. The Red Cross also set up their headquarters in its basement to make surgical dressings and acted as agents for sales of war bonds and stamps.

Through a myriad of programs and projects, the library continues its mission "to advance the quality of life in the community of Westfield by providing unrestricted access to information and by offering materials geared to user wants and needs. The library provides collections, services and programs that support the development of an individual's full potential, and assists users of all ages in the pursuit of knowledge."

The Chautauqua Society of History and Natural Science was organized in 1883, with Samuel G. Love as its first president. In 1935, the name was changed to the Chautauqua County Historical Society. When Dr. William J. Moore, James McClurg's grandson, died in 1938, the old mansion in the center of the village was set to be razed. Samuel Nixon, with great foresight, halted the process, and in 1950, the society obtained a 75-year lease from the Village of Westfield and authorized $15,000 to convert the residence into a museum.

Richard Wright, Ralph Norton, Christopher Hanks, and numerous other committed individuals deserve special recognition for their efforts to save and maintain what is now known as the McClurg Museum. In 1984, Sam Nixon's daughter-in-law Priscilla Nixon, "a tenacious and charming grass-roots preservationist," received one of the six New York State

Historic Preservation Awards from Gov. Mario Cuomo for her longtime leadership in her efforts to preserve the Chautauqua County Historical Society. Her husband, Roderick Ard Nixon (1924–2005), also exemplified a lifetime of community service to the Chautauqua County Historical Society and his native Westfield.

Over 120 years, the museum has evolved into a history center that houses materials for genealogical research and also emphasizes education for county residents. James O'Brien, the society's current president, is a graduate of the prestigious Rhode Island School of Design. He accepted an award presented to the museum by the Western New York Association of Historical Agencies for the 2004 exhibit The Lincoln Legacy: Chautauqua County Connections to the Great Emancipator.

Through various activities including children's enrichment programs, featured speakers, demonstrations, historic tours, and daylong outings, the society's ultimate goal is to inspire children by discovering the achievements of their ancestors and "to find pride in Chautauqua County."

On August 22, 2003, county executive Mark Thomas, in a letter to O'Brien, commended individuals who have endeavored to preserve the area's history: "Chautauqua County's local municipal historians deserve, I believe, a great deal of praise for their tireless efforts to promote, and preserve, an awareness of our county's history. And I would be remiss, if I did not add to this mix, our tremendous county historian Michelle Henry. To paraphrase Winston Churchill, 'the more you learn about the past, the more you know about the future.' Learning about the challenges and achievements Chautauqua County has witnessed in the past, only helps our resolve to build an even brighter future."

County residents have accessed the Patterson Library as a reference source, including Library School students at the Chautauqua Institution. For the past 20 years, under the leadership of current librarian Deborah Williams, the library has also partnered with local schools to enhance their programs. (Jane Nelson.)

Hon. George Washington Patterson (1799–1879), of Scotch-Irish ancestry, and his wife, Hannah W. Dickey, moved to Westfield from Livingston County in 1841 to succeed William H. Seward as the Holland Land Company agent. Patterson "rendered invaluable service" to the Presbyterian church and to Westfield as town supervisor and president of Westfield Academy. The "natural-born leader" was elected lieutenant governor of New York State in 1848.

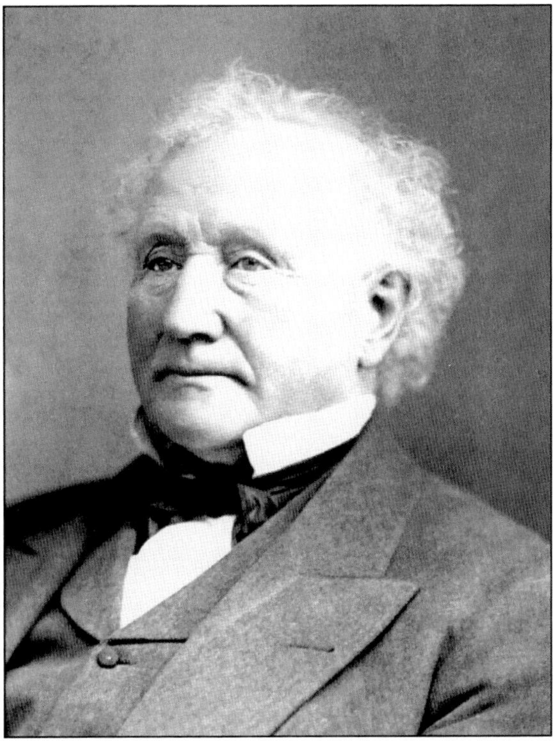

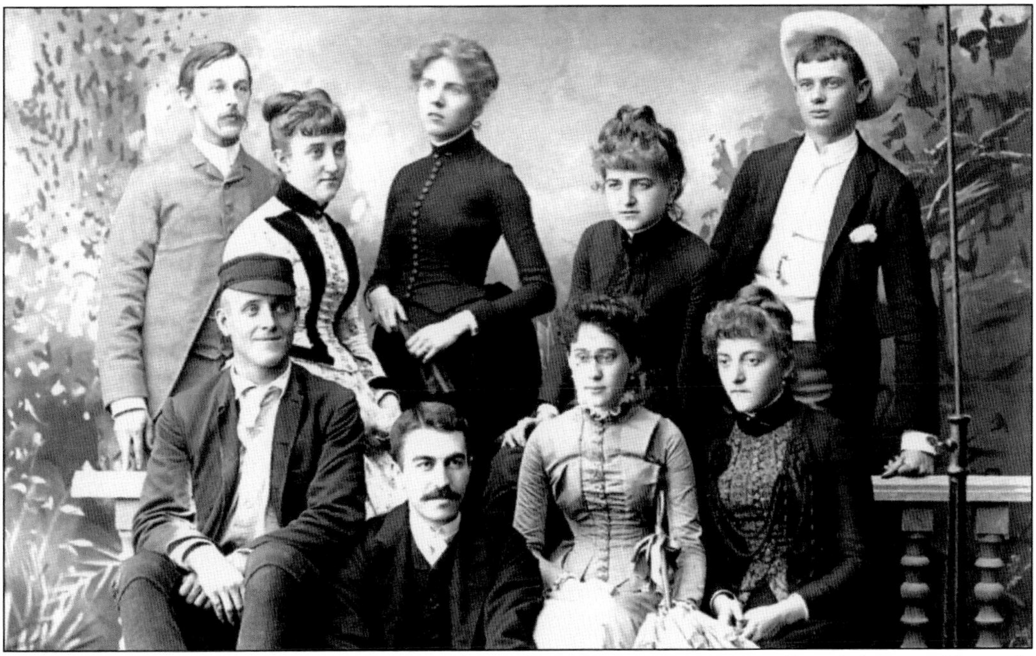

Standing from left to right in 1886 are York Patchen, Frances Patterson, Rose McLean, Hannah Patterson, and Louis Sessions. Seated are George W. Patterson III, Frank Crandall, Cora Packard, and Kittie Patterson. Hannah, whose portrait hangs in the reading room, willed $100,000 "to found a library in the Village . . . to be called the Patterson Library, dedicated to the memory of [her parents] George W. Patterson and Hannah W. Patterson."

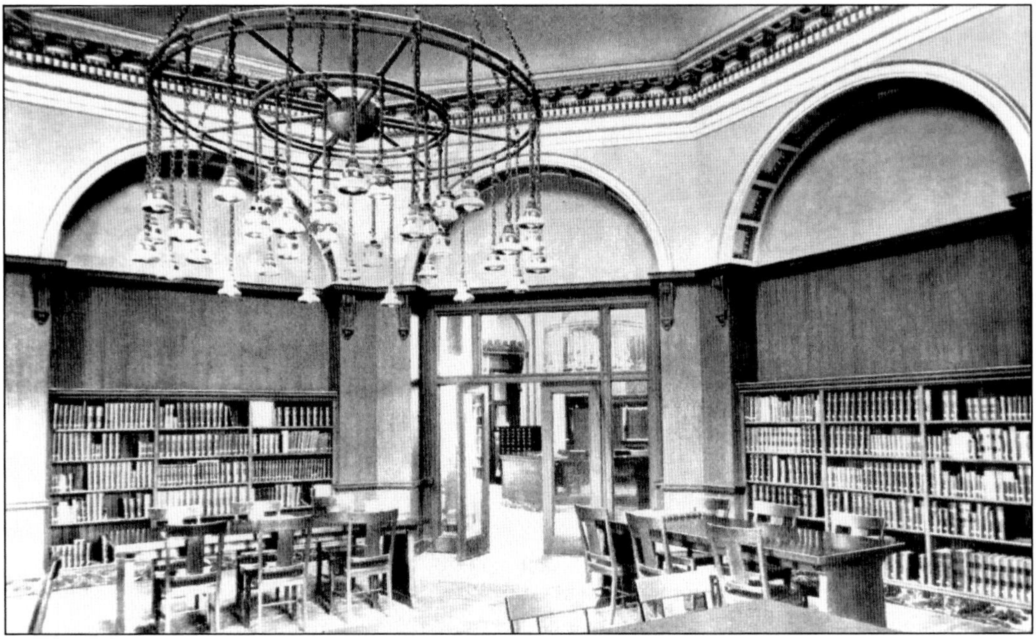

Hannah Patterson (1835–1894) envisioned a library of great beauty and excellence for northwestern Chautauqua County. The two rare images on this page illustrate the ornate interior of the Patterson Library. The skylights in each reading room and above the clerk's desk provide additional lighting. At one time, authentic bronze chandeliers with favrile glass shades made by Tiffany & Company of New York City made the interior even more glorious.

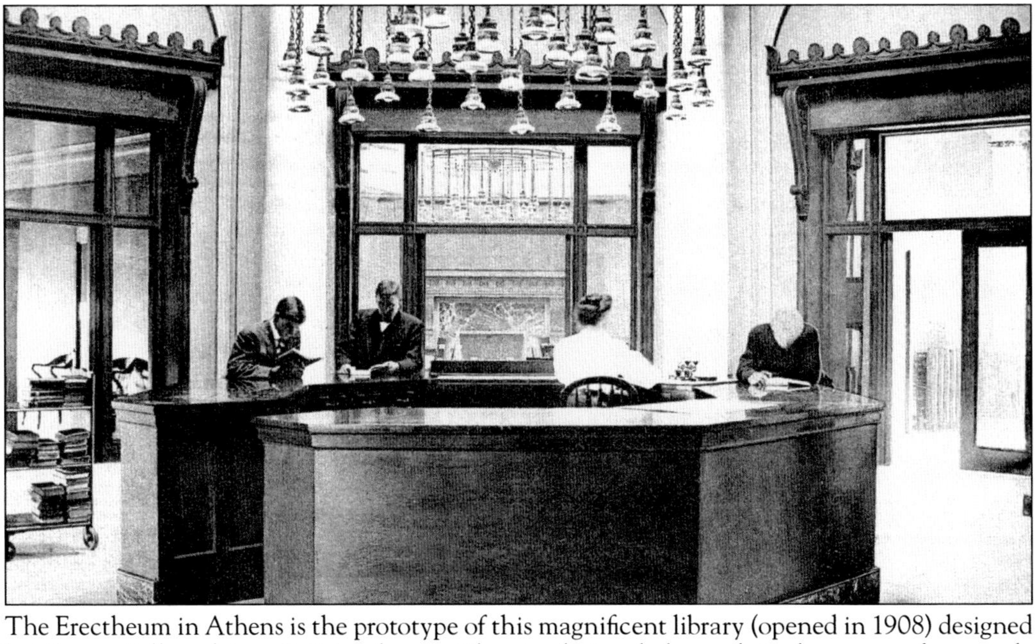

The Erectheum in Athens is the prototype of this magnificent library (opened in 1908) designed by Niagara Falls architect E. E. Jarolemon. The circulation desk stands in the center of a rotunda from which the "stacks radiate toward the rear like spokes of a wheel." Its main dome is supported by eight Corinthian columns. Green-brown oak and green marble mantels complement the white marble floor.

Siblings Evelyn and Earl Dascomb appear to be reluctant subjects for this photograph shoot. In his adult years, however, Earl and his wife, Jenny Hunt, were enthusiastic donors to the Children's Library of Westfield, housed in the Patterson Library, and also to the Minerva Free Library in Sherman, New York, Jenny's childhood home.

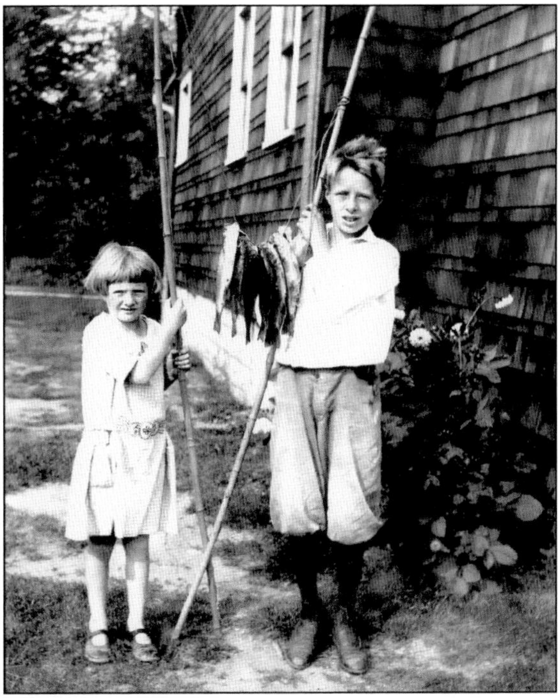

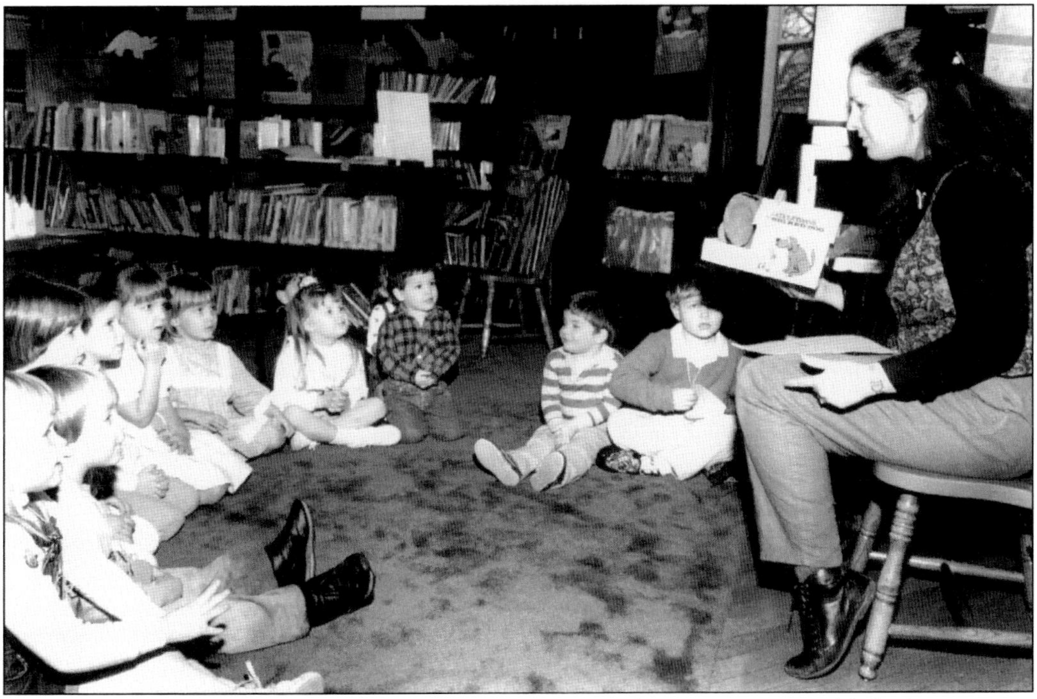

Patterson Library's E. M. B. Children's Literature Memorial Program was established in memory of Elizabeth Myers Brown (1915–1991), whose family founded *Highlights for Children* magazine. The endowment is used to invite a young people's author to meet with children on a biennial basis and support the continued development of a collection of fine children's literature. Children are encouraged to use the collection and to attend story hours, as seen above.

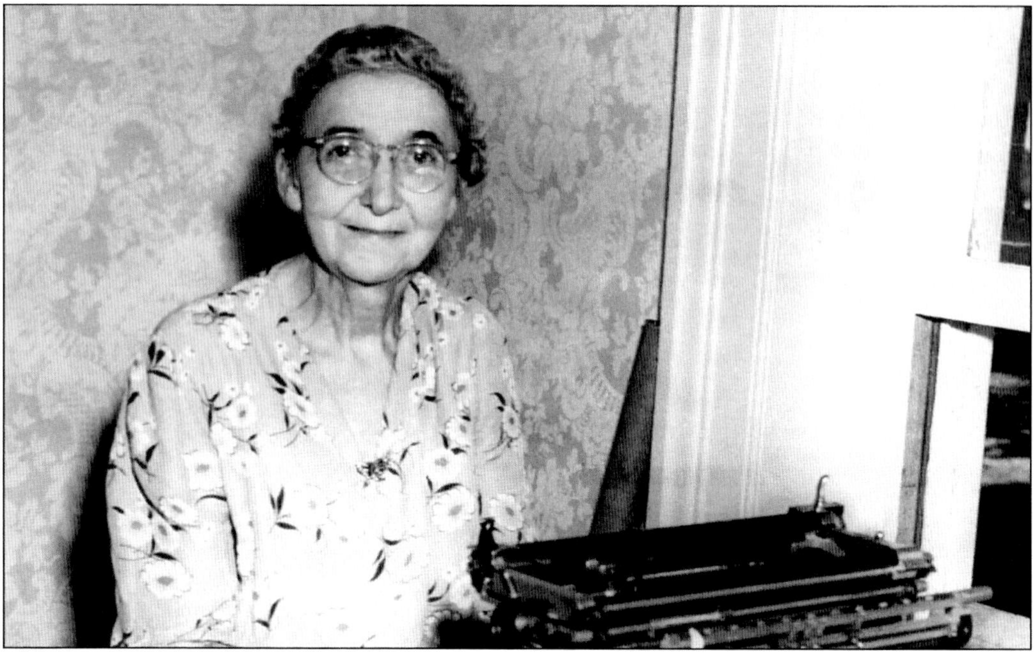

Emma Wilhelmina Piehl, at her desk at the historical society in 1952, was the town historian and also a no-nonsense librarian at Patterson Library for half a century. A graduate of Albany Library School, she left a lasting impression on the youngsters of Westfield. Nonagenarian Billie Dibble, below, recalls Piehl's severe warnings regarding "clean hands, tiptoes, and whispers." (Chautauqua County Historical Society.)

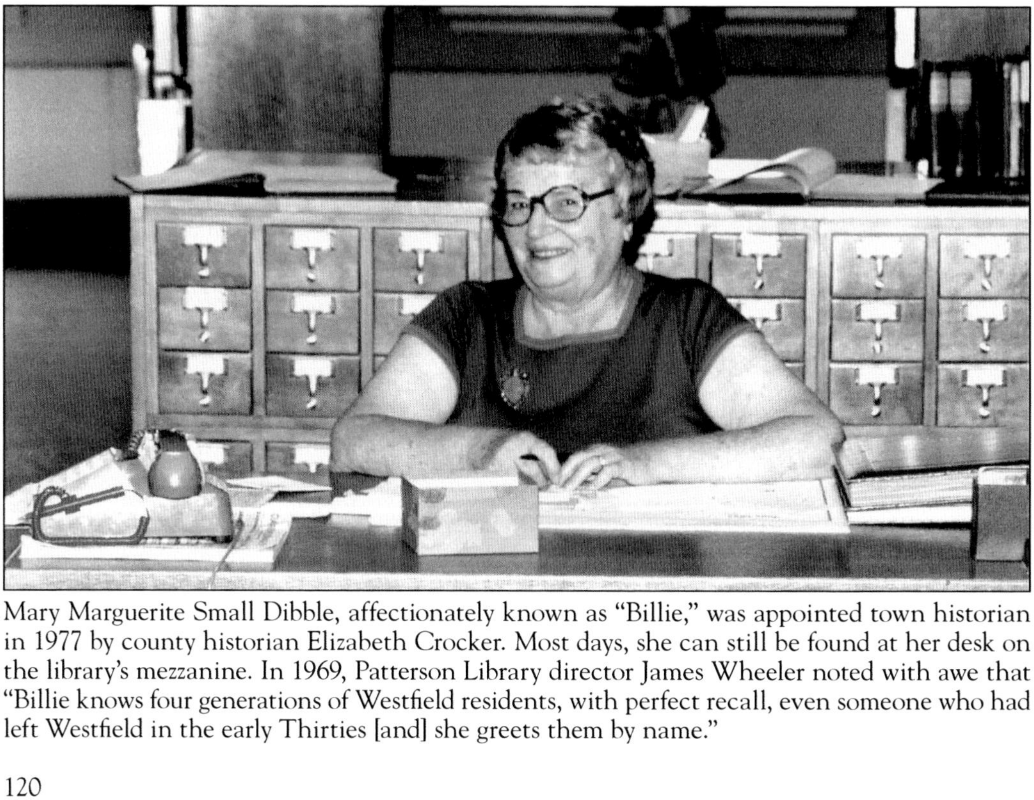

Mary Marguerite Small Dibble, affectionately known as "Billie," was appointed town historian in 1977 by county historian Elizabeth Crocker. Most days, she can still be found at her desk on the library's mezzanine. In 1969, Patterson Library director James Wheeler noted with awe that "Billie knows four generations of Westfield residents, with perfect recall, even someone who had left Westfield in the early Thirties [and] she greets them by name."

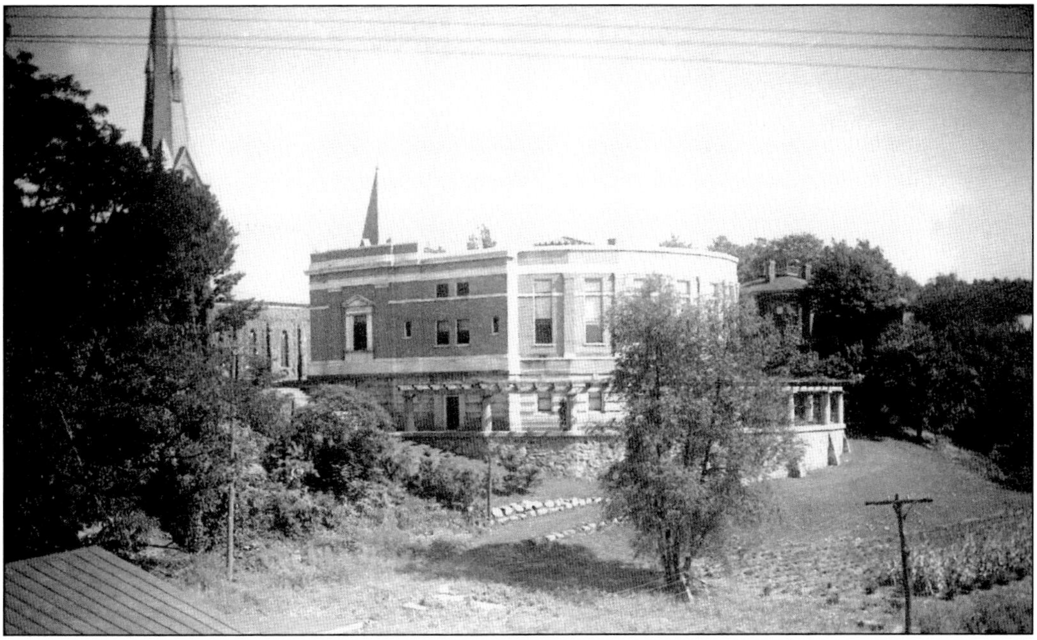

The rear view of the Patterson Library is equally beautiful as its pillared front steps. A pergola encircles the rear of the white marble and gray brick library building. A 20-foot-wide grass terrace lies between the library and the colonnade of stone pillars that support an arbor of trelliswork. It is not uncommon to see people reading in the cool vine-shaded lower level. (The Gollnitz family.)

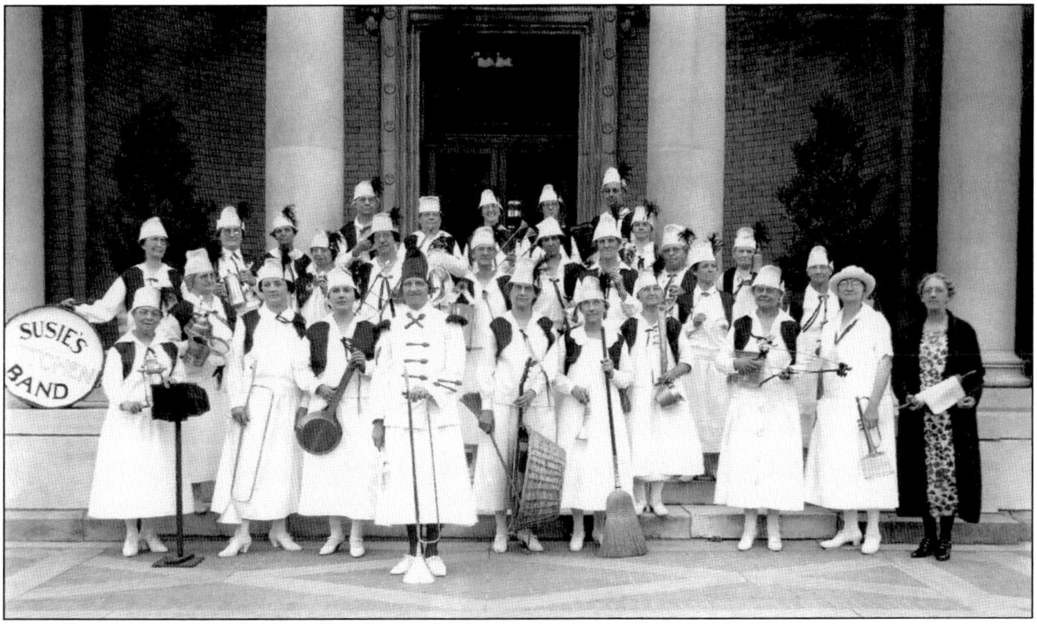

On March 3, 1926, a crowd of 850 people were entertained at the Grand Theater by Susie's Kitchen Cabinet Band. Spirited members of the Methodist church, posed on the Patterson Library steps, donned white uniforms while director Amy Caldwell (front row middle) added red stockings and a red plumed hat. Although kitchen utensils appear to be the instruments, music was actually made by kazoos accompanied by piano and drums.

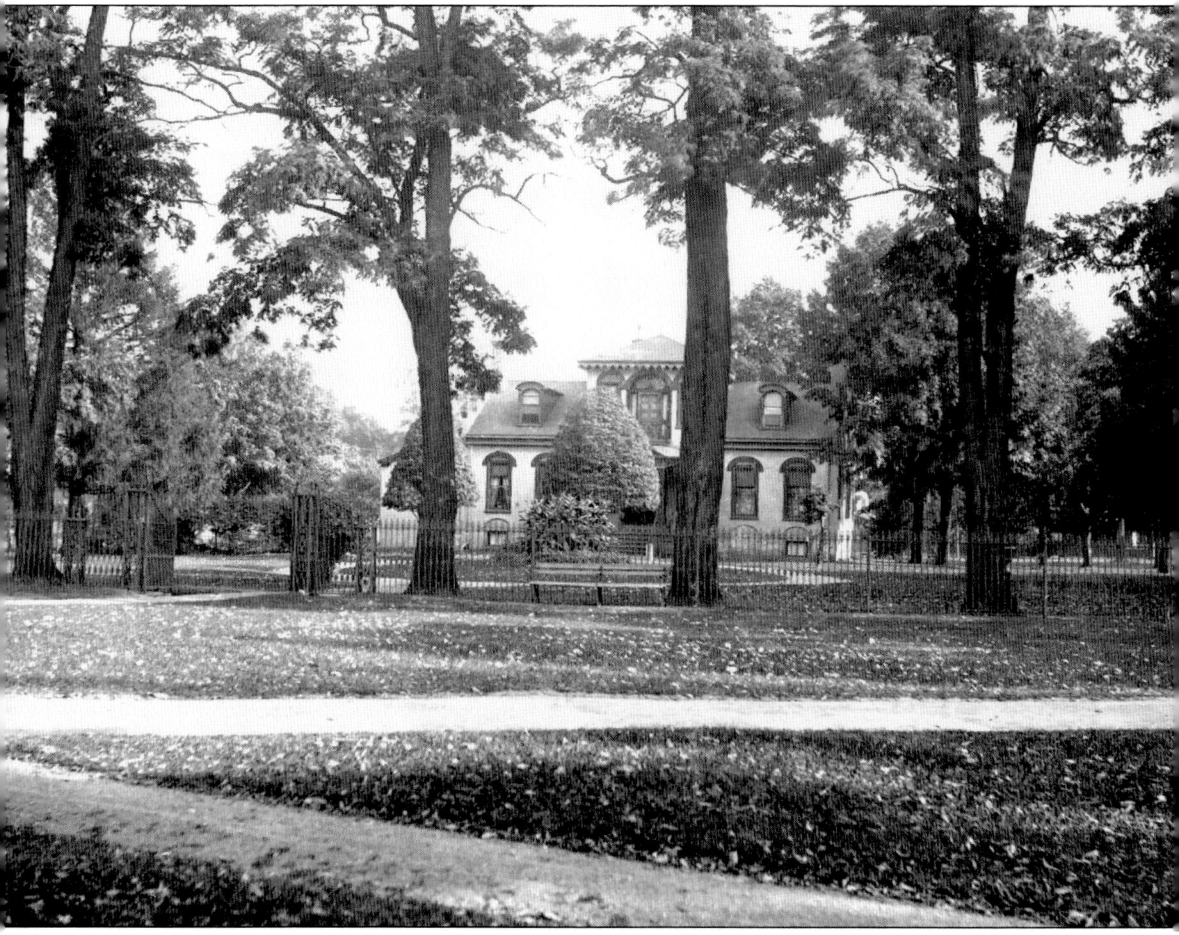

James McClurg bequeathed land adjacent to his house on the west for a Presbyterian meetinghouse and on the east for St. Peter's Episcopal Church (see opposite page). His grandson Dr. William J. Moore reconstructed the home in 1935. After his death, the removal of the iron fence from the estate provided the land for Moore Park or "the Commons," which has been the hub of community activities ever since. On summer evenings, band concerts have drawn townsfolk and many summer people too. In years past, during intermission, people would "cross the street to Julia Poole's, Tony's, or the Ellis Brothers for an ice cream or a soft drink if [they] were lucky enough to have a nickel."

Called the Chautauqe Church, the First Presbyterian Church was founded in 1808 by Rev. John Lindley, who organized the first congregation in the county. The present brick church, designed by architect Aaron Hall, was dedicated in 1879 and is already preparing for its 200th birthday in 2008. It is readily identified by two Gothic spires and its bell, whose peal served as the town crier.

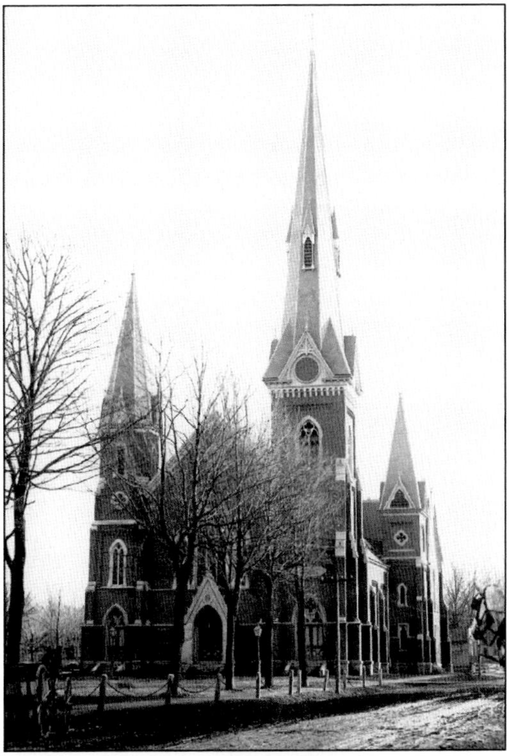

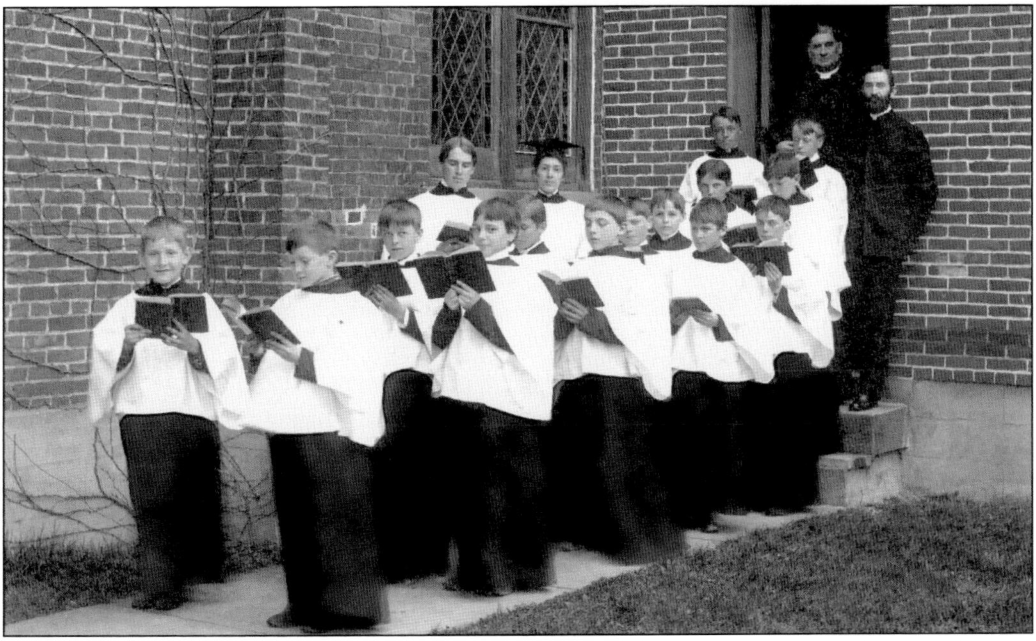

St. Peter's Episcopal Church, consecrated in 1833, is one of the oldest churches in New York State. "Built not only on a solid foundation of brick and mortar, but also on a spiritual foundation . . . [it is] representative of Westfield's finest old landmarks," the site of William H. Seward's baptism and confirmation. St. Peter's choir poses with Bishop Walker and Rector John McKinney on April 6, 1899.

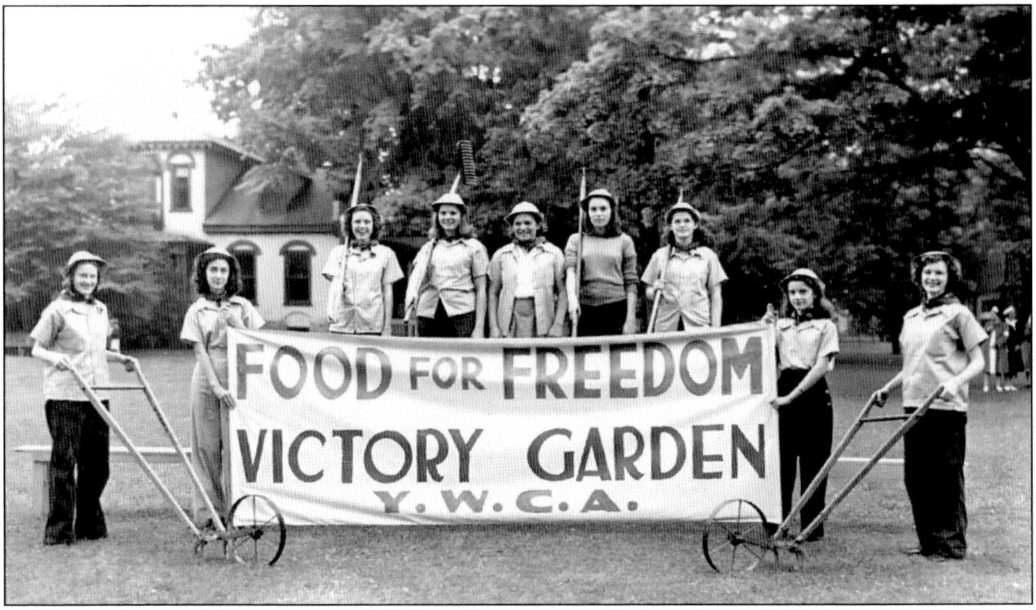

Members of the YWCA, organized in 1894, tend their victory garden near Moore Park during World War II. Their headquarters, at 58 South Portage Street, doubled as a first aid center. Girls were taught embroidery, home nursing, cooking, Bible study, and gymnastics. After 1938, with an endowment from Dr. William J. Moore, they provided classes in English to Italian, Scandinavian, Puerto Rican, and Laotian community members.

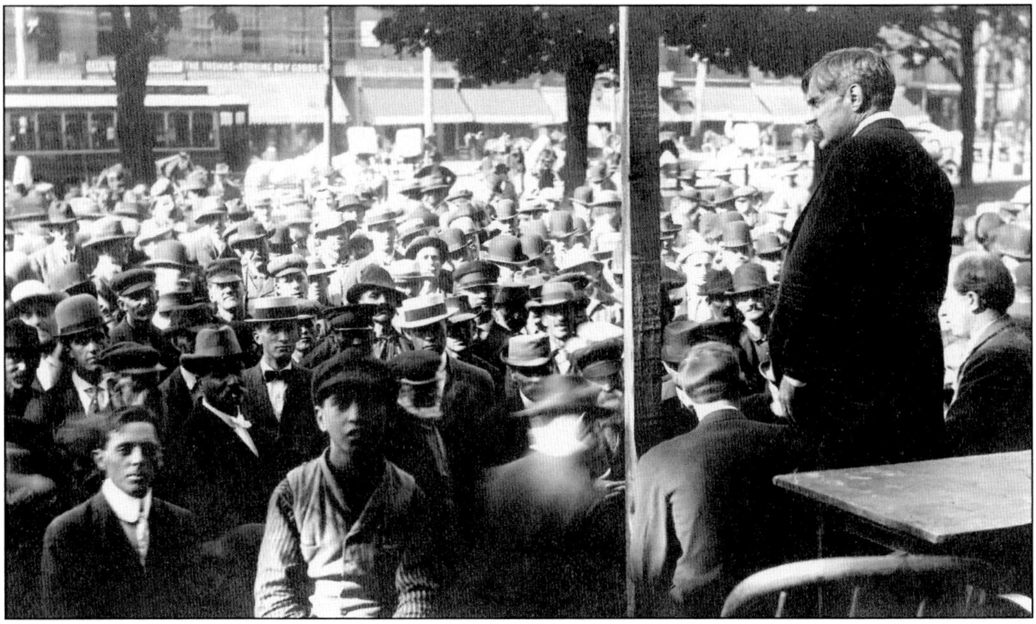

The "public-spirited progressive, aiding in every way to further the interests of Westfield and to advance the cause of the public good," county judge Arthur B. Ottaway was one of many political activists who held forums at Moore Park. From one of the oldest families in the county, Ottaway was elected district attorney in 1884 and, in 1906, began an 18-year distinguished career as judge of Chautauqua County. (Sydney S. Baker.)

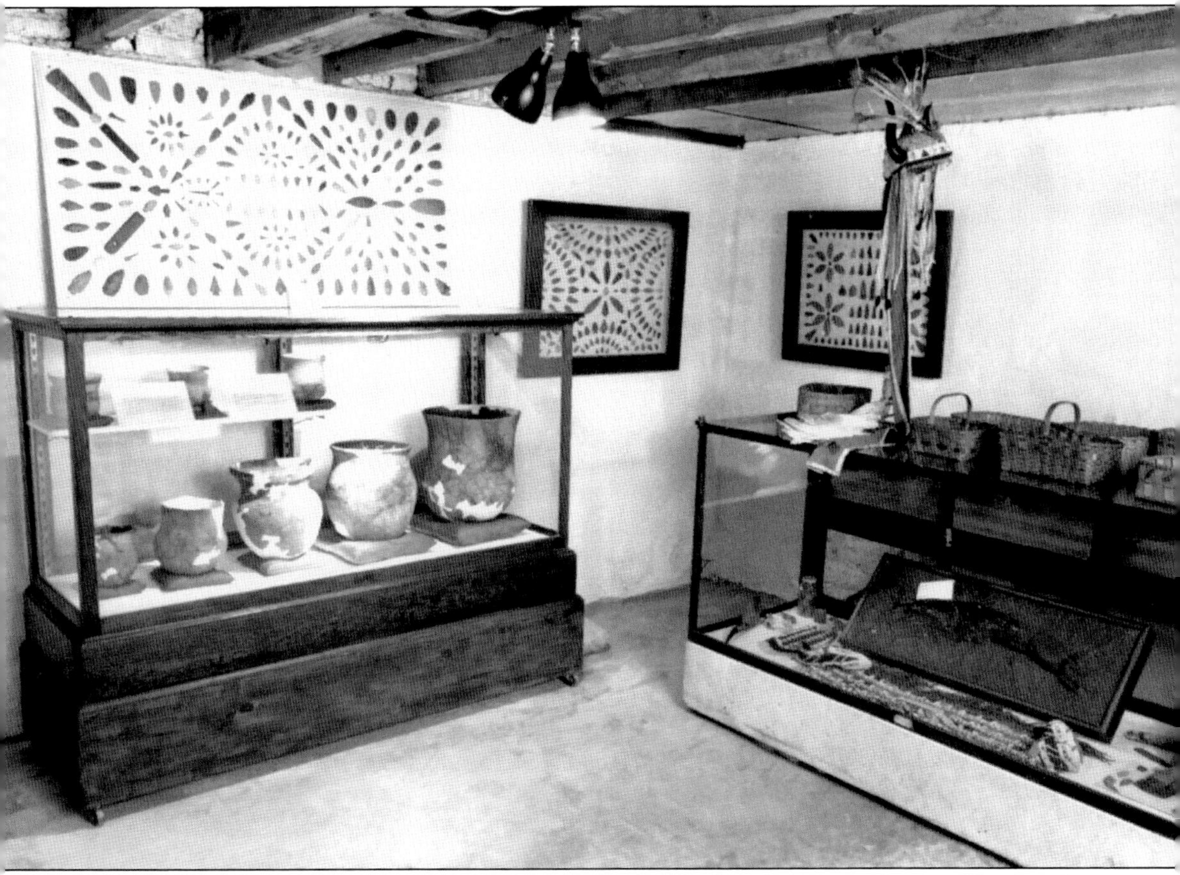

In the 1920s, Ross Pier Wright, longtime administrator for the Pennsylvania Historical Commission, and his sons unearthed a prehistoric Iroquois Indian village at South Gale Street on the outskirts of Westfield. During their noteworthy archeological excavations, clay pipes, "projectile points" or arrowheads, mortars, pestles, hammerstones, and various primitive implements were found in fire, storage, and refuse pits. Many of these Native American artifacts are on display at the McClurg Museum, as is Civil War memorabilia. The collection also includes rare county-related papers; out-of-date publications; diaries; family and individual histories; school, church, and cemetery records; maps; and miscellaneous photographs and files. This priceless treasure trove is accessible to the public to acquaint themselves with the county's rich 200-year history. (Chautauqua County Historical Society)

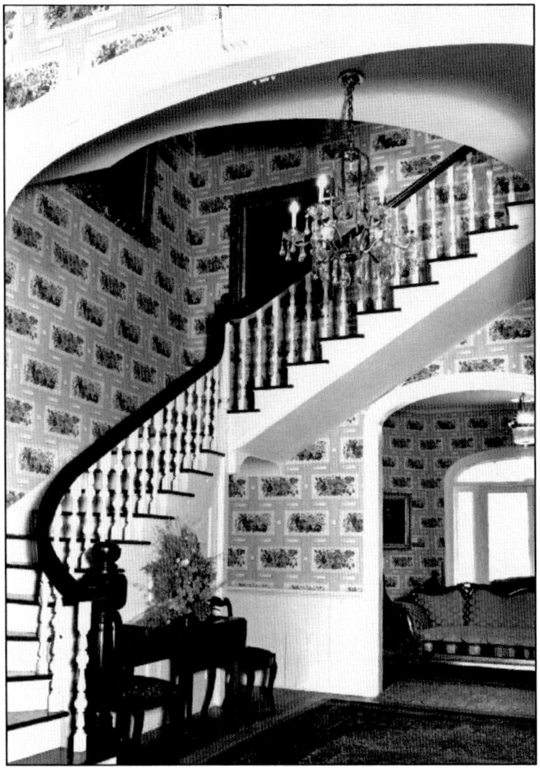

The grand staircase in the foyer of the McClurg Museum in Moore Park is indicative of the lavishness of the entire residence built by James McClurg around 1820. The first brick house between Buffalo and Erie, it was dubbed "McClurg's Folly" because of its pretentiousness in comparison with his neighbors' log cabins. In reality, the Federal-style house symbolized Westfield's increasing prosperity. (Chautauqua County Historical Society.)

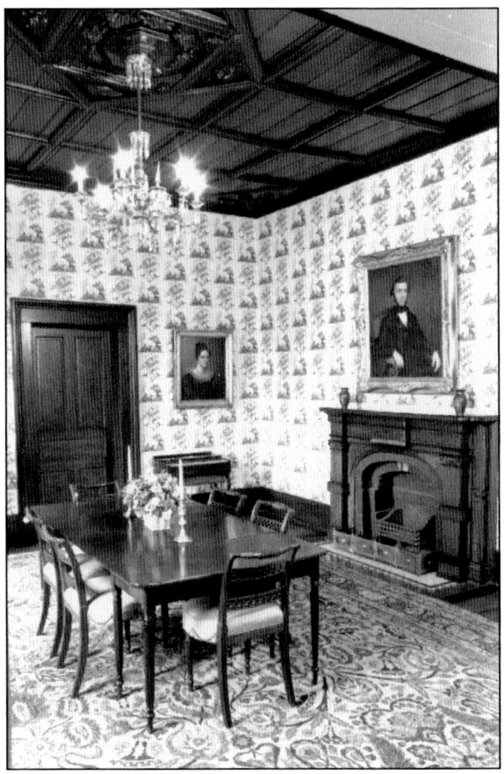

The restored 16-room frontier mansion is listed on the National Register of Historic Places. Its exquisite dining room is one of many rooms in this "gem of a small museum" with period furniture, fine art, and collectibles. The former office of land company agent William H. Seward, who resided there from 1836 to 1838, contains his desk, record books, and two safes.

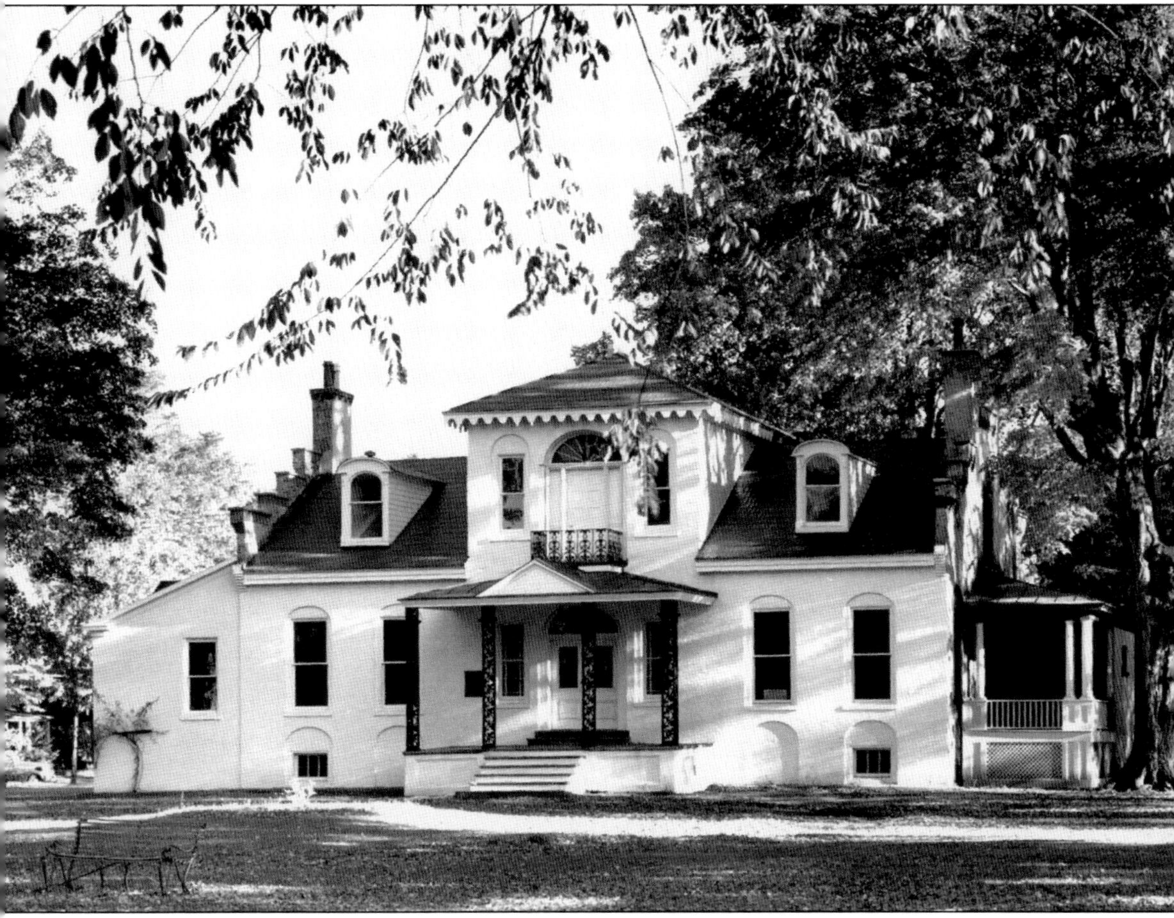

"The Chautauqua County Historical Society (CCHS) was formed in 1883, making it the oldest historical society in Western New York. Its mission is to foster an interest and knowledge of the history of Chautauqua County through the collection, preservation, and interpretation of archives and objects of local significance." The society maintains its collection at the McClurg Museum in Westfield "which has everything: great beauty, architectural significance, and strong cultural connections. The society's holdings within it include valuable objects and documents that are important and rare. All of it needs to be preserved and protected. As Westfield's premier cultural asset, we owe it to the next generation," states president James O'Brien. (Chautauqua County Historical Society.)

Partial Bibliography

Brown, Kent L. A *Medical History of Westfield, NY.* Westfield, NY: W. Publications, 1992.

Bush, Paula H. *History of Barcelona and Its People During the 1800s.*

The Centennial History of Chautauqua County, Vol. 1. Jamestown, NY: Chautauqua History Company, 1904.

Chautauqua County's Bicentennial Era: A Commemorative Book, 1802–2002. Jamestown, NY: The Post-Journal, 2002.

Chazanof, William. *Welch's Grape Juice: From Corporation to Co-operative.* Syracuse, NY: Syracuse University Press, 1977.

Curtis, Dorothy Hopkins. *History of Westfield, Part I, 1802–1952.* Westfield, NY: Long & Holbrook Printers, 1979.

Dibble, Mary "Billie." "Dibble's Dabbles" column for the *Westfield Republican*, 1981–1990.

Doty, William J., ed. *The Historic Annals of Southwestern New York*, Vols. I and II. New York: Lewis Historical Publishing Company, Inc., 1940.

Hutchins, Porter. "Early History of Barcelona." *Westfield Republican*, April 1922.

Lindquist, Marlene, and Therold Lindquist. *Architecture in Westfield: An Historical Survey.* Sponsored by the Lakeshore Association for the Arts, 1976.

McMahon, Helen G. *Chautauqua County: A History.* Buffalo, NY: Henry Stewart, 1958.

Meyer, H. Harold. A *History of the Grape Juice Industry and Growers of the C & E Belt, 1917–1926.* Cincinnati, OH: 1965.

Powers, Mabel (Yehsennohwehs). *The Portage Trail.* East Aurora, NY: The Roycroft Shops, 1924.

Richardson, Virginia. *Telling Our Stories, 1883-2000.* (History of the Chautauqua County Historical Society and Individual Biographical Essays).

Severance, Frank H. *An Old Frontier of France*, Vol. I. New York: Dodd, Mead and Company, 1917.

Taylor, Devon. *The Chautauqua Gorge.* Mayville, NY: Mayville Library Association, 1995.

Trump, Fred. *Lincoln's Little Girl: A True Story.* Honesdale, PA: Boyds Mills Press, 1977.

Trump, Clara K., ed. *History of Westfield, Part II, 1955–1977.* Westfield, NY: Long & Holbrook Printers, 1979.

Turner, O. *Pioneer History of the Holland Purchase of Western New York and a History of Pioneer Settlement.* Buffalo, NY: George H. Derby and Company, 1850.

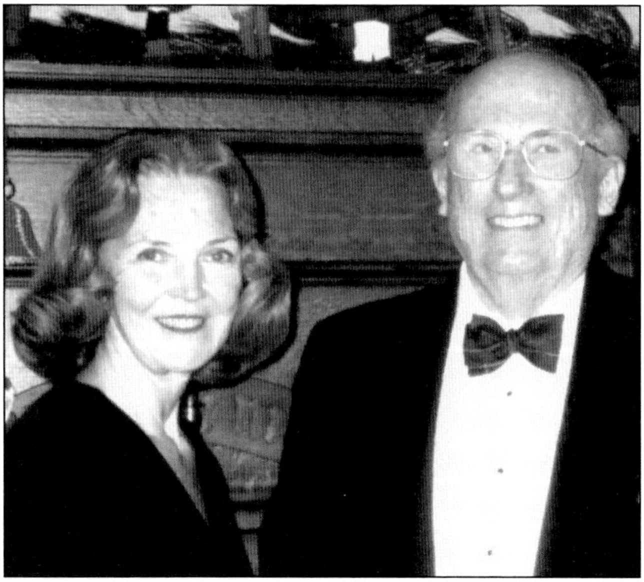

In 2002, James O'Brien, the newly elected president of the Chautauqua County Historical Society, praised Priscilla and Rod Nixon: "The community owes a great debt to [them]. Their vision, their leadership, and their sheer hard work over the past 50 years have left Westfield and Chautauqua County an invaluable legacy." For their stalwart stewardship, the authors' highest praise. (The Nixon family.)